THORNRIDGE

THORNRIDGE

The Perfect Season in Black and White

Scott Lynn

[signature: Scott Lynn]

authorHOUSE®

AuthorHouse™
1663 Liberty Drive
Bloomington, IN 47403
www.authorhouse.com
Phone: 1-800-839-8640

First published by AuthorHouse   12/3/2009

ISBN: 978-1-4490-4091-8 (e)
ISBN: 978-1-4490-4089-5 (sc)
ISBN: 978-1-4490-4090-1 (hc)

Library of Congress Control Number: 2009912327

Printed in the United States of America
Bloomington, Indiana

This book is printed on acid-free paper.

TABLE OF CONTENTS

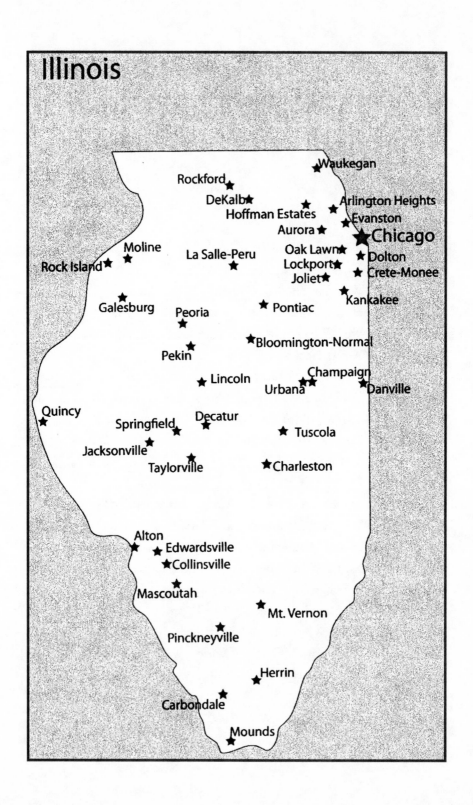

FOREWORD

THE HIGH SCHOOL BASKETBALL COACH's character in the 1973 Pulitzer Prize-winning play "That Championship Season" tells his players: "You were a thing of rare beauty, boys. Life is a game, and I'm proud to say I played it with the best."

Those guys from Thornridge must feel that way. By far, they were part of the best high school team I ever saw.

Quinn Buckner once told me, "I'd rather be a good player on a great team than the other way around."

I asked his coach, Ron Ferguson, what that Thornridge team would have been like with Buckner and four ordinary players.

Fergie said, "With Quinn Buckner around, how long do you think the other four would be ordinary?"

I was an eyewitness to, oh, probably two dozen of Thornridge's 58 wins in a row. Buckner was the best scholastic athlete I ever saw, a man among boys. I visited his house and met his parents. I even sold a story about him to Sports Illustrated which had recently put another high school kid, Rick Mount, on its cover. I wish they had done the same for Quinn, but the magazine couldn't make space for it before his senior season came to an end. The story never ran.

"Bewitched" was a popular TV show of that era. Lockport's coach Bob Basarich told me, "That Buckner, he's like Samantha the witch. He wiggles his nose and the ball that you had in your hand disappears."

A lot of people forget that he was called Bill Buckner through his sophomore year. Quinn is his middle name.

Buckner wasn't all that tall. He couldn't run the fastest, jump the highest or shoot the straightest. All he could do was beat you. And beat you. And beat you.

Over a 24-month period, those Falcons teams played 69 games and won 68.

In their undefeated 1971-72 season, only four teams came within 20 points of them. They won the state championship game 104-69. I was there in Champaign that day. Quincy couldn't have won that game if Thornridge had let it use 10 players instead of five.

They beat Peoria Manual by 47 points, Richards by 53, St. Francis de Sales by 54. The closest game all year came against St. Patrick -- they only won that one by 14.

I can still recall some colorful comments about that team.

Thornton's coach, Tom Hanrahan, thought Thornridge "should be awarded an NBA franchise."

Wes Mason, the coach from my alma mater, Bloom, once said Thornridge's pressing defense was so tough, "Even our guys without the ball had trouble crossing the 10-second line."

Do you know how the greatest teams often have somebody questioning their greatness? I remember something Mike Bonczyk told me five years later. Thornridge hadn't dazzled some of the spectators in the state semifinals because it only got a 19-point victory over a Peoria Manual team that it had already beaten by 47 and 27.

Bonczyk said, "That's how fans treated us. If we beat a team by less than 20, we weren't as hot as we were made out to be. If we won by more than 20, we were humiliating them."

Bonczyk was kind of the John Paxson or John Stockton of that team. He was that unselfish kid who knew how to get the ball to the guys who could score.

He was born in Canada, but I don't know how Bonczyk's family ended up living in that Dolton area. Some people mistakenly remember Bonczyk as the only white kid on the team. On the starting five, yes, but a team photo shows that six of Thornridge's seven reserves were white. And the school's 1971 championship team had an unfairly forgotten 6-5 center named Mark McClain in the middle -- that kid was a big factor in that championship.

What I remember most about Greg Rose was that he excelled at defense at a time when most kids cared only about offense. He played drums at night to make some money to help his family pay its bills. Before a trip once, Ferguson told the players not to to show up without a necktie. Rose didn't own a necktie, so he didn't show up. He took it literally. A sportswriter ended up driving Greg 100 miles to the game.

I felt sorry for Ernie Dunn. He wanted to go to a major college, but the big ones didn't call. He didn't have much of a career after Thornridge, and that kid could play. When I found him five years later, he was 23 years old, watching Quinn Buckner on national television while Ernie was working in an office for unemployment insurance. He told me, "This is no kind of job for a young person to live with. I bring home too many people's personal problems from the office. It's too much a strain on me."

Boyd Batts was a puzzle. His older brother Lloyd was as huge a talent as ever set foot on a high school court -- a Kobe Bryant caliber talent. Boyd could have been, too. He had gigantic games, like 37 points and 15 rebounds in the 1972 state championship game. He could have become an NCAA superstar. But he wasn't as mature or grounded as Buckner was. He went to a junior college, then to Hawaii, then to Nevada - Las Vegas. He averaged, like, 11 points a game for that UNLV team, which scored 90 or 100 a night. He was just a nice player there, not a star.

One other thing I remember about Thornridge was how, just across the state line, in East Chicago, Ind., there was a sensational team at the same time. They had guys like Junior Bridgeman, who went on to play in the NBA, and Tim Stoddard, who played for North Carolina State and ended up in Major League Baseball as a pitcher.

For a few weeks of our lives, everybody wondered what would happen if somebody could arrange a game between those two teams, Dolton Thornridge and East Chicago Washington. It never came off because, well, why would the loser want to go out that way?

I've been to Olympic basketball games, NBA Finals games and NCAA championship games, but that's one basketball game I would have killed to see.

--MIKE DOWNEY, Former Sports Columnist--
Chicago Tribune and Los Angeles Times
September 23, 2009

INTRODUCTION

I GREW UP ON A farm in central Illinois at the same time the Thornridge High School basketball team was kicking everybody's butt. I played on the Lincoln team that won its first 17 games and did not lose a road game all season. I thought we might beat Thornridge if we met in the state tournament. We never got the opportunity, but I realize now that I was wrong. My Lincoln team was very good. Thornridge was spectacular. In the 33 years I have worked as a radio and TV sportscaster in Illinois, Florida, and Oregon, I have never seen a high school team as great as the 1971-72 Thornridge Falcons.

A few years ago, I was at a Portland Trail Blazers game talking with Indiana Pacers Vice President Quinn Buckner who was one of the captains of the Thornridge state champions in 1971-72. I told him I was the captain of the Lincoln team that ranked second in the state behind his team a majority of that season. I also told him I would have been assigned to guard him had our teams played. I suggested he probably would have kicked my ass. I am now six-five and weigh 240 pounds which prompted Quinn to say "No, it looks to me like you could have played." I told him that I was six-five back in the day, but added that I only weighed about 160 pounds. Buckner, who as a high school senior was six-three and weighed between 200 and 220 pounds, replied matter-of-factly and without a moment's hesitation, "Oh *yeah*. I'd have kicked your ass." Close to four decades later, Buckner still had the confidence of a champion.

I know for a fact that he was not being arrogant or boastful. You see, I was one of more than 16,000 fans at the Assembly Hall in Champaign the night his team laid 104 on Quincy to win by 35 and claim a second straight state championship. It wasn't like Buckner and his pals beat a bad team that night. Quincy had scored a tournament record *107* in its state semifinal victory.

Some said Thornridge wasn't perfect. Coaches and sportswriters of the era said the Falcons' full court press ranked only second best --- behind *collegiate* national champion UCLA. Now, we all know a mere high school team could not have defeated John Wooden's Bruins led by a sophomore named Bill Walton. However, Thornridge was not a typical high school team. If you ever saw Thornridge play, you know it might well have been an entertaining game.

The Falcons were unstoppable on the basketball floor. But what few of us realized at the time was the impact the Thornridge basketball team was making *off* the court. This book is my humble attempt to tell the story of how a high school sports team brought together black and white communities in the early 1970s.

I began the project because I wanted to learn what had happened to the Thornridge players in the decades since they made Illinois sports history in my senior year of high school. As I spoke to each of the players, I realized there was a more significant story to be told. *THORNRIDGE* is about sacrifices and friendships. It is also about a group of teenagers whose success on the basketball court changed the way blacks and whites felt about each other in the south suburbs of Chicago.

I wanted those who had experienced the Thornridge basketball phenomenon to share their memories with you. In *THORNRIDGE*, players, coaches, broadcasters, and sportswriters remember the Falcons and the unforgettable 1971-72 season. I believe you will enjoy hearing the story from those who lived it.

The men and women interviewed for this book spoke in terminology that was politically correct for the time. An African-American was a Negro, a minority, a black, or a brother. A Caucasian was a white. Those interviewed for this book, including the African-Americans, are quoted speaking in those terms. I wrote in those terms, not to disrespect African-Americans reading the book today, but simply to be true to the time period.

Unless specifically noted, all quotes are from interviews conducted in 2008 and 2009. Because nearly four decades have passed, recollections of specific events sometimes vary slightly. In every case, those interviewed tried their best to recall events accurately. I thank them for sharing their memories and for being forthcoming with intimate details of their lives.

This book is very personal to me. I began the project in July of 2008, making a trip from my home in Oregon to Illinois to spend a day with former Thornridge coach Ron Ferguson at his home near Peoria. I stayed at my father's house in nearby Lincoln. For a full week, I went through Ferguson's scrapbooks and began doing some preliminary writing. I spent many hours that week typing on the computer while my ailing father watched TV in the next room. I remember feeling guilty that I was spending more time with the scrapbooks and my laptop than with Dad. His health was poor, and I knew it was probably the last time I would see him. But, I was anxious to get started on the book. I also could sense that he was proud of me for taking on the project. Before heading home to Oregon, I promised him that I would complete the book, no matter how long it took.

After Dad died just before Thanksgiving, 2008, friends and relatives told me how excited he was that I was writing a book about the famous Thornridge team. Dad, as you and Mom look down from heaven, I hope both of you are proud. I dedicate this book to you, my parents. You were my biggest fans when I was playing basketball and in the years that followed.

This book is also personal to me because I wrote much of it while undergoing chemotherapy for colon cancer after undergoing life-saving emergency surgery in December, 2008. It was a blessing to have something to take my mind off the chemo treatments. There was a sense of urgency as I wrote the book because I came to understand there are no guarantees in life. (Talk about a writer working under a deadline!) My latest test results are promising, although I now live my life one day at a time. I give special thanks to my loving family Sharon, Adam, and Kelsey. Without their support I could never have made it through chemo or finished writing the book.

I'm sure you can understand why this book has a special place in my heart. I've been told it also means the world to the players and coaches featured throughout the book. It was my pleasure to do the research and writing. I hope you will find great pleasure in reading it.

--Scott Lynn (Betzelberger)--
October 25, 2009

CHAPTER 1

We'll Be Back

THEY WON A STATE RECORD 54 straight.

They were black and went to a white school.

They won by an average of 32 points a game.

One was white and played on the black playgrounds.

They averaged 87 points a game *before* the 3-point-line.

They were thirteen when their lives changed with the assassination of Doctor King.

They had the national high school player of the year.

His mom led the fight for desegregation.

They travelled the state playing in the north, the south, and when it counted most in central Illinois for the state championship. And they won it. Again.

They survived the '60s and matured in the '70s.

They played in historic high school gyms and in front of 16,000 in the state title game.

Some wore Afros. One had a mop top with Elvis sideburns.

Broadcasters, sportswriters, coaches, and players say they were the best. Period.

They grooved to the hits from Motown.

They became a broadcaster, a telecom executive, a high school coach, a cook, and an R&B singer.

But in 1972, they were the perfect basketball team.

They were THORNRIDGE.

***

Longtime basketball fans in Illinois remember the names -- Quinn Buckner, Boyd Batts, Mike Bonczyk, Greg Rose, and Ernie Dunn. They are forever linked in legend as the starting five on the greatest high school basketball team in the state's history, a team once ranked as one of the top five high school teams in the nation's history. The Falcons did not exactly come out of nowhere. Nearly everyone expected them to win the 1972 Illinois state championship. Most confident of all were the Thornridge players. One of them willingly posted a target on their backs exactly 364 days prior to the 1972 title game.

It was March 20, 1971. Chicago's Top 40 AM radio stations WLS and WCFL were playing the hits. Janis Joplin belted out *"Me and Bobby McGee"*, the number one song on the Billboard Top 100. One of the hottest selling 45s in America, The Temptations' *"Just My Imagination"*, played on transistor radios throughout Illinois as blacks and whites grooved to the sounds of Motown. The new issue of TV Guide included a story on the 1970-71 All-America Basketball Team featuring Austin Carr of Notre Dame and Sidney Wicks of soon-to-be-again champion UCLA. On television that Saturday evening, viewers around the nation tuned in to action-packed episodes of "Mission Impossible" and "Mannix." However, basketball fans in Illinois dialed their TVs to Chicago's WGN Channel 9 or to one of the other stations on the statewide network that televised the Illinois High School Association (IHSA) state tournament live from the Assembly Hall in Champaign.

Thornridge of Dolton and Oak Lawn Community, south suburban schools located just nine miles apart, had followed Friday quarterfinal round victories with semifinal wins Saturday afternoon, setting the stage for Saturday night's first all-Chicago-area final in the history of the 64-year old state tournament. With the entire state watching, the Falcons, playing their third game in 24 hours, survived a late Oak Lawn rally to win 52-50 and claim the school's first state basketball championship. Victory wasn't assured until two Oak Lawn shots bounced off the rim in the final seconds. When Thornridge sophomore Greg Rose hauled in the defensive rebound as the final horn sounded, the Falcons sprinted up and down the court while leaping high into the air in jubilant celebration. For the Thornridge players and coaches, it was a richly deserved championship. The only blemish on their record was a stunning loss to tiny Mounds Meridian in the 1970 Carbondale Christmas tournament. Thornridge won its next twenty-one games to finish with a record of 31-1.

Moments after becoming the 1971 state champions, the Thornridge players continued to celebrate on the floor of the Assembly Hall. They hugged and mugged for the cameras while savoring the fruits of their labor. Junior point guard Mike Bonczyk (pronounced BAHN'-zick) enjoyed the moment but was already dreaming about winning another championship. During the postgame television interviews, Bonczyk calmly looked into the camera and issued a warning to the teams around the state that would try to dethrone the champions the following season.

"I'm a junior, and we've got four or five guys coming back next year," said the confident Bonczyk. "And we're gonna be just as tough next year."

39-year-old Thornridge coach Ron Ferguson, who said he felt like he was 60 after surviving the grueling tournament trail, immediately began to dread the challenges his team would face the following season. While relieved to have finally won a coveted state title, Ferguson knew the pressure to win another championship would become overwhelming over the next twelve months.

"The first thing I felt inside was the pressure that was going to be on us after winning and having pretty much everybody back," says the now 78-year-old coach at his home near Peoria, Illinois. "I said, 'God, you know everyone is going to be gunning for us, and we're going to have to play so much better to overcome it.'"

There was little question that Thornridge would be the team to beat in 1971-72. From the championship team's core, only starting center Mark McClain and sixth man Mike Henry would graduate. Four starters from the 1971 championship team would return. Bonczyk, the pass-first point guard, would be back to orchestrate the offense. Also returning would be Boyd Batts and Quinn Buckner. They were already considered two of the most athletic and talented players in Illinois. Buckner had just become the first junior ever to be named the Chicago Sun-Times Illinois Player of the Year. Thornridge fans would also have a chance to again savor the marvelous skills of Greg Rose, who was a starter as a sophomore on the 1971 championship team. But that would be next season. First, the Falcons would celebrate a state championship with their fans.

On Sunday morning, March 21, 1971, the Thornridge players packed their bags into the trunks of the brand new 1971 Buicks that had been provided by Bauer Buick in Harvey for the team's trip downstate. After the Falcons made the long drive north from Champaign, they were met by an estimated 15,000 fans who lined the streets from Illinois State Highway

57, through Phoenix and Harvey, all the way to the school in Dolton. A motorcade of some 600 cars was led by two fire engines from the Dolton Fire Department. The Falcons' cheerleaders rode on the first fire truck while the Thornridge players waved to fans from the second fire engine. The team started out at 172nd and Halsted Street and paraded through many local communities. The players waved at fans while they wound through the streets of Harvey, Phoenix, South Holland, and Dolton before arriving at Thornridge High School which is located in Dolton. The 3000 seat gymnasium was packed with more than 5000 raucous students and fans. Thousands more waited in the school parking lot to welcome the team home. Not wanting to draw attention to himself, the man who had guided the team to the state title was not to be found on either fire truck.

"I wouldn't ride on the damn thing," says coach Ferguson. With a laugh, he adds, "I told the other coach, (varsity assistant Dave Lezeau), 'That's your assignment. I'm not gonna ride.' They were lucky to get me to make a speech at the [championship celebration]."

Ferguson was somewhat concerned about the safety of his players. He knew something bad could happen if teenagers were allowed to fool around without adult supervision. Ferguson gave his assistant coaches an explicit order.

"I said, 'You guys get on there and don't let any of them fall under the fire engine or anything like that.'" laughs Ferguson.

Because he rode apart from his players, the head coach was late for the championship celebration at the school. The open convertible in which Ferguson was riding became separated from the rest of the parade by a train that slowly rolled through Dolton at a most inopportune time. By the time the train rolled through the middle of the parade, the fire trucks, and most of the fans that had lines the streets, were nowhere in sight. Fans had abandoned their positions along the parade route to follow the players to the school gymnasium. Due to the unfortunate timing of the train, Ferguson rode the rest of the way to the high school in relative solitude.

Inside the gym, the Thornridge pep band played. Students and fans of all ages, both black and white, stood as one to deliver a five minute standing ovation as the players entered the gym holding the prized state championship trophy which was adorned with a basketball net from the Assembly Hall draped over the top. Buckner and Batts proudly took turns carrying the golden trophy while receiving countless congratulatory pats on the back.

Batts addressed the fans and declared, "If I do my job and Quinn does his job, ain't nobody gonna stop us."

Considering the possibility of back-to-back state titles, the crowd was whipped into an absolute frenzy as Bonczyk stepped to the microphone and announced, "We'll be back next year."

Buckner then praised his teammates and thanked the fans and students for their support. He indicated that with their help, the Falcons could again be champions the following year. Nearly four decades later, Buckner explains why he didn't feel comfortable making any *guarantees* about the next season.

"That's not my nature. That bravado, that's Mike," laughs Buckner. "I'm tellin' ya. Mike has always been like that. You know, just short of saying a little too much. Boyd had the same kind of bravado, so they could say that."

Bonczyk admits he was a rather cocky high school junior who made his prediction of a second straight championship while still feeling the euphoria of becoming a state champion less than 24 hours earlier.

"Well," laughs Bonczyk, "that was the youth, the exuberance. You're sixteen or seventeen years old and you know, we were just having fun the first year. We didn't understand what was to come the following year. You're so excited about everything and you just say things. It just comes out."

In the packed gymnasium that memorable Sunday afternoon in March of 1971, black and white fans celebrated in unison. It was remarkable to see how everyone had come together to support the team during the final weeks of the Falcons' championship run. It had not been that way much of the season. Many fans had been slow to jump on the bandwagon, a surprise considering the basketball team was ranked number one in Illinois. Some Thornridge fans felt the Falcons would fall flat at tournament time considering they had never won any postseason trophy. With the fans taking a wait-and-see attitude, the Falcons rarely played before capacity crowds during the regular season and in the early rounds of the state playoffs.

Illinois was changing to a two-class (large-school, small-school) system in 1972, so the 1971 tournament was the final time all high schools in Illinois played for a single state championship. To win the 1971 title, the state champion had to win nine consecutive playoff games. The champion had to win three games in a regional and two more in a sectional just to reach the "Sweet 16" and be considered a "state tournament" team.

Eight "super-sectional" games, most played at college arenas around the state, determined the eight quarterfinalists. The "Elite Eight" advanced to play in the Assembly Hall on the campus of the University of Illinois in Champaign. Every game played in Champaign was televised live on a statewide network which gave an Illinois high school player maximum exposure in the days prior to ESPN, the regional sports networks, and the internet.

Thornridge had the advantage of hosting its own regional tournament in 1971. The Falcons easily won their first two games downing St. Francis De Sales 86-44 and Quigley South 102-41. Despite the blowout wins, many wondered if Thornridge would be able to get past rival Thornton of Harvey in the regional final. The Falcons had never advanced out of the regional because the Wildcats had always blocked their path. In the ten years of Thornridge's existence, Thornton had won the regional championship each year. Thornton was the area's powerhouse high school basketball program. The Wildcats had won a pair of state championships and had played in five state championship games through the years. You could understand if the Thornridge players and fans had an inferiority complex. They were not accustomed to being considered one of the state's elite. Being ranked number one in the state was a new experience for Thornridge and its followers.

Ten years of frustration ended in March of 1971 when the Falcons defeated Thornton 66-58 in the regional final. Even so, there were still some fans hesitant to give their hearts to the team. During the state tournament, participating schools were given tickets to sell to their fans. Thornridge was unable to sell its allotment and had to return 350 unsold tickets for the Falcon's next game against Marist in the sectional tournament at Joliet. However, the fans' excitement grew after Thornridge came from behind in the second half to beat Marist 66-55 in the school's first-ever sectional appearance. Thornridge then posted a 66-63 win over one of the state's best teams, Joliet Central, in the sectional final to reach the "Sweet 16" for the first time. At that point, people began to realize Thornridge might well win the state championship. By the time Thornridge defeated Chicago Harlan 73-63 in the Crete-Monee super-sectional to earn a trip to Champaign as one of the "Elite Eight", fans were scrambling for a seat on the bandwagon. For the next twelve months, Thornridge High School basketball tickets would be one of the toughest tickets in Chicago area sports.

As the Falcons prepared to play Kewanee in the IHSA quarterfinals at the Assembly Hall, they knew they had been somewhat fortunate to get to

Champaign. Thornridge needed a 23-point performance from sixth man Mike Henry to overcome a halftime deficit in the win over Marist in the sectional opener. Then in the sectional final, the Falcons were challenged by the host team, the Joliet Central Steelmen. Joliet Central was a very good basketball team with an excellent young coach in Dale Glenn. Joliet Central had finished third at state the previous season. Future Illinois State University standout Roger Powell was back for the Steelmen and proving to be a difficult matchup for opposing players. The packed gym at Joliet Central was quite intimidating for most visiting teams. The boisterous Joliet Central fans were extremely close to the action and seemed to be situated right on top of the players. It was so loud fans could be seen putting their hands over their ears. Joliet, a tough industrial city, was proud of its Steelmen, and many of the area's rabid basketball fans expected Joliet Central to win the state championship after coming close the year before. Thornridge was fortunate to survive at Joliet. Powell, a first team all-state swingman, moved down to the low blocks and scored a game-high 34 points. But the Falcons survived when Powell missed a potential tying basket late in the game, and Henry again came to the rescue for Thornridge making three free throws in the final 21 seconds to clinch the win.

The Falcons dodged another bullet against Harlan in the super-sectional. The score was tied at halftime, and Thornridge was in serious foul trouble. Four Falcon starters (Buckner, Batts, Bonczyk, and Rose) would each finish with four fouls, one short of disqualification. But Rose scored 11 of his team-high 23 points in the fourth quarter to lead Thornridge to its 18th straight win.

In the state quarterfinals, a Buckner steal in the final seconds denied Kewanee the opportunity for a potential game-winning shot. Rose scored four points in the final five seconds to seal the Falcons' 63-58 victory. The Saturday afternoon semifinal game against Danville was a relative breeze. The defensive-minded Falcons held the Vikings to just 28% shooting from the field in a 57-47 win. Buckner was again the hero finishing with 20 points, 9 rebounds, and 8 assists.

But it was back to nail-biting time in the state championship game against Oak Lawn. Buckner led the Falcons to the two point win by scoring 18 points. Mike Henry again came off the bench to play a pivotal role. Henry scored 13 points, pulled down a team-high 10 rebounds, and scored what turned out to be the winning basket on a put-back of a Buckner miss with just under a minute to play. Helping his team win the state championship was the perfect way for Mike Henry to cap his Thornridge career which had its ups and downs. As a junior, Henry had been kicked off the team just prior to the regional tournament. He was not allowed back on the squad until mid-season in his senior year. Reflecting back on his team's 1971 state championship run, Ron Ferguson says without Henry's contributions down the stretch, Thornridge would have never won the last Illinois single-class championship.

"He got in trouble," says the Thornridge coach. "They had something over a black cheerleader not making the squad in the fall. He got suspended from school. Then I had to suspend him from the basketball team. He was allowed to come back in the second semester [of the 1970-71 school year] with a lot of terms he had to meet. I don't know how many games we had left, but I'll tell you this. We wouldn't have won it without him. He came back [after his suspension] and really rebounded and played defense and was a model guy."

"Of all of us Mike Henry may have been the most skilled player we had," says Thornridge star Quinn Buckner nearly four decades later. "Mike Henry could really play. He was six-four, six-five, great body, and could rebound. [He was] not a great ball handler but was a very good scorer and a good defensive player with long arms. There's no question we don't win it without him."

Henry and fellow senior Mark McClain had both moved on when the Falcons began looking ahead to the 1971-72 season. With McClain no longer around, the defending state champs would have one starting spot open. Most people expected the position to go to Chuck Hogan. However, Hogan surprised the coaches by moving during the summer.

"Chuck Hogan moved back to Mississippi," recalls Coach Ferguson. "He was like six-five. I thought, 'Oh boy! He's going to be a starter.' I mean there was no question. He'd have been a starter."

When Ferguson found out Hogan was leaving, he began to look for another player to work into the mix. Most fans expected junior Nee Gatlin to be in the starting lineup on opening night. However, a transfer from rival Thornton High School arrived on the scene. Junior Ernie Dunn stepped in and brought added quickness and intelligence to the team. Dunn was the perfect complement to Buckner, Batts, Bonczyk, and Rose. He was the final piece of the puzzle.

The Thornridge players achieved rock-star status during their remarkable 1971-72 season. Every game was broadcast on a Chicago area radio station. The Falcons' game highlights were shown on evening sports reports in one of the nation's largest TV markets. Each contest, home and away, was played before a sellout crowd. Home games were even piped in to the school's cafeteria via closed circuit TV for fans that couldn't get tickets to enter the packed gymnasium. Thornridge basketball was a happening in 1971-72. Just a few years earlier, no one could have anticipated that the primarily white high school would be setting records on the basketball court featuring a team led by minority players. In the early 1960s, black students did not attend Thornridge High. But times had changed. The previously all-white high school in the south suburb of Dolton now had black students in its classrooms. Some of those black students were outstanding athletes who played key roles in changing the landscape of Illinois sports history. Without desegregation, Thornridge would never have won a state basketball championship. Once the school integrated, Thornridge became a high school basketball power the likes of which Illinois had never seen.

CHAPTER 2

It All Was About Text Books

THORNRIDGE WAS FORTUNATE TO HAVE assembled such an outstanding collection of basketball talent. Fans around the state did not know that not a single one of the six players who saw regular playing time during Thornridge's perfect 1971-72 season would have attended the Dolton school if Mike Bonczyk's family had not moved into the district during the summer prior to his freshman year and had boundaries not been adjusted in the late 1960s and then changed again in the early '70s. The first boundary change led to the integration of previously all-white Thornridge High School and resulted in four talented basketball players being bused to Dolton from the tiny village of Phoenix. Quinn Buckner and Boyd Batts were part of just the second class of minority students to enter Thornridge in fall of 1968. Fellow Phoenix residents, Greg Rose and Bill Gatlin, came in the next year. Like Buckner and Batts, Rose was a starter on both of the Falcons' championship teams. Gatlin was the first player off the bench in the perfect 1971-72 season. The other starting player on the undefeated team, Ernie Dunn, came to Thornridge because of another boundary shift that went into effect starting with the 1971-72 school year. One can assume that without those two boundary changes and the Bonczyk family's move to South Holland, Thornridge would have won neither of the state championships it captured in 1971 and 1972. Gatlin, known as Nee to his friends, says it was quite a shock for the blacks from Phoenix to be bused to school in predominantly white Dolton.

"Phoenix, that community, it was predominantly black. 95%," recalls Gatlin. "You had Coolidge [Elementary in Phoenix] that was 95% black.

Now you go to Dolton or any of the schools in that area, Brother, you're talkin' about 99.9% white. Thornridge [High] was 99.9% white."

Gatlin recalls it was not an easy time for blacks or whites. Both were forced out of their comfort zones by desegregation.

"In the era of the Sixties, [Martin Luther] King had just got assassinated," remembers Gatlin. "The Kennedys had got assassinated. It was all kinds of marches and demonstrations and Civil Rights movements. The Vietnam War was going down. It was a hot era in America. Integration was a big thing too. There was a lot of hatred goin' on, especially when the leaders got assassinated. A lot of riots was goin' on in major cities."

Gatlin was a Coolidge Elementary student when MLK was killed. The ghetto on the west side of Chicago was one of the many urban areas across America torched in fury. In Chicago alone, eleven blacks died. Hundreds were injured, thousands arrested. As the 1970s began, things had improved, but only marginally. Americans were still dying in Viet Nam. Anti-war demonstrations continued on college campuses. The integration of schools was happening at such a slow pace that the U.S. Supreme Court unanimously ruled that busing of students may be *ordered* to achieve desegregation. Racial conflict remained in Chicago and throughout the country.

"So when we came together as one at Thornridge, sports brought everybody together," says Gatlin. "I know that for a fact."

Gatlin never dreamed that he would one day play a key role on the Thornridge basketball team. When the black children of Phoenix reached high school age, they attended Thornton High in Harvey. It had always been that way. It was where they were accepted. Blacks were not entirely welcome at Thornridge, the school that had opened its doors to students from the white neighborhoods of Dolton and South Holland in February of 1960. Attitudes would change, but it was a slow, painful process.

Quinn Buckner's parents, William and Jessica Buckner, were well-educated African-Americans who spent their adult lives as teachers. Growing up, Quinn attended Coolidge Elementary, where Mrs. Buckner taught for many years before becoming the school's Principal and eventually the first African-American Superintendent of Elementary School District 151. While teaching at Coolidge in the 1960s, Jessica Buckner wanted to see that her son and the other children in the primarily black school received a good education. Therefore, she was adamant that they received the same quality in the classroom that the white children were getting in the neighboring communities. Jessica Buckner came to realize that Coolidge students were being forced to learn from hand-me-down textbooks. The used textbooks likely came from a white school in the same school district. Mrs. Buckner remembers thinking that wasn't fair to the black children of Phoenix.

"We felt that the kids were not getting the things that they needed for a quality education at that time, and one thing led to the other," says 86-year old Jessica Buckner more than 40 years later. "There were hearings before the school board. There were hearings before the State Board of Ed. Over the years, we ended up with hearings with the Education Committee of the State Legislature. And then after that we went into court. We went into Federal Court."

The Buckners joined other Phoenix parents and marched in protest trying to force desegregation. The demonstrations produced results, but change did not come swiftly.

Kamala Buckner, William and Jessica's daughter, has for the past eleven years been the Superintendent of High School District 205. Since January of 1971, the district has consisted of three high schools, Thornridge, Thornton, and Thornwood. Like Elementary School District 151, High School District 205 was under great pressure to desegregate in the '60s.

"It was contentious," says Superintendent Buckner, who attended Thornton High during the desegregation debate. "All the children in Phoenix went to Coolidge. This was our K-through-8 experience. What occurred was our parents were taking a look at the text books that we had to utilize and realized that they came from another school. They were *used* books. We rarely got new books. It all was about the text books. It was not having equal access to quality materials that began to burn deeply into my mother's soul, but not only hers, also many other people within Phoenix."

She says with a chuckle, "I think one day some of them got angry and just said, 'We won't take it anymore.'"

Turning serious, Kamala Buckner adds, "So the actual activism began when some community members in Phoenix signed a petition and went to federal court to have School District 151 desegregate. A judge named Julius Hoffman forced the desegregation which was a very contentious piece [of legislation]."

Hoffman would gain national notoriety when he presided over the Chicago Seven trial following the protests at the 1968 Democratic National Convention. But before meeting Abbie Hoffman, the judge helped bring change to the south suburban schools. However, High School District 205 did not wait for Judge Hoffman's July of 1968 ruling in which he ordered the desegregation of Elementary School District 151. After years of heated debate, High School District 205 boundaries were altered in 1967. As a result, freshmen students from Phoenix were bused to Thornridge beginning with the 1967-68 academic year. Each year that followed, another freshmen class of minority students from Phoenix was bused to the Dolton high school.

"Within the community, they looked around and [saw that] Thornridge had not had any minorities," says Kamala Buckner. "I think the natural progression was, 'Okay [Phoenix students] should have a right to go to that school too.' The school board found a way to integrate the schools. It was not easy. It was '67 [when] the first group went in [to Thornridge], and that was very difficult on those young people. Then Quinn's class came in [the next year] and that was difficult on them."

Perhaps the school board sensed integration was inevitable so the Thornridge boundary lines were redrawn to include Phoenix. Or perhaps enlightened members of the school board understood integrating the high school was simply the right thing to do.

With 86 years of life experience, Jessica Buckner briefly considers that notion, then laughs and says, "I hope so, but you have to understand the prevailing wind at the time in America."

The battle between whites and blacks over desegregation in Elementary School District 151 had raged for years. A federal law had mandated that schools be integrated both in terms of students and teachers, but District 151 had remained segregated. Whites in South Holland and Dolton resisted desegregation. So, when the black students from Phoenix began attending Thornridge in the fall of 1967, the transition was not easy for anyone. Black and white students struggled to co-exist, and the situation was especially traumatic for those white residents who had fought long and hard to keep blacks out of Thornridge High.

"When they made the change it was a culture shock for South Holland and Dolton," says former Thornridge basketball coach Ron Ferguson. "Dolton was a working, labor union [town], but they were very prejudiced. They didn't want the blacks in there any more than the man in the moon. In those days, if you were black and you lived in that community, you were harassed. South Holland didn't have any [black residents]. South Holland was a little more upscale property-wise. Dolton was very, very unreceptive [to minorities]. They loved the basketball team, but they were glad [the blacks] lived in Phoenix and didn't come [to Dolton]. I was surprised to see how so many people felt."

Ferguson, who had coached the Falcons since the school opened in 1960, remembers an ugly incident that occurred during the early years of integration at Thornridge.

"Somebody came out with, I don't know if they were posters, flyers, or handouts," recalls the coach. "But they put on there, 'The Thornridge Fal-COONS'. The Fal-COONS! That really upset the people in Phoenix. It was just uncalled for. I can't remember if they ever found out who did that, or why they did it, but it was just ridiculous. I didn't want to make a big fuss. A lot of people probably didn't see it, and [there was] no sense calling anybody else's attention to it. I tried to downplay it somewhat and not make a big deal out of it [even] as much as it bothered me."

Nee Gatlin remembers emotions ran high during the early days of integration at Thornridge High.

"Man, when we initially went there, our parents used to have to ride the bus," says Gatlin. "It got so bad, police had to protect us."

It was indeed a shock for those basketball players from Phoenix who now played for Thornridge after once dreaming of playing basketball for Thornton High. Thornton had a storied tradition. Baseball Hall of Famer Lou Boudreau had played basketball at Thornton and helped the Wildcats win a state basketball championship in 1933. Boudreau and Thornton also played and lost in the 1934 and 1935 finals. The Wildcats also dropped the 1961 championship game before capturing the school's second state title in 1966.

As youngsters, Nee Gatlin, Quinn Buckner, Boyd Batts, and Greg Rose shot baskets on the outdoor courts in Phoenix and fantasized about playing for the Thornton Wildcats. But as high school students, they were being bused to Thornridge and asked to represent a school that did not seem to want them. Buckner admits he and the others had to overcome disappointment when they first learned they would not be going to Thornton.

"It was where the balance of the people you grew up with [attended high school]," says Buckner. "We all thought about going to Thornton. [But, the decision to send us to Thornridge] wasn't nearly as much of a problem for me because my mother was involved [in the effort to desegregate the schools]. I got the sense it was coming, so I had more time to deal with it."

However, Buckner remembers the other players from Phoenix were unhappy about having to attend Thornridge where they were harassed by some of the white students.

"Sure they were," he says. "I didn't know about how narrow-minded people could be. My ignorance actually helped me. I wasn't as concerned about it."

One of Buckner's friends was concerned. He didn't know how Quinn and Boyd would handle the move to Thornridge.

"I think it was a bit disappointing because of not knowing how they would adjust to the racial change and playing with white kids instead of playing with black kids," says Boyd's older brother Lloyd, who as a senior was named the 1970 Illinois High School Player of the Year.

"Would he be able to fit in?" Lloyd Batts remembers wondering about Quinn. "He had only been coached by a black coach in the community he grew up in. Every time when he went to play, he always played against the black kids until he started playin' at Thornridge."

Many whites in Dolton and South Holland had made it quite clear that they wanted blacks to stay in Phoenix or Harvey. The black Thornridge players generally observed the unwritten rule. Yet, their presence in the white neighborhoods could not always be avoided. Gatlin recalls one occasion when the black players were forced to race home on foot after a practice lasted longer than expected. The experience went from terrifying to comical.

"I remember a time we missed the bus after practice," laughs Gatlin. "From Dolton to Phoenix was approximately six miles. Man, we was runnin' through [white] neighborhoods takin' shortcuts. [House] lights was clickin' on. People was chasin' us. As we was runnin' Boyd was lookin' back, and when he turned around, he got *clotheslined* by a clothesline! We [were] in a backyard laughin' hard. All these lights [were] clickin' on, man. We got up and run some more. It was one of those eras. It was just that time."

Boyd Batts remembers that journey homeward and says with a laugh, "We were runnin' so fast. I turned around, and I turned back around just in time to hit the clothesline, and [I] flipped over. I got up and said, 'Let's get on home, man.'"

Terry Wells is now the Mayor of Phoenix, the village in which he was raised. Wells, an African-American, says those Phoenix kids had to endure plenty of hardship before eventually gaining acceptance once they achieved success in sports.

"If you've seen the Disney movie [Remember the Titans] with Denzel Washington, they could have made that movie about Thornridge," says Wells. "You bused these kids into an environment, and the white kids were there and the white coaches and everything. These black kids came in, and there were some issues. There was turmoil, but what turned it all around was athletics. Suddenly this anger and this hostility, it all kind of went out a window with this team."

Buckner says he learned a lot about life from his time at Thornridge.

"What I learned very simply was how sports could galvanize people when they have a common goal," says Buckner.

"I think he's accurate there," says Thornridge coach Ron Ferguson. "It was tough for some of those guys to come to Thornridge to begin with. They grew up loving Thornton. They had the tradition at Thornton."

A realist, Ferguson knows Thornridge would never have won a state championship if the school district had not changed the boundaries to make students from Phoenix a part of Thornridge High School.

"If they had never changed the boundaries, Thornton might have won three or four state championships in that time," says Ferguson. "If Buckner had been there with Lloyd Batts, and Boyd Batts, and some of the other good players that Thornton had, I mean, they had a *ton* of them. If you put all those guys together for about four or five years, they would have been just a super power. But it worked out [at Thornridge], and eventually [the minorities] were well accepted by the community and everything. But it wasn't easy for them."

It was initially quite a challenge for that small group of black teens from Phoenix, but it certainly turned out to be rewarding. While starring for Thornridge, Buckner, Batts, and Rose defeated Thornton three times during the 1970-71 championship season. Then in 1971-72, the Falcons beat their chief rival three more times. The Thornridge basketball program no longer took a back seat to tradition-rich Thornton.

Once the Falcons began winning state championships in basketball and football, there was a drastic change in attitude at Thornridge High. No longer were the black student-athletes from Phoenix disparagingly called the "Thornridge Fal-COONS." They were the "Falcons", accepted and respected by basketball fans black and white.

CHAPTER 3

A Man Among Boys

BASKETBALL FANS ACROSS AMERICA KNEW of LeBron James long before he reached the NBA. LeBron was a prep legend even before several of his high school games were nationally televised (on ESPN and ESPN2). James was on the cover of Sports Illustrated while a junior in high school and he was featured on SportsCenter in the days leading up to his nationally televised games.

Thornridge star Quinn Buckner might have received similar attention had he been born one generation later. Buckner was the Lebron James of the early 1970s. In December of 1971 Buckner appeared on the cover of *Letterman* magazine. The national publication named the six-three, 200 pound Buckner the National High School Athlete of the Year. It was no contest. Buckner was All-America in both basketball and football. He was considered to be a man among boys. Buckner's thick body was ripped with muscles. His wide shoulders and huge thighs looked like they might have belonged to an NFL running back. As a result of his impressive physique and athletic accomplishments, most sports fans in Chicago and throughout Illinois knew Quinn Buckner.

In the early 1970s, it was not easy for a high school player to gain notoriety outside of his local area. There was no ESPN. Instant access of information via the internet was still decades away. Nobody knew much about the players outside of their respective regions. In many cases, college basketball recruiters did not even know if a player was black or white. College scouts had to attend games to see if potential recruits were as good as advertised. At the time, there was no VHS or Beta Max tape. The first videotape and video recorders were reel-to-reel, and the relatively new technology was considered a luxury few high schools could afford. Many schools shot silent black & white film of their games so the coach could determine what his players needed to practice.

It was hard to find news about high school basketball players in the early 1970s. A few national sports magazines compiled lists of the premier players in the country, but the names were often accompanied by only the player's height, year in school, and town in which he lived. Local newspapers provided the best and most consistent coverage of high school basketball and the standout players in the region. If a prep player hoped to drum up interest from college recruiters, he might have mailed out some of his newspaper clippings. Today, players can post edited video highlights of themselves on My Space, You Tube, or Facebook.

High school recruiting services were in their infancy at the time Thornridge was rolling to back-to-back state championships. Unlike today, high school players in the early 1970s did not travel around the country all summer competing on AAU teams. Players generally were known only in the region in which they established their reputations by representing their high school teams in the winter months. Even so, most college coaches in America were familiar with the name Quinn Buckner. Buckner was the 1971 Player of the Year in basketball-mad Illinois. He would receive the same recognition in 1972.

Buckner's basketball skills were considerable, but his greatest asset was his ability to lead. At Thornridge, he led an extremely talented group of players. Each of the five starters on the 1971-72 Thornridge basketball team could handle the basketball. Coach Ron Ferguson has always said that was one of the keys to the Falcons' success. Just as important, though, were each player's unique abilities and character traits. Blended together the Thornridge players formed the consummate team.

Six-one junior guard Ernie Dunn, an extremely intelligent young man and an outstanding athlete, was willing to sacrifice his own game in order to fit in with the established Thornridge players. A capable offensive performer, Dunn became a defensive stopper once he realized there was little need for him to be a big scorer.

Five-ten senior point guard Mike Bonczyk was the playmaker. The only white starter on the Thornridge team, Bonczyk was a wizard with the basketball and preferred the dazzling pass to the ordinary. Bonczyk also played with the good of the team as his top priority. He often passed up open shots to give the ball to teammates that he knew had a more desperate need to score.

Six-three junior forward Greg Rose was one of those who loved to get his touches at the offensive end. The most athletic player on the team, Rose was an offensive machine, capable of scoring inside the paint or from the perimeter. More importantly, he was the point man defensively on the Falcons' tenacious 1-2-1-1 full court press. Few teams had anyone who could match up physically with Rose.

If any Falcon loved shooting the ball more than Rose, it was senior center Boyd Batts. Batts had grown to six-seven over the summer giving the Falcons an athletic and extraordinarily gifted player with the size to compete against the state's other top big men. When he put his mind to it, Batts could dominate at both ends of the floor. A talented shot blocker on defense, Batts was the Falcons' chief inside threat on offense. A former guard converted to center because of his size, Batts could also shoot effectively from the perimeter. However, Batts was a true enigma. He sometimes lost focus on and off the court. He was a free spirit and in his early years at Thornridge had been rebellious. His teammates were aware Boyd could be led astray.

The person who took it upon himself to keep Batts on the same page with his teammates was senior Quinn Buckner, a 17-year old whose understanding of the game was exceeded only by his maturity and understanding of the ways of the world. Buckner was the one Thornridge basketball player who commanded the respect of his classmates on and off the court.

"The thing that gave me credibility [was] my mother and father," says Buckner. "At Coolidge my mother taught Boyd, myself, all of [the players from Phoenix]. So they knew where I came from. They knew, generally speaking, that I was on the *right* side of right and wrong. That's how I really became somewhat the leader of the team. It was easy to follow me because I wasn't putting it to the test, because in those days you got corporal punishment from the teacher, then my mother [while still] in school. Then I'd get it when I got home."

"I had no interest in that *at all*," laughs Buckner. "So they knew if they stayed and hung out with me they weren't going to get in trouble because *I* wasn't going to get in trouble."

"He just kept them playing basketball all the time." says Quinn's mother Jessica Buckner. "They did not get too far afield because he could always figure out how they would get out on a court and play basketball. That was pretty much what kept them going. And I think they looked up to Quinn because they knew Quinn's parents were backing him."

Nee Gatlin acknowledges that the players knew they would stay out of trouble if they followed their teammate's lead.

"Quinn's parents were educators." says Gatlin. "It was kind of difficult for him not to do what he was supposed to do in school. That direction was a lot more scrutinized in his house than in mine. I don't know if you heard about him, but Mister Buckner was a big ol' dude, man. That was a big man."

"Oh, that's putting it mildly," laughs Quinn's sister Kamala. "He was about five-eleven and probably 300 pounds, a former football player at college. He was an absolute no-nonsense, take-no-prisoners kind of person. He did not believe that you were supposed to quit. [He felt] under any adversity, you are to stand. [His philosophy was] don't say you want to start something and then [you] do not finish it. But to balance that was my mother who was just absolutely adamant that 'C' was not good enough [in school], so you better find a 'B' and an 'A' to remain on a team. My father's point was you were *gonna* remain on the team, so you were kind of like in a vice. You *had* to make grades because you *had* to stay on the team, because either *one* of them, or *both* of them, would create havoc in your world."

Coach Ron Ferguson remembers thinking William and Jessica Buckner were a terrific one-two punch in terms of parenting.

"She was kind of a spokesperson," says Ferguson. "The dad was one of those guys who would just fold his arms over his chest. He was short on a lot of words, but when he did speak, [his words] meant something."

Gatlin was not the only one of Quinn's teammates who was intimidated by the head of the Buckner household. Ernie Dunn spent a lot of time in the Buckner home. Dunn says the players made sure to act properly when William Buckner was around.

"Oh yeah, his dad, Mister Buckner, was mean," remembers Dunn. "You know, let's put it this way. He had a mean demeanor. But when you talked to him, he's okay as long as you're stayin' within limits and you're doin' the right thing. He didn't have tolerance for people that didn't want to do right or wasn't going to school. He didn't want Quinn around those kinds of people either. They definitely protected Quinn, which is what I would do too if I had a son."

Boyd Batts laughed when told Dunn had been scared of Mister Buckner. Although Boyd was eight inches taller, he was intimidated by William Buckner.

"Me too, yeah, me too," says Batts. "No joke. He was a big fella. See it's different today. When we grew up, if one of them parents saw us out there doin' something wrong, we'd get a whippin' from them."

"Yes, most of the fellas would come in [and say], 'Hello Mister Buckner.' and try to *move* out [of] his way," remembers Kamala Buckner. "No, he did not play [around]. [But he was] very respectful. He loved them. He made sure we ate [with the players] and gave them milk. He did all those things, but he [was] old-school. He was in World War II, so he was an old military guy."

Quinn believes his disciplinarian father was tough on the Buckner children because he was preparing them for a challenging life in a nation that continued to be slow to accept minorities.

"My dad was very demanding, but he was fair," says Buckner. "He's a former athlete that had played [football] at Indiana. In retrospect, God rest his soul, he was about making sure I was going to be a good man --- a good, tough man. He knew how difficult it was going to be in society, so he was about making me just a tough, tough guy."

Since the players understood Quinn would not lead them astray off or on the court, Buckner was the team's glue. With due respect to the coaching staff, the person perhaps most responsible for keeping the Falcons on task and making sure they won each game was Buckner. Coach Ron Ferguson acknowledges Buckner deserves credit for keeping things together when times were tough.

"In the first place, they all respected him. He was big enough he could have whipped any one of them if he had to," laughs Ferguson. "He was such a good leader in every way. On the floor, he was a leader. Off the floor, he was a leader. And his mom and dad helped. He comes from a well-educated and a well-organized and disciplined family."

The Buckners also provided a sense of family for the players who did not have ideal home situations. Boyd Batts and Greg Rose were among the players who benefitted from the thoughtfulness of Mr. and Mrs. Buckner. The Buckners treated each of the players as their own. They gave Quinn's friends food to eat and comforted them in times of distress.

"Well, I really felt that I needed to be there for my own [kids] when they would get bad," chuckles Jessica Buckner. "I just kind of felt that I would be there for the kids, you know, in particular for my own. I felt then, and I feel now, that parents need to be involved with their children and help them with whatever experiences they're having. Since both of us were teachers, we were aware of that, and we championed our kids and any of the others that were there with us. It wasn't one of those overt kinds of things. It just happened."

Kamala Buckner remembers Quinn and her family tending to the needs of the other Thornridge players.

"Quinn was very protective of his teammates," says Kamala. "He was always [their] big brother. He once said, 'Man, are you eating? Come on by the house. Don't forget to eat before the game.' I remember I used to go into the kitchen and go, 'Who [are] these people Mom?' She goes, 'I'm feeding the team. Just go on to your room.' We always had that. That's the spirit [we received] from my father. My father always believed that you would help young people because they're our future, and they're our neighbors, and that's what you do."

"They had individual [bad] situations, but basically they [were] all good," says Jessica Buckner. "They were good kids. They really were."

No one ever questioned the character of young Quinn Buckner. Quinn received countless accolades for his athletic accomplishments while in high school, yet he kept his ego in check. His mother saw to it that the pride of Thornridge kept his head out of the clouds and his feet on solid ground.

"Well, I could always say, 'Quinn, it's your time to take the garbage out.'" laughs Jessica Buckner.

Continuing to laugh, she adds, "He never got too big for *that* now. He had to do what he had to do."

Quinn listened and obeyed when his parents issued marching orders. Buckner was mature beyond his years, and the maturity was clearly evident when he was on the basketball court. Blessed with a terrific understanding of the intricacies of the game, Buckner didn't care which of his teammates scored or got the newspaper headlines. Winning the game was the only thing that mattered to Quinn. In typical Buckner fashion, he always credited his teammates for their roles in a victory and downplayed his own contributions.

"No, no, he never wanted attention," says his mother. "He had some soul-searching to do when he went on to Indiana, and they became quite good and in the press all the time. It just was not his thing. He was good at what he did, and he enjoyed it, but he didn't want any fanfare with it."

That personal philosophy would help make Buckner one of the most successful players of all time. Buckner played on winning teams throughout his career. He is one of only three players in the history of basketball (along with Hall of Famers Jerry Lucas and Magic Johnson) to have won championships at every level, in high school, college, the

Olympics, and the NBA. His teams won in no small part because he did whatever necessary to prevent his teams from losing. One of the original "Play them one at a time" guys, Buckner says he made sure to never look beyond the next game on the schedule.

"It becomes a mindset," explains Buckner. "It's a mindset where success breeds success. It's not arrogance. [Success] just breeds [success]. You just try to do whatever you can to carry it forward. All I know is we got a game, and I'm tryin' to win it. It's the one we got, and I'm tryin' to win it. To prepare for our championship series in high school and college, it was all the same to me. We got a game. The next game is the game we gotta win. That's all I know. That's all I care about. It's funny about my athletic career. I've always played 'em that way. [I] never cared who the opposition was. If the opposition didn't have on the same colored jersey I had, I was trying to do whatever I could do to make them *not* be able to do what they wanted to do."

"You know it's weird to have this conversation," chuckles Buckner. After pausing for three full seconds he says, "I hadn't lost. Honestly. I hadn't lost. I didn't know how to lose. All I knew is that if it didn't work, you worked harder at it. If it wasn't working, you figure out a way to work harder at it. If *that* didn't work, you figure out how to work *smarter* at it. My dad was always a big one [to say] 'Son, now work harder, work smarter.' So that's what I always tried to do. My first year of high school as a freshman I played [on the] sophomore [team], and I think we lost seven games. I think I lost five games on varsity as a sophomore, and I lost one game after that [as a junior and senior]. My high school and college careers were comparable in terms of wins and losses. Seriously, I don't think I lost more than thirty games in the eight years [of playing high school and college basketball]."

Hall of Fame basketball coach Bob Knight, who recruited Buckner and convinced him to play at Indiana University, says the thing he most admired about Quinn was his ability to lead his team to victory game after game.

"Yeah, what he wanted to do was *win*," says Knight. "What we got him for [at Indiana] was to *win*. And that's what he did."

After leading his high school team to consecutive state titles, Buckner played four years for Knight at Indiana. In his senior season with the Hoosiers in 1976, Buckner co-captained the most recent undefeated NCAA Division One champion. Buckner won a gold medal playing for Team USA in the 1976 Olympics. He won an NBA championship ring with the Boston Celtics in 1984. Those who saw Buckner in high school remember the physically-mature Buckner as a man among boys. His college coach, who won more games than any men's basketball coach in NCAA Division One history, says Buckner's impressive physique was not his best attribute.

"Don't get carried away with the fact that he was a man among boys," says Bob Knight, now a college basketball studio analyst on ESPN. "You know he was six-two, six-three at the most, [and] weighed 195 pounds. There are a lot of kids like that. Where he was a man among boys was the way he *thought,* and the way he handled himself on the floor, and the things that he brought to the game that maybe only he and I understood. That's where he was a man among boys."

"Buckner was the best player I've ever coached at making sure that what I wanted done on the court got done," says Knight, before adding a qualifier, "With maybe the exception of Mike Krzyzewski. But they were the two best."

Those who saw Buckner play at Thornridge High School remember him as the total package. Knight was more impressed with his intelligence and understanding of the game, but Buckner was always more mature-looking than his peers. It created problems at times.

"It got to a point for Quinn," says Quinn's sister Kamala, "particularly in elementary school we used to have to take his birth certificate with us to prove to people his age. Because he was such a mature athlete, they just wouldn't *believe* when he was twelve, or wouldn't *believe* when he was fourteen, or wouldn't *believe* when he was fifteen. In fact, I think they had to do that when he was in high school."

Quinn learned the subtleties of basketball from his father while quite young. His sister says Quinn was always hanging around with their dad watching games on television.

"My father tells the story," says Kamala, who is four years older than Quinn. "They were out rakin' leaves, and all of a sudden Quinn starts doin' these flips, flips, flips. My father looks at him and goes, 'Well, he's an athlete. I need to redirect his energy or he's gonna hurt himself.' It was at that point they would sit down in front of the TV, and Daddy would talk him through the game. It was just amazing how they would tear a particular game apart. When you're young, you want to be with your dad anyhow, [jumping] all over his head [and] in his lap, so you were going to listen. You're a sponge. Yes, our father taught the game and taught the game from a point of intelligence."

Kamala Buckner believes those instructional sessions between father and son laid the groundwork for Quinn to become one of the game's most cerebral players.

"Usually some of your smartest athletes can be better than most natural athletes because they'll stop and think the game through," she says. "Quinn was really brilliant. He understood the game."

It was that understanding of the game that allowed Buckner to do whatever his coach asked him to do for the benefit of the team. That was true when he played for Ron Ferguson in high school and true when playing for Coach Knight at Indiana.

"I was in tune [with Knight]," says Buckner. "I absolutely trusted him. [Knight is] a hell of a coach but just a great *man*. I trusted him. I knew he knew what he was talking about. I knew his motives were pure. I knew the guys would have trouble trying to deal with him sometimes. It was different than Coach Ferguson, but it was [somewhat] the same. This is where I was very fortunate. Anytime you work with good people, you can give, and this was my nature. You could give whole heartedly, completely. So, whatever it took to help them get what they needed in order for us to be successful, that's what I tried to do. I always wanted to be a person that could play with whatever combination of people you put on the floor. I listened more intently to make sure I understood the purpose of whatever it was we were doing, so [that] if somebody wasn't doing it, I wasn't guessing at what the coach wanted done. I *knew* what coach wanted done, because I listened. I wanted to be prepared to play with any and every body."

It is clear that the male authority figures in his life were extremely important to Quinn. His desire to please Coach Ferguson and Coach Knight was exceeded only by his intense desire to please his father. Quinn looked to his dad for guidance whenever he needed a voice of reason. William Buckner played a key behind-the-scenes role when tension between blacks and whites boiled over at Thornridge High School during Quinn's junior year. Coach Ferguson remembers the ugly incident.

"They were trying to get blacks into cheerleading for basketball," recalls Ferguson. "A lot of the blacks had a [protest] march. Michael Henry, a basketball player, was in on it. His sister was one of that ones that wanted [to cheer]. I'm not so sure she eventually didn't make the cheerleading squad. It was a real [bad situation]. They suspended a lot of [black] students, and they suspended a lot of white students too. The [white students] were harassing the blacks who were protesting. [Authorities] were trying to prevent having a free for all, so it wasn't easy."

Henry was suspended from school for a time for walking out of school to demonstrate his support for his sister. Other Thornridge basketball players considered joining the walkout, but Buckner calmed his teammates after receiving sound advice from his dad.

"My father helped me understand at a fairly early age, that I could be able to deal with this stuff and help my teammates, my friends, deal with it," recalls Buckner. "[Henry's sister] Rowena should have made the cheerleading team. She was clearly good enough to make the team. The walkout was because there were no black cheerleaders. I was having a conversation with my father, and he said, 'Quinn, not only can you *NOT* walk out, you can't let your teammates do that.' He was very adamant about that because he knows the stigma that's attached to that. My dad was educated, but he also had great street sense."

Buckner remembers there was at least one player who might have considered joining Henry in protest.

"The one guy that could have potentially done it would have been Boyd," says Buckner. "Boyd had the most difficult family life of any of us. I knew Michael Henry was strong-willed, but I didn't realize how strong-willed until that happened. But if Boyd walks out, we really got a bad situation."

Quinn realized he needed to act to keep Batts from following Henry in the walkout.

"[I had] that ability," says Buckner, "to be able to talk to those guys and say, 'Hey, I'm not doin' it. I am *not* doing that.' I just told them, 'My daddy will *KILL* me.' I didn't have a real inkling to do it anyway, but it was because my father had been so adamant about not doing it, I had an excuse not to do it."

Quinn's mother shared with her husband the belief that walking out of school to protest the lack of black representation on the cheerleading squad was not something Quinn or his teammates should do.

"No, that was not the way to go," says Jessica Buckner nearly four decades after Mike Henry led the walkout. "I mean, you have to pick your hill to die on, and at that time, that was not the way to go. Those children had good intentions, but unfortunately, they didn't have any adults that were helping them come to deal with that. Of course, with me, I was family first. I had to make sure that my family was on the right path."

Quinn's father also played a key role in helping his son cope with his first real taste of racism at Thornridge. Heading into his sophomore year, Quinn was practicing with the varsity football team. Everyone assumed that he would be on the squad when the season started. Most agreed Buckner was more talented than the other players at his position. The previous season a sophomore player had made the jump to the varsity. Buckner assumed that he would likewise make the varsity. However, there was a difference. The sophomore who made the varsity team the previous season was white.

"The week before the season started I was told I didn't make the team," says Buckner. "I effectively quit football for a week. This is one of the lessons I learned. My dad stayed on me every day about why I was quitting. He gave me all of the logic, sound as it was. [He said], 'Quit now [and] it's easier the next time. Don't let people take your spirit.' So I kept asking him, 'Why didn't I make it?' My dad told me the head coach of the football team told him that the community was not ready for a black player to be moved up [to the varsity as a sophomore]."

Although 40 years have passed, the pain is still evident in Buckner's voice as he continues, "I was either 14 or 15 years old. That was my first experience, my first personal experience with that. But my parents were both college educated. What my dad kept telling me was, 'The people that think that way will take your spirit.' So that really drove me. It drives me to this day."

Jessica Buckner remembers Quinn feeling the emotional sting, but says he did not let it take his spirit.

"Quinn took it pretty well," says his loving mother. "I know that he had instances where people said and did things that hurt him. But he took it pretty well."

"It doesn't matter about the racial issues," Quinn says philosophically. "It's about people who don't care for you for some reason. People don't like you because you're too short [or] you're too tall, the whole nine yards. [It's important] not to let somebody take your spirit. It was a life lesson that happened to be at *that* time which was a turbulent time obviously. [It was an incident] that happened to be racially motivated."

Quinn was extremely close to his father who passed away in 1986. For many years, Buckner had even shared his dad's name. His first two years at Thornridge High School, William Quinn Buckner was known to the media as Bill Buckner. But prior to the start of his junior year, in a sign of his growing independence, Buckner had Coach Ferguson tell the media that he wanted to be known by his middle name, the name his friends called him.

Buckner had become one of the best high school basketball players in the country. He also was an incredible football player who utilized his athleticism to dominate on the gridiron. In his last two years of high school football, Buckner returned kicks 85, 86, and 89 yards for touchdowns. Also while playing safety on defense he had 69, 88, and 95 yard interception-returns for scores. He led his conference in scoring one season while playing primarily on defense. Success on the football field and the basketball court helped Buckner and the other minority students gain acceptance from the whites at Thornridge High and in Dolton and South Holland. The barrier between the blacks and whites began to break down after Buckner led the Thornridge football team to a mythical 1970 state championship. There were no postseason football playoffs in Illinois at that time, but after finishing undefeated, Buckner and the Falcons were voted the number one team in the state. When Quinn led the Thornridge basketball team to its first state championship the following winter, attitudes about Buckner and the other student-athletes from Phoenix dramatically changed at Thornridge.

"Yes, they were accepted because of that," says Quinn's mother. "They were accepted and revered because of their winning in athletics."

Even so, Jessica Buckner knows it wasn't always easy for Quinn. She believes her son and his black friends had been subjected to racist name-calling.

"I am sure that they were," says Mrs. Buckner. "But they didn't tell me because that kind of went with the territory. They handled it."

Buckner could have played football or basketball for any college in the country. Indiana offered him the chance to play both sports. National power UCLA wanted him but only to play basketball. Legendary Bruins' basketball coach John Wooden never saw Buckner play in person but was interested in bringing the young Buckner to Westwood.

"Wooden wrote me and said, 'We don't recruit unless somebody really wants to come here and they write us first,'" remembers Thornridge coach Ron Ferguson. "I wrote him a letter and said I think he's interested."

Wooden recalls setting up a meeting with Buckner to see if the Thornridge star was serious about wanting to become a UCLA Bruin.

"I never initiated contact with any recruit," says the Hall of Fame coach, who turned 99 in October of 2009. "Even [Lew] Alcindor (later known as Kareem Abdul-Jabbar), I never initiated [contact]. Their coach or someone initiated for them showing an interest. Quinn's coach had called me. He knew I was being back there [in the Midwest] for something, and

[he] told me about Quinn. Of course, I had heard about him. So they arranged to meet me in the airport in Chicago while I was changing planes. I visited with him there, and I liked him personally. I'd already found out he was a good student [and that] he would be able to meet our entrance requirements. I definitely would have liked to [have] had him."

Wooden, whose UCLA teams had at that time won six consecutive national championships and eight of the last nine, nearly always had his choice of any player in the nation. Yet he could sense that he would not be able to convince Buckner to play for the Bruins.

"I liked him very much as a person and obviously he was an outstanding athlete," remembers Wooden. "I was very impressed. [But] I wanted him to *want* to come [to UCLA]. I didn't want to have to talk to him [to convince him]. I got the impression just from that one short time that he was going to go to Indiana, and [that was] probably because of the parents. I don't know that, but that was just the feeling that I had."

Wooden's analysis of Quinn's relative lack of interest in UCLA was right on the mark. Jessica Buckner remembers meeting Wooden that day at the airport. Quinn's mother laughs heartily when told that Wooden had a good idea that Quinn would attend Indiana.

"Yes, I was there," laughs Jessica Buckner. "[And] ultimately [Indiana is] where he ended up. He was recruited several places, but evidently that is where his father was quietly steering him all the time."

William Buckner definitely had strong feelings about where he wanted his oldest son to go to college. Quinn's brother, Lorin, was two years younger and still developing as an athlete. His athletic future was yet to be determined. But Mr. Buckner made it clear that he wanted Quinn to play football and basketball at Indiana University. It was, therefore, a momentous occasion when Coach Bob Knight, shortly after completing his first season at Indiana, showed up at the Buckner home to try to convince Quinn to sign with the Hoosiers.

"I was there when we first met him," remembers Jessica Buckner. "But I let my husband do most of the talking and assessing what he thought would be best for Quinn. We do have to recognize that Quinn's father graduated from Indiana University. Although Quinn might have wanted to go to some other places, and I kind of thought he might go someplace else, his father very quietly steered him to where he wanted him to be. [His father] thought it would be best for him. At that time Coach Knight was just starting out. He was recruiting, and he was recruiting someone who tended not to create havoc, you know? And that was the kind of person Quinn was."

Quinn remembers a young Knight coming to his house to talk with him and his parents.

"Oh, yeah, I remember it because my dad, God rest his soul, Man, my father was a trip," laughs Quinn. "We have this small house in Phoenix. First of all, my mother kind of figured out pretty early that Coach Knight was going to be all right. My mother is the one that Coach sold. That's what Coach is good at. He sold my mother. Basically, Coach has to sell [parents] that [he is] gonna take care of their kid."

Quinn remembers his father having a long conversation with Knight. The talk lasted into the evening.

"My dad and I were sitting there, [and] my dad would talk," remembers Quinn. "We used to have this chair, and we had an oblong ottoman that my dad always used to turn on its oblong side, and [he would lean forward and] put his elbows on it. Coach Knight reminds me that we sat there 'til it was almost dark in there."

Quinn, laughing so hard he can barely continue, says, "My dad and I are both dark complected, so Coach Knight almost couldn't see my father 'cause it's dark, and we won't turn on a light. My dad was like that. He wouldn't turn on the light [because] he was comfortable."

Quinn once told reporters that he had seriously considered signing with Michigan. However, when it came time to sign on the dotted line, he signed to attend Indiana where he would play for Coach Knight.

"Here's the thing that will surprise you." says Knight. "I never saw them play. I'd seen films of *him* play. I knew he was going to be very good. He wasn't a kid that was a great scorer or great shooter, but he was a tremendous addition to a team from a *mental* standpoint. He was a very tough kid and a very smart kid."

Knight says while he never asked Buckner to be a big scorer, Quinn was able to contribute at both ends of the court.

"He had to adjust from the standpoint of scoring and shooting, and he was able to do that," says Knight. "But he was such a good player defensively that he created a lot of offense out of his defensive play. He could rebound. He really wasn't a guard. He was a really good *player*. He could do a little bit of everything. Then on top of that, he really got done on the floor what you have to have somebody do. Very often, you don't have somebody that can do that."

"By the same token Coach says he never saw me play," says Quinn, "I never saw Coach *coach* either. I had no idea what I was getting into. I had absolutely no idea that he was the way he was until I got there. Truthfully, I don't know if scared is the word, but it took me aback. Coach Ferguson didn't coach that way. Every now and then [Ferguson] would get ticked off. Coach Knight *stayed* at peak [intensity] level. That's how he was trying to get us to practice because that's the way you gotta play. That was the difference."

Although Quinn played basketball for Knight, William Buckner made sure Quinn also played football for the Hoosiers. Quinn played two years of football in Bloomington, but then made a decision to stop. According to legend, Buckner gave up football after Knight advised him to make a choice between the two sports. The story is true, but Quinn says there are details that not everyone has been aware of until now.

"Here's the story," says Quinn. "We were 2 and 9 my first year under John Pont. We were 1 and 10 under Lee Corso my second year. We played at either Ohio State or Michigan [my sophomore year]. It was one of those teams. I don't remember which one. We were playing in the game, and it becomes apparent to me that I'm playin' the wrong game because they play for real, and I got my brains beat out. [As a punt returner], I got a punt that hung, and when punts hang, you're gonna get creamed, and they blitzed me."

Even before Buckner had his bell rung, he had already considered giving up the sport.

"I wasn't going to play [football] my sophomore year," says Buckner. "I was literally in Bloomington and not going to play. I remember walking down [the aisle of] a Krogers [store] on the east side of Bloomington and my dad saying, 'You got a new coach. Give him a chance.' And I gave in because my dad was a football player. He wanted me to play. As you can tell, I have a great respect and love [for] my father. So I played. But I knew after this one game [I got creamed that I was done]."

"I told him, 'Daddy, Buckners don't quit, right?' He says, 'Right.'"

"I said, 'Daddy,' and I said it like this," his voice dropping to a near whisper. "Daddy, I don't *quit*, but I'm not playing anymore either. I'm not playing after this year.'"

"So I had effectively made up my mind during the season," Quinn continues. "What I did not do is tell anybody. [Former Indiana teammate] Scott May is one of my dear friends, and we were roommates. I was closer to Scott at IU than anybody, but I never said a word to him."

While he didn't share his secret with anyone at Indiana, Quinn's actions on the field made it rather obvious to some that he no longer desired to play football. His high school basketball coach remembers travelling to Bloomington to watch Buckner play football for the Hoosiers. Ron Ferguson came away with the impression that Quinn seemed anxious for basketball season to begin.

"I went over to a game, and he was back catching a punt," says Ferguson with a laugh. "He caught the punt, and he couldn't wait to get out of bounds. I think it was close to the end of the season and he wanted to make sure he was making it to basketball [season]."

Buckner finally completes the story about talking with Knight and making a decision to give up football.

"Later, we play a basketball game, and we either lose or come close to losing to Toledo or one of those mid-majors in Ohio," recalls Quinn. "I think we're headed to play Michigan. Coach is miffed. He brought me to the front of the plane."

"We talked about it," says Buckner. "Then [Coach] finally said, 'You know, as long as you play football and basketball you'll be good at both. But as long as you play football and basketball, you'll never be *great* at either one.' He never forced me to make a decision in that regard. It wasn't like 'Choose football or basketball.' It was basically 'Choose what you want to be' which is what any father or surrogate father should tell anybody. That's what he did."

Quinn continues, "You know [Coach Knight said], 'What do you want to be? Do you want to be good? You'll be good at both, but you'll never be great at either as long as you're doin' both.' The guy is a genius. You cannot tell a kid anything any better than that. The kid has to make a decision."

Interestingly, Buckner never told Knight he had already decided to stop playing football.

"I'll never forget it. I was on that airplane, but I didn't tell him I had made up my mind [to quit football]," says Buckner. "I don't know why it was I wouldn't tell him that day, but I never said anything to him. I just listened to what he said. But I had already made up my mind."

Buckner ultimately experienced most of his success on the basketball court. He is understandably proud of having won championships at every level of the sport. Although he is hesitant to admit it, he is also proud that as time passed, people better understood the sacrifices he made so that his teams could be successful.

"I just had one of my teammates who said the most interesting thing to me," says Buckner. "He said, 'I came to realize that what you did was never about you.' That's really what I was hoping everyone understood. It was never about me. It was about us winning a game. I don't care what jersey you got on. If you got on my jersey, okay, we're all right. But if you don't, I'm trying to do everything I can to beat you. This goes back to my dad again. My ability [was] to understand and translate and share with people. My dad knew that that's a form of leadership. I didn't know what the heck it was. I just did it. That's what I did because that was part of the contribution I could make to the overall success of what the heck we were trying to do."

The contributions Buckner made led to a pair of state championships at Thornridge. He says winning that first championship with his boyhood friends was truly special.

"I do remember the first time we won," says Buckner, now in his mid-50s and a Vice President of the Indiana Pacers. "I screamed so loud I almost passed out. I remember that distinctly. We were at this hotel not far from the Assembly Hall, the Urbana Howard Johnson. I screamed so loud that I got lightheaded and had to sit down in the elevator. The [elevator] door closed. I was in there, and there were players in there. That I do remember."

After four years at Indiana University, Buckner played ten seasons in the NBA and later served as head coach of the Dallas Mavericks. He became a nationally-known broadcaster. Buckner covered the NBA for NBC, was an analyst for NBA games on ESPN Radio, and worked on college basketball broadcasts for CBS. Buckner was named Vice President of Communications for Pacers Sports & Entertainment in 2004 and continues to serve as a color commentator on Pacers' games.

Buckner's passion for the sport has never waned. You could see early in his career that Buckner was all about competition. Once he won a state high school championship as a junior, Quinn would not be satisfied until he and his teammates did it again the following year.

Buckner knew there were questions that would have to be answered. After going 31-1 and winning the last of the single-class Illinois state tournaments in 1971, what would he and his friends do for an encore? Could they win the inaugural Illinois Class AA state championship, and even if they did, would the second state championship taste as sweet as the first? There was only one way it could possibly be better.

The Falcons would have to win every game.

CHAPTER 4

We Were The Fab Five

AFTER MIKE BONCZYK THREW DOWN the gauntlet following his team's 1971 final win at the Assembly Hall, it would be months before Thornridge could begin defense of its state championship. While the time passed slowly for the players, it was an eventful period in our nation's history. Between the Falcons' championship in March of 1971 and their season opener the next November, there were many newsworthy events in America and around the World.

Month after month, Walter Cronkite sat at the CBS Evening News anchor desk and delivered the most important stories into our homes. In April, more than 500,000 people flocked to Washington, D.C. to march in protest of the Vietnam War. Also, the U.S. Supreme Court upheld the use of busing to achieve racial desegregation in the nation's schools. The next month, rail service became a popular mode of transportation when Amtrak began passenger service throughout the United States. Also in May, the price of a first class stamp climbed 33% from six cents to eight. In June, the *New York Times* began to publish sections of the "Pentagon Papers" which led to an erosion of the American public's confidence in their country's Cold War foreign policy. Then in July, the standardized voting age in the United States was officially lowered from 21 to 18 with the certification of the Twenty-sixth Amendment to the Constitution. Also in July, Apollo 15 astronauts James Irwin and David Scott toured the moon in a lunar rover. Construction of the Louisiana Superdome in New Orleans began in August, and bloody prison rioting in Attica, New York, led Cronkite's news reports in September. In October, at the same time Thornridge players began seriously anticipating the start of the basketball season, Disney World opened in Florida. One era ended when *Look* magazine published its final issue. Another era began when baseball played its first World Series night game. The Pittsburgh Pirates beat the Baltimore Orioles 4-3 in the first World Series game in TV's prime time. And in November, with the start of the basketball season only days away, a relatively unknown company called Intel trumpeted the creation of the world's first microprocessor.

Some news made headlines, such as the passing of jazz musician Louis Armstrong and Soviet leader Nikita Khrushchev as well as the untimely deaths of World War 2 hero-turned-actor Audie Murphy and rock star Jim Morrison. The births of Lance Armstrong, Pete Sampras, Mariah Carey, Winona Ryder, Jada Pinkett, and Noah Wyle were not news to anyone outside of their respective families, but those birthdays would later be celebrated by their fans when the future celebrities achieved fame as adults.

Like most teenagers, the Thornridge players were somewhat oblivious to the news of the day. In the summer of 1971, they spent much of their free time on basketball courts on area playgrounds. They wanted to be prepared for the challenge ahead. The players understood they would need to play even better if they wanted to repeat as state champs in the 1971-72 season. Al Holverson, an assistant coach of the Falcons' 1971 state championship team before leaving to Chair the Math Department at Thornwood HS in 1972, remembers the Thornridge players were not about to rest on their laurels.

"Those guys used to just get in their car and go play wherever they could get a game," recalls Holverson. "They would go down to Chicago Heights and play. They'd go up to La Grange and play. They'd go to Lockport and get on the courts in the summertime, and they just played, played, played."

Throughout the summer the players hopped in Greg Rose's Pontiac to search for a pickup game.

"I had a jalopy," laughs Rose. "I had a '63 Grand Prix and that thing would smoke so bad. I think I paid $300 for it. But I was proud that I was able to buy it. That was my first car."

Many high school students in the '70s owned an 8-track tape player, but Rose says he had only an AM radio to listen to the hits of the day.

"Man, I couldn't afford an 8-track," laughs Rose.

No problem. As Rose drove around with his teammates in search of a game, he simply turned up the radio and grooved to such Motown hits as Marvin Gaye's *"Mercy Mercy Me"* and The Undisputed Truth's *"Smilin' Faces (Sometimes)"*.

"We knew guys that had cars," recalls Mike Bonczyk. "I had a car at my disposal every once in a while. We could get to wherever it was needed to go play. We were listening to AM radio. It would be something out of Motown. [We listened to] WLS with Larry Lujack, and there was another [station] out of Chicago, WCFL. Those were the two stations that were playin' the pop music coming out of Detroit and all that other stuff."

"We were playing basketball at different parks," continues Bonczyk. "We would go on the weekends, and we'd play up at Coolidge Park. We'd play at Bryant Grade School. We'd play at Ivanhoe Park. We went all over and played. We just enjoyed *playin'*."

When the Thornridge players found a game in Phoenix or Harvey, Bonczyk was often the only white player on the court. Other black players occasionally directed racial comments at Bonczyk. Buckner says it was important to make sure the Falcons' point guard knew his teammates had his back.

"I wanted to make sure that the guys that I played with never allowed Mike to be uncomfortable," says Buckner. "I knew he was making a sacrifice. Mike would come over to Phoenix and play, and I knew what they were calling him. I mean, Mike would tell me. He didn't care then, and he doesn't care now. He'd come over in the neighborhood and play. Some [black] guys would go crazy and say stupid things, [and we Thornridge players would say], 'No man, you can't say that to him.' He was protected, not only by me, but by the balance of the group because Mike had endeared himself to the group. We supported him because it was easier for him to come over and play with us than for us to go over [to the white towns] and play with him. You know [in] South Holland and Dolton that really just was *not* the thing to do."

While keeping an eye on Bonczyk to ensure his safety in the black neighborhoods, Greg Rose and his Thornridge teammates fended off challenges from players who came to test themselves against the Thornridge group.

"Man, that court would be so jam packed," says Rose. "[It was] *so* jam packed. It was like people were coming from everywhere to play against us."

Summer eventually turned into fall and fall into winter. Football season ended, and the focus shifted to basketball in suburban Chicago and throughout Illinois. Once the pads and cleats were put away, the excitement grew at the school and in the surrounding neighborhoods. The Falcons were at last preparing to open defense of their state title.

Since Thornridge had four returning starters most fans around the state believed the Falcons were likely to win again. While small schools would compete for the Class A title, the Thornridge players were looking to become champions of Illinois' first Class AA title for schools with enrollments of 751 or more students. Thornridge would also be attempting to become the first school to win consecutive state championships since Rockford West accomplished the feat in 1955 and 1956. Buckner recalls thinking the Falcons could repeat and perhaps go undefeated.

"I figured frankly because we'd won it and we were bringing a majority of the people back, we'd be good," says Buckner. "I wasn't sure about the undefeated part. [In '70-'71] we lost to a team in Mounds Meridian who we were better than, but we were clearly too cocky and [we] should have gotten beaten. I thought we would have something good [in '71-'72]. I just didn't know it would be *that* good."

Although the Falcons were the clear favorite, there were a few skeptics. Some people felt Thornridge had been fortunate to win the 1971 title. They pointed out the Falcons had won three of their last five games during their championship run by five or fewer points.

It was true. The Falcons had dodged some bullets along the tournament trail including the state championship game. Like several of their other tournament victories, the title game had been decided in the final seconds. Thornridge had squeaked past Oak Lawn 52-50 in a game that probably should have gone overtime. Seconds after Buckner missed the front end of a one-and-one, time was running out when Oak Lawn star C. J. Kupec missed a difficult fade-away jumper on the right baseline. Oak Lawn's Bob Carr grabbed the offensive rebound, but his hurried shot clanged off the rim and into the hands of the Falcons' Greg Rose as time expired. Oak Lawn fans, looking for a foul call, complained that the officials had swallowed their whistles in the final seconds.

"We *were* lucky to win that championship game," says Thornridge coach Ron Ferguson. "Of course, Buckner missed the one-and-one at the end. [If he had made a free throw] we wouldn't have had to worry about it. And there *may* have been a foul there at the end. You couldn't really tell for sure. I could see where Oak Lawn had a legitimate gripe."

Ferguson admits his team had a healthy supply of good fortune during its 1971 championship run.

"We were pretty much a better than average basketball team, but we weren't a *great* basketball team and anybody could beat us," acknowledges the coach. "We won some close ones, beating Joliet Central at Joliet Central and a couple close games like that. So that was kind of lucky. And even that championship game, that last shot, I'm not so sure we didn't foul. But they just don't call it I guess at that stage [of the game], at least most times they don't."

"There were like three or four games in the state tournament we could have easily gotten beat and not won the state title," says point guard Mike Bonczyk. "One would have been the finals where we could have gone into overtime. Another was the quarterfinals against Kewanee with Tommie Smith who played at Kansas. They had us on the ropes (Thornridge prevailed 63-58). We had to beat Joliet *at* Joliet when they had that great team coming back that had finished third the year before, and we only won by three (66-63). There were three games right there that we could have very easily got dumped and never won the state title our first year [in 1971]."

Though Bonczyk admits the Falcons were a little lucky to win a state title his junior season, he says the Thornridge players looked forward to taking care of business his senior year.

"I don't want to say we had a chip on our shoulder, but we didn't want to leave any doubt that we were good," says Bonczyk. "We didn't want people to say, 'Well, you know, they barely got by.' That was the thing after our junior year. There had been some talk. You'd hear skepticism. 'Well, Thornridge was lucky. If this guy would have made the bucket they'd have been in overtime, and maybe they would'a got beat.' You hear all that stuff, so the next year it was like, 'Okay we're playing. And we're going to leave no doubt.' It wasn't where we tried to go *kill* people, although the outcome seemed to be that way. But I mean we *played*. We enjoyed playin' on the court. That was the biggest thing."

Coach Ferguson was a nervous wreck as he thought about the many outstanding teams that would be trying to dethrone his team and become the King of Illinois high school basketball. In the north, Waukegan, Hinsdale Central, La Salle-Peru, and Aurora East all figured to be powerhouses. In central Illinois, Quincy, Lincoln, Danville, Champaign Central, and Springfield Southeast hoped to get a shot at the Falcons. In the southern part of the state, East St. Louis Lincoln, Collinsville, and Benton were among the schools that believed they could contend for the first Illinois Class AA state championship. The list of challengers was long, yet every coach and player in the state understood Thornridge was the team to beat. And Thornridge had improved in one critical area. The

Falcons' players now had the collective confidence of a champion. Mike Bonczyk recalls a team meeting in which Quinn Buckner, the reigning Illinois Player of the Year, interrupted the head coach and delivered a message to Ferguson and the rest of the team.

"Before the season started, Coach Ferg had a meeting, and he puts on the board all of the *goals*, you know. Win the conference. Win the regional. Win the sectional, and get back to state," says Bonczyk. "Quinn raised his hand and said, 'Coach, if we're going to go undefeated, don't we accomplish all our goals?' And Fergie goes, 'I guess we would.' Quinn says, 'End of meeting.' So the meeting only took about five minutes," says Bonczyk, laughing hard.

"It was very simple," recalls Ferguson. "He just said all we gotta do is win them all, and then we don't have to worry about anything. I don't know the exact words how he said it, but in essence that's what he meant."

"I was probably arrogant enough to say something like that, but that's arrogance," says Buckner. "That really is arrogance. It was an innocent arrogance is what it was."

Perhaps, but the team's leader might also have been sending a subtle message to his coach and teammates. Never one to boast in public, Buckner chose the privacy of a closed door team meeting to deliver a telling statement. The young man who considered winning one of life's great pleasures was not about to let his team stumble in his senior season. He wanted his teammates to be focused, striving to win each game, never looking back, always looking ahead to the next challenge. Exuding confidence, Buckner understood that if he led, the others would follow. So, Buckner planted the seed that would sprout into an unforgettable season. He interrupted his coach to work the math in front of his teammates. Even the players who were not math whizzes understood that if the Falcons won every game, they would be the state champions. That was their goal. Finally, after months of anticipation, the wait was over. It was time to play.

***

GAME 1 (Friday night, November 19, 1971)
Rich East (Park Forest)

Armed with a chip on their shoulders and a firm belief in their abilities, the Falcons prepared to tip off the season against Rich East High School of Park Forest on Friday, November 19, 1971. Before heading to the game, one of the players tuned in WLS on the radio. The number one hit in America, Isaac Hayes' hit *"Theme from Shaft"*, played through the speaker of his tiny transistor radio.

Rich East had a new head coach, Steve Fisher, who would later serve as head coach at the University of Michigan and guide Chris Webber, Juwan Howard, Jalen Rose, and the rest of the heralded Fab Five into the 1992 and 1993 NCAA championship games. Now the head coach at San Diego State University, Fisher recalls playing Thornridge on a cold November night in the south suburbs of Chicago.

"That was the first game of my head coaching career," says Fisher. "I remember it vividly. I was so excited we were playing the defending state champions in my first game. As a rookie first year coach, you think you're going to win the game by yourself. We played at Thornridge, and I had become good friends with Fergie. I was best friends with Wes Mason, who was coaching at [Chicago Heights] Bloom. He and Ron Ferguson were best buddies, so I really got to know Fergie."

The two head coaches believed they had their teams ready to play, but it was the defending state champion Falcons that came out of the starting gate quickly. Wearing its home white uniforms, Thornridge took command from the opening tip and scored the first nine points of the game. The atmosphere was electric in the crowded Thornridge gymnasium. Students and fans jumped to their feet to cheer after each Falcons basket. Buckner, who had only practiced for three days after turning in his gear at the end of the football season, missed his first three shots but still scored nine points in the first quarter en route to a game-high 22.

Fisher says, "At the time, we were all in awe [of Buckner]. As much as it was really a team and they were all great, Buckner was so good and so physically and mentally mature. It was incredible."

Thornridge led 20-7 after one quarter and 42-22 at halftime. In the second half, the Falcons struggled to execute their fast break but were never threatened and won with relative ease 70-52. Fisher remembers thinking the Thornridge coach eased off the throttle after the Falcons had the game under control.

"To be honest with you, Fergie had empathy for me as a first-time ever head coach," says Fisher decades later. "We were down twenty at [the] half. He kind of had mercy on me. But they were unbelievable, and obviously it was more than Buckner and Batts. Mike Bonczyk and [the others], I mean they had a phenomenal team."

Thornridge committed an uncharacteristic 29 turnovers but forced Rich East to turn the ball over 24 times. The Falcons would become more dominant as the season progressed, but they were off to a good start. Boyd Batts scored 17 points and pulled down 15 rebounds. Greg Rose scored 16 points. Mike Bonczyk dished out 10 assists. In his first game at Thornridge, Ernie Dunn played excellent defense and scored 7 points with 4 rebounds and 4 assists. Nee Gatlin played well off the bench and scored 6 points to solidify his spot as the Falcons' sixth man.

"I didn't realize at the time they were gonna do what they did, you know, with that kind of dominance," says Fisher. "I knew they were really, really good. I wanted to maybe rethink whether I was in the right profession. I said if this is what it's gonna be like, I'm not sure I'm destined to be in this business."

Despite the loss, the Thornridge game holds a very special place in Fisher's heart and not just because it was his first game as a high school head coach.

"My dad saw me coach one game, and that was it," says Fisher. "He drove up from southern Illinois with another dear friend of the family. My dad was superstitious about everything. He thought he jinxed me when he came to that game. He never came back. We even played at the Centralia tournament, and he didn't come to that [even though he did not live far away]."

Fisher notes that basketball had always provided a special bond between father and son.

"My dad was my first coach," Fisher explained. "He coached our Catholic grade school team. He wanted to be a coach and teacher, but World War 2 got in the way of him finishing student teaching. He did everything except student-teach to have an education degree. Then [he had] four kids and the family. He worked at a job that he hated. But he loved sports, so he coached me."

Throughout his coaching career, Fisher made sure to share details about his games with his father.

"We talked after every game," he remembers wistfully. "I'd go back to the office, call him, replay the game, and talk about it."

Fisher did not need to telephone his father after the game against Thornridge. His dad was there to offer his son words of encouragement after the 18-point loss in his head-coaching debut.

"My dad was always the optimist with me," says Fisher. "He just said, 'Stay in there. You're gonna have a good team. They have a *great* team. You were just out-manned.' You know how parents are, 'You weren't outcoached. You were outmanned.' He was complimentary about the potential for our team and said what everybody was saying, 'Boy, Thornridge has the players.'"

Yes, Thornridge had the players. They also had a 22-game winning streak dating back to the previous season. Coach Ferguson wondered if his team could remain mentally prepared for every game throughout the long high school basketball season. He need not have worried. Only two teams came as close as Rich East over the Falcons' next 32 games.

Buckner, Batts, Bonczyk, Rose, and Dunn were a simply fabulous starting five. Bonczyk boasts nearly four decades later, "We were the Fab Five before the Fab Five became the Fab Five up at Michigan."

"Well, he's probably right," laughs Fisher, the Fab Five's coach. "He's probably right. We just played on a little bigger stage than they did."

Fisher spent eight years as head coach at Rich East High School before heading to Western Michigan University to serve as an assistant. In 1982, he became an assistant coach at the University of Michigan. Fisher was named interim head coach of the Wolverines just prior to the 1989 NCAA Tournament after head coach Bill Frieder accepted a job at Arizona State University. Athletic Director Bo Schembechler immediately replaced Frieder with Fisher because he wanted a "Michigan man" to coach the Wolverines in the tournament, not an "Arizona State man." Thrown into the job on the spur of the moment, Fisher guided Glen Rice and the Wolverines to an NCAA title and was awarded the job on a permanent basis. It wasn't long before Fisher found out that no college coaching job is permanent. He was let go by Michigan in 1997 and worked the next year as an assistant coach with the Sacramento Kings in the NBA. Fisher became the head coach at San Diego State University in 1999. The former high school math teacher has posted some impressive numbers as a collegiate head coach. Fisher won 184 of 266 games at Michigan and won 173 games in his first ten years at San Diego State. His first Aztecs' team went 5-23, but he quickly turned the program into a winner. His San Diego State teams have won 20 or more games in each of the last four seasons. San Diego State played in the NCAA tourney the first of those four seasons and in the National Invitation Tournament the past three years. The Herrin, Illinois native considers it an honor to have been the first victim in Thornridge's perfect season.

"We were a good high school team that had the privilege of starting them off on their undefeated, never challenged season," says Fisher. "I watched in awe as it unfolded. As the season went on, I'm saying, 'Oh my Gosh! They beat 'em by *how* much?' They have to go down as the best team in the history of Illinois basketball."

***

GAME 2 (Friday night, November 26, 1971)
Batavia

After beating Rich East, Thornridge had a full week to prepare for the Thanksgiving Holiday Tournament at Rockford Guilford High School. Coach Ferguson had guided Thornridge to Rockford tourney championships the two previous years and wanted to make it three in a row.

The coach constantly worried about things he could not control. One of those things was game officiating. Ferguson wanted his players prepared for anything they might encounter on the basketball court including differences in officiating styles. Ferguson scheduled games throughout Illinois so his team would know what to expect at during the state tournament when officials from all parts of the state were assigned to work games.

"In those days there was always the perception that southern Illinois officiating was different from northern Illinois officiating," says Ferguson. "I picked Rockford for Thanksgiving so we could go up to the north, then Carbondale down south [for the Christmas tournament] to get lots of the [various styles of] officiating."

"I never noticed there was that much difference in the officiating," Ferguson adds with a hearty laugh. "I didn't think anybody was any good wherever you were."

On Friday, November 26, much of America was talking about a man named Dan Cooper who two nights earlier had jumped out of a hijacked jetliner over southwestern Washington near Portland, Oregon. People were speculating whether the man (who later became known as D.B. Cooper) had gotten away with the $200,000 in ransom money or if he had died in the jump from the back of the Boeing 727. The FBI has yet to solve the case.

The Thornridge players were paying little attention to the drama playing out in the Pacific Northwest. The Falcons were opening the Thanksgiving Tournament against Batavia High School, the alma mater of long-time professional player Dan Issel. The Bulldogs could have used Issel against Thornridge. Batavia struggled against Thornridge's full-court pressure and committed six quick turnovers as Thornridge pulled out to a 31-19 lead after

46

the first quarter. When the Falcons opened the second period by scoring the first 10 points, they were on their way to a 23ʳᵈ straight win. Batavia managed to stay within 11 points at halftime, but when Thornridge exploded for 33 points in the third quarter, the only thing left to be determined was the final score. The Falcons breezed to a 97-71 victory. Point guard Mike Bonczyk played a solid game with 6 points and 9 assists. He remembers fans in Rockford, and everywhere that Thornridge played, turned out in huge numbers to watch the state's number one team.

"The crowds we played in front of were fantastic," recalls Bonczyk. "The fans that supported us, especially the high school student body, and no matter where we went we always played in front of a full house. It was like you were on display to put on a show, and that's what we did. We put on a show."

Buckner laughs when told Bonczyk considered the 1971-72 Thornridge basketball team a group of showmen expected to deliver exciting basketball for fans at home or away.

"That's Mike," says Buckner, laughing hard. "I never had to put on a show. I'm not thinkin' about puttin' on a show. I'm tryin' to figure out how to win a basketball game. But that's Mike," Quinn says, laughing even harder.

Buckner played his typical magnificent game against Batavia. The prep All-American had 20 points, 10 rebounds, 8 assists, and 7 steals. Ernie Dunn, the newest member of the Thornridge team's Fab Five, led the Falcons with 24 points. Batts added 21 points and Rose scored 19. After the game, Coach Ferguson urged his players to get some rest. They would be playing two more games within the next 24 hours.

***

GAME 3 (Saturday afternoon, November 27, 1971)
Manual (Peoria)

The next afternoon in the second game of the four-team, round-robin tournament, Thornridge faced the always dangerous Rams of Peoria Manual. A perennial power out of central Illinois, Manual had surprisingly lost to host Guilford 91-77 in its first game in the tourney. Even so, Ferguson worried that his team might have trouble against Manual. It appeared his fears were well-founded early in the game. Despite a knee injury that slowed Manual star Mike Davis, the score was tied at 18 after one quarter. But just when it looked like the Falcons might be challenged, they outscored the Rams 32-16 in the second quarter, 32-8 in the third, and 25-18 in the fourth quarter.

When the final buzzer sounded, Thornridge had scored a school-record 107 points and had defeated Manual 107-60. Boyd Batts scored 12 points in the first quarter and 16 more in the second. Batts finished with a career-high 40 points. He made 15 of 25 shots from the field and 10 of 12 from the charity stripe. The senior center also pulled down 14 rebounds, 11 at the offensive end. Ernie Dunn, with 19 points and 11 rebounds, also delivered a "double-double" although the term had not yet become part of basketball lexicon. Ferguson was able to rest his starters in the fourth quarter and give the reserves significant playing time. Dave Anderson scored 7 points and Joe King added 6 to lead the bench brigade that was responsible for helping the Falcons reach the century mark for the first time in the 1971-72 season. Most high school teams are fortunate to score 100 points even once in a season. Thornridge reached the century mark seven times during the 1971-72 campaign. That is remarkable when you consider this was prior to the implementation of the 3-point line and since high school games last only 32 minutes. Thornridge averaged 87.4 points per game for the season and never had the benefit of playing additional minutes in an overtime game. No team ever came close to forcing Thornridge into O.T. Although Thornridge had pulled away for an easy win, Falcons' coach Ron Ferguson believed Peoria Manual was a better team than it showed that Saturday afternoon.

"Back in those days, Peoria always played those Thanksgiving Day football games, and several of their key guys were football players," says Ferguson. "So they had not been on the basketball court for [even] two or three days when they went up there for that tournament. That was certainly a disadvantage. The score was completely misleading, because they certainly weren't ready to play basketball at that time."

Manual's senior captain Wayne McClain scored a team-high 13 points in the lopsided loss. McClain recalls that the Rockford tournament tipped off the day after he had hung up his football cleats. McClain had tried to get himself in basketball condition even while he was still playing football.

"I was comin' in after football practice," says McClain. "It's so different with your muscles and stuff, so what the football team did allow was for us to come in after practice. I would come in and just do things on the side, you know, tryin' to get some basketball legs. But incorporated [into practice], running plays and things like that, no, [I hadn't practiced with the basketball team]."

McClain says even though the Rams were facing the defending state champions, he and his teammates entered the game believing they had a chance to upset the Falcons.

"We had seen them every year [at the Rockford tournament]," says McClain, now an assistant coach at the University of Illinois. "Quinn started as a sophomore, [and] so did I. I played against them sophomore year, and they beat us. As a junior, they beat us and went on to win the state. So coming in we knew they were really good. We thought *we* were going to be really good because we started five juniors [the previous season]. We came back with a senior-laden team. I don't remember the score, but I think they handled us pretty well. The only thing that you could think was hopefully some of our guys were still in football shape. But they just kind of toyed with us."

The early season 47-point defeat to Thornridge is still remembered by Dick Van Scyoc, who coached Manual for 45 years and retired in 1994 with 826 victories, at the time more wins than any coach in Illinois high school basketball history. Van Scyoc says Manual not only had several football players still adjusting from football to basketball, the Rams also had two key players battling injuries.

"If I remember right, I had two of 'em that played but were hurt," recalls Van Scyoc. "We were running a drill in practice, and I had one drill where they were taking a charge. My two big guys collided and went down. I thought I might lose them for the season. That was Mike Davis. He was about six-six, and Paul Maras, the other kid [was also] six-six. Both of them [were] 200 pounders. I know they weren't healthy. But I'm not taking anything away from Thornridge."

McClain remembers the day Maras and Davis were hurt during the practice drill.

"Yes, Yes," remembers McClain. "Line up people on both sides. One had to go stand in front of the other. You know *beat* him [to the spot on the court]. You sprint. One guy is with the ball, and the other guy is sprinting to beat him outside the lane. And [the collision] hurt Mike Davis' leg. [We] never did that drill again. I'm not jokin'. After that [incident we] never did it again."

Davis played against Thornridge with a heavily taped leg and was clearly hampered by the injury. He scored only six points which would be far below his season average. Davis, an All-State player by season's end, would get two more cracks at Thornridge later in the season. With his leg injury healed, Davis was significantly more effective in the following matchups. However, he and his teammates would continue to be frustrated by the high-flying Thornridge Falcons.

***

GAME 4 (Saturday night, November 27, 1971)
Guilford (Rockford)

On Saturday night, November 27, in its third game in 24 hours, Thornridge played the host school for the tournament championship. Coach Ron Ferguson admits he was worried. He thought Guilford might benefit from some home cooking.

"Any time you have to play in somebody's home gym you're a little concerned," says Ferguson. "We didn't really know too much about the Rockford schools because that's the only time we were ever near there."

Once again the Thornridge players promptly put their coach's mind at ease. Rockford Guilford had no answer for Quinn and company. Buckner scored 17 of his game high 27 points in the first half. He also pulled down 11 rebounds while leading Thornridge to an 88-57 victory. Boyd Batts scored 18, while Greg Rose (14) and Ernie Dunn (11) also scored in double-figures.

Heading home after the tournament, Thornridge fans listened to WLS as the *"Theme from Shaft"* played on the car radio. It was still the number one record in America. And even though no Associated Press poll had been taken in the new season, Thornridge was unquestionably the number one high school basketball team in Illinois. The Falcons were 4-0 as they looked ahead to the next week's game against highly-regarded Waukegan and its six-eleven center Bill Rucks.

While Thornridge was winning in Rockford, Aurora East, Rock Island Alleman, and Hinsdale Central all stayed unbeaten with early season wins. Lincoln won the Washington Thanksgiving Tournament with wins over Rantoul, Peoria Spalding, and Washington. Quincy captured its own Thanksgiving Tourney championship with a 1-point victory over Ottawa, a 2-point win over Pekin, and a 4-point victory over Champaign Central in the title tilt. Aurora East, Rock Island Alleman, Hinsdale Central, Lincoln, and Quincy were all quality teams that would be near the top of the state rankings throughout the season. Each school wanted a shot at Thornridge, but only one of those teams would ever get the opportunity to play the defending champions. That would come in the state championship game inside the Assembly Hall at Champaign in the middle of March. The title game was still three months away which meant Coach Ron Ferguson had many sleepless nights to come.

CHAPTER 5

How Can I Screw It Up

BECAUSE HE WON CONSECUTIVE STATE championships at Thornridge, Ron Ferguson is remembered as one of Illinois' most successful high school basketball coaches. The truth is Ferguson's Thornridge teams did not always win. His first year as a head coach, he really had to pay his dues.

"Yeah, we were 2 and 20," says Ferguson. "We opened the season at Bremen [of Midlothian]. The [opening] jump-ball, the ball was tipped back, and one of our kids got it and went in and made a basket… at the *wrong* basket!"

"That was my first experience as a head coach. And the first play, the first basket we got, was for the other team," Ferguson laughs.

When Thornridge opened in 1960, Ferguson was the perfect coach to direct the new school's basketball program. He knew the area and was aware of the challenges he would have trying to compete in the same school district with state power Thornton of Harvey.

Ron Ferguson was born in Chicago in 1931. He lived in the city at 79th and Evans until he was seven years old. Then, in 1938, the family moved to Homewood. From 1945 to 1949, Ferguson attended Thornton High School where he played baseball and was the quarterback on the football team. His junior and senior years, he also played basketball for legendary coach Tommy Nisbet. Ferguson got his first taste of state tournament basketball while playing for the Wildcats. Ferguson was a starter on the Thornton team that played in the 1948 Illinois High School Association (IHSA) tournament. At that time, all 16 teams that reached the "Sweet 16" travelled to the state tournament in Champaign. In his team's first

51

game in Huff Gym, Ferguson scored 8 points in Thornton's 57-50 loss to Springfield Cathedral. Pinckneyville eliminated Springfield Cathedral in the next round and went on to win the state championship.

Ferguson attended the University of Illinois from 1949 to 1953, and while in Champaign, was enrolled in the ROTC program. Upon graduation, he was a 2nd Lieutenant in the U.S. Army. Ferguson was promoted to First Lieutenant in 1955 becoming Battery Commander for the 513th AAA Battalion at Headquarters Battery near Bremerton, Washington. After serving two years in the Army, Ferguson went back to the U. of I. to get his Masters' Degree. He earned his Masters and soon began his coaching career at his high school alma mater. He assisted his former coach Tommy Nisbet in the 1956-57 season. Bill Purden then became Thornton's head basketball coach, and Ferguson worked three years under him. Purden eventually left Thornton to coach in college, but not before making a lasting impression on Ferguson.

"I learned a lot from him," says Ferguson. "He was way ahead of a lot of people in terms of things he did. Had he stayed at the high school level, he would be one of the guys we're talking about in terms of [legendary prep coaches]. He was only there about eight years. He would have had a great record."

Purden was still at Thornton when Thornridge opened in 1960-61. Believing Purden wasn't going to leave any time soon, and looking for a chance to lead his own program, Ferguson accepted the job as the head basketball coach at Thornridge. One of the things he learned right away was it was going to be difficult to win with no minority players on the team.

"If you knew what I went through at Thornridge to start with," says Ferguson. "When they divided the school district, they moved me over [to Thornridge] in 1960 as the head coach, but what they didn't do was integrate the district. [At] Thornton, at that time, most of their great players were minority kids. We played the first six or seven years [at Thornridge] with no minority in the lineup."

Since every other team in the conference was integrated, Thornridge was at a distinct disadvantage those first seven years. Ferguson's early teams included some good athletes, but many were probably more suited to football than basketball. A relative lack of quickness hurt the Falcons as they tried to keep up with the other teams in their league.

"We played in a league that, outside the city of Chicago, probably had as many good minority teams as anybody," recalls Ferguson. "We had Bloom, Thornton, Argo, Joliet, Lockport, Kankakee, Blue Island Eisenhower. We just had to struggle like hell to stay up with them because we didn't have the quickness. By the third year, we competed well. We just didn't win enough."

Despite losing records in each of Ferguson's first four years at the school, the basketball program showed gradual improvement. Ferguson believes the effort of the players in the early and mid-1960s helped the Falcons get better each year. He remains very proud of those less-celebrated players who sacrificed blood, sweat, and tears in his first years as a head coach.

"We had great, hard-working kids during those early years," says Ferguson. "They helped me develop a philosophy in coaching and showed me that hard work and good attitude will go a long way in athletics."

The first two years were a struggle, but the gap between Thornridge and the other teams in its league began to close. Several of those early Falcons' players, including Ken Smith and Mike Vuletich, received all-conference honors as Thornridge began to gain respect. And once the 1964-65 squad went 16-8, Ferguson's Falcons never again suffered through a losing campaign.

"We gradually got better and better," says Ferguson, who coached a total of twelve years at the school. "The last two or three years before we had the integration, we had good basketball teams without any minority kids. We had a pretty good team in '65-'66. We were 20-5. We beat some good teams, and we were ranked tenth or something like that. We beat [the] Thornton [team] that won the state championship that year."

All-State guard Al Armour was the leader of that 1965-66 Thornridge team. He averaged 24 points per game and went on to play collegiately for Dean Smith at North Carolina.

Though Thornridge was competitive in the mid-1960s, Ferguson grew increasingly frustrated that his teams were unable to consistently beat Thornton and the other schools featuring minority players. The Falcons' fans, too, were disappointed. Some even complained to the coach. Ferguson, perhaps feeling the pressure of unfulfilled expectations, talked about needing minority athletes in order to have greater success.

"I almost lost my job just before [Thornridge] integrated," says Ferguson. "Every school's basketball team in our league was primarily made up of minorities. I made that a little too much of a deal and shouldn't have done that. It should not have been made public. People recognized that without me trying to tell them."

"That made some of the parents of the white kids uneasy," continues Ferguson. "So, that got me in trouble with the parents. We were struggling to get over [a] .500 [winning percentage], even though there was a good reason why. They didn't want to lose. Thornton's winning, and we can't win. The fans are so used to seeing Thornton win over there, and here we were [not as successful]. Naturally, they're going to blame it on the coach most of the time. But, you're not going to win big with some of the kids we had in the early years at Thornridge. I was surprised we won as many as we did. However, they were great kids and worked their butts off."

Ferguson was understandably excited to learn that black student-athletes would attend the school starting in the 1967-68 academic year. That first year of integration, only freshmen were bused from Phoenix to Thornridge High. Because those minority freshmen players were young and inexperienced, the varsity basketball team remained 100% white. Even so, the Falcons had one of the best seasons in school history. Proof of how far the program had come under Ferguson, Thornridge won 20 games that year and lost only 9. Six-four forward Wally Michna, a future standout at Augustana, was the Falcons' top player.

Though no blacks played on the varsity in the first year of integration, history was made. Minorities, for the first time, represented Thornridge on the freshmen basketball team. James Loggins and Tony Jackson, two players that would be part of Thornridge's first state championship team in 1971, were among the seven minority players on the freshmen squad. While not a great deal was made about the integration of the freshman team, there was certainly a buzz about the 8th-grade team at Coolidge Elementary. Two young guys that would later play key roles in both Thornridge championships were lighting it up at Coolidge. Though they would not enroll at Thornridge until fall of 1968, the high school's varsity basketball coach had already heard about Quinn Buckner and Boyd Batts. He wanted to see for himself what all the excitement was about. Ferguson took freshman coach Ron Bonfiglio with him to Phoenix to watch the two future Falcons' greats play at Coolidge. It did not take long for the two coaches to see that big things were in store for Thornridge basketball.

"Fergie said we got something special coming in," remembers Bonfiglio. "On the opening tip, Buckner and Batts combined for a <u>dunk</u> – in *eighth grade!* I said, 'Holy Cow!' Obviously, we were very anxious for them to become freshmen."

The story has become part of Thornridge legend. The two coaches had barely settled into their seats when Batts tipped the ball to Buckner, who promptly threw an alley-oop pass to Batts streaking down the floor. Batts caught the pass and hammered the ball through the basket. Remember, this came at a time dunking was not even allowed in high school or college.

"I think nobody told [them the rules]," laughs Ferguson. "I'm not sure *I* knew any of the rules in grade school at that stage."

But the point, like the basketball itself, was hammered home. Thornridge was going to have two spectacular players when Buckner and Batts arrived the following year.

"Yeah, I sorta got excited," remembers Ferguson. "But then, also being kind of the pessimist that I am sometimes, I said, 'You know what'll happen, don't you? A couple of those guys won't [show up at Thornridge].' Because Thornton was living high off the hog at that time, [I said], 'There will be a couple of those guys [who] are gonna move back into [the] Thornton [district]. They'll find an aunt or an uncle [in the Thornton district to live with], or their family will move.' I said, 'I'm not gonna count on it until I actually see them enrolled, and then we'll go from there. There's no sense worrying too much about it at this stage because something's gonna happen. They'll change the boundaries again, or they'll do something else.' I was just hoping that nothing would fall through and [that] those guys wouldn't petition to go to Thornton. If the talent would have all been at one school, it would have really been something else. Thornton could have very easily had a dynasty in those next several years if all those kids from Thornridge went to Thornton. But it turned out the other way because Ernie Dunn transferred [from Thornton] into our district."

Bonfiglio, who later served for 16 years as Thornridge's Athletic Director, was the freshmen coach when the two Coolidge players showed up as freshmen at Thornridge. Bonfiglio coached Batts on the freshman team but never had the pleasure of coaching Buckner.

"When they became freshmen, Quinn went right to the sophomores," says Bonfiglio. "He went and played for [sophomore coach] Frank Nardi. Fergie said, 'He's not going to play freshman ball, Ron. He'll go right to the sophomores, and we'll evaluate it from that point.'"

"As a freshman, he played on the sophomore team," says Ferguson. "Then, he played three years on the varsity. He could have played varsity his freshman year, but we had a pretty good sophomore team, and I thought we'd have success there."

Trying to remember back more than 40 years, Ferguson recalls Buckner played on the sophomore team all season and then was allowed to dress with the varsity for the Thornton regional tournament. Ferguson and Nardi both say that was the first time a minority player wore a varsity jersey at Thornridge. But according to Nardi, Buckner did more than simply don the uniform. He went right into the starting lineup for the postseason tournament. Even with the addition of the talented freshman, Thornridge failed to advance out of the regional. It would take two more years for the Falcons to cross over that hurdle. But, Ferguson achieved his goal of building a winning program from the bottom up.

Frank Nardi, Buckner's coach on the sophomore team his first year at Thornridge, says Ferguson did the right thing by keeping Buckner on the sophomore squad rather than elevating him to the varsity for the entire season.

"He was not going to bring him up to the varsity until the tournament at the end of the year," remembers Nardi. "I give Fergie a whole lot of credit for sticking to that. We never had a real, real good sophomore team. He wanted to establish a winning tradition, if at all possible, with one of our lower-level teams. He stuck to his word."

With the talented Buckner starring for the sophomore team, fans flocked to the Thornridge High School gym well before the varsity games were scheduled to start. Nardi's team, which played just prior to the varsity game, was just as popular as Ferguson's varsity squad.

"For all of our sophomore games, it was jam-packed," recalls Nardi. "The crowds at the sophomore games [were huge]. It was already jam-packed because of the type of team that we had."

Ferguson was able to establish a winning tradition at the lower levels of his program. Nardi says the sophomores, led by freshman Quinn Buckner, experienced a near-perfect season.

"Bloom beat us by one point 37-36, a low-scoring game for both teams considering both teams had great personnel," says Nardi. "[Now go] to the end of the season, Bradley High School always had an end of the year 16-team sophomore tournament. We happened to end up playing each other because we were the two best teams of the sixteen. I remember we beat them by 38 points. At the conclusion of the game in the locker room, I told [my players], 'If you guys stick together [and] keep your heads on straight, you're gonna win a state title.' And, of course, that's (now) history. I had a great team, just a great team. We had a wonderful season. I'm gonna say (our record) was 28-1."

Nardi adds, with a laugh, "I remember the one loss because it was at Bloom, and I'm a graduate of Bloom."

Not everyone thought it was a good idea to play Buckner with the sophomores. Dave Lezeau, who worked with the Thornridge freshmen during Buckner's first year in high school, says Ferguson heard complaints from some fans who thought Buckner should have been playing on the varsity from day one.

"There was some pressure on Ferg about how come he didn't put Quinn on the varsity that first year," says Lezeau. "Everybody knew Quinn was head and shoulders above anybody else [in talent]. And it was, 'Why you messing with him on the sophomores?' But Fergie understood, in the long run, it was better to not [put him on the varsity]."

Lezeau believes there was also another reason Ferguson kept Buckner on the sophomore team rather than promote the freshman up to the varsity. It was just the second year of integration at Thornridge, and Lezeau thinks Ferguson wanted to keep the peace with white fans who were upset that blacks were taking roster spots previously held by white players.

"It was an interesting situation," says Lezeau. "At that time, Thornridge was primarily a white school. Then we had the integration thing start. I think part of Fergie's realization [was] that he just didn't want to create unnecessary waves right away. Fergie was smart about [his] handling Quinn his freshman year."

With Buckner playing sophomore ball a majority of the 1968-69 season Ferguson's varsity team went 17-12. Six-foot six-inch Mark Nordin had an excellent season and would sign after the season to play at the University of Miami in Florida.

The following year, Buckner was a varsity starter. Fellow sophomore Boyd Batts also saw significant playing time as the Falcons went 20-7.

Ferguson was aware there were white fans upset with him for picking minority players for his varsity squad. In reality, the coach could have chosen even more blacks for the team. But, he knew the white community would rebel if the entire team consisted of minority players.

Former Ferguson assistant Frank Nardi says, "I remember saying, 'Fergie, okay if that's what they want, let's put a few guys on the team that are white [and] satisfy whoever the complainers are and go from there.' But Fergie knew what the situation was. [Selecting white kids for the team] is something that he had to do."

"It was bad, the black and white thing," says Ferguson. "You could hear the complaints [about utilizing too many black players]. Different comments were being made. When we won though, all of a sudden it made a lot of people happy."

Through it all, the coach tried to make sure his players stayed focused. He wanted them thinking about basketball and avoiding controversy off the court. Ferguson also knew that his players were so talented they would likely repeat as state champions as long as he didn't make any major coaching blunders.

"I was just trying to figure out how I could screw it up," says Ferguson. "I know they had all the confidence in the world which was fine. I didn't want them to be worried about everybody. But fouls, injuries, there's lots of different things that can happen in a basketball game. There are things that can turn games the other way if they're close."

When reminded that no team got closer than 14 points during the 1971-72 season, Ferguson laughs, "We didn't have too many close games, but they were close at the beginning. They're always tied when you start."

The players insist they felt no pressure during the perfect season even if their coach was tied up in knots.

"We didn't. We were playin', just havin' fun which is the way you gotta do it," says Buckner. "I think once you start getting pits in your stomach, [you become less effective]. I understand why Coach Ferguson got it because it's a lot of pressure for a person who influences the game, but in terms of actually being out on the court, doesn't really impact the game. I understand how he got that way, but we just enjoyed doin' what we did. We enjoyed each other."

Still, Ferguson worried that his players might succumb to the pressure since every opponent targeted its game with the defending state champions as the biggest game of the year.

"Going in [to the season], I think the pressure was on," says the coach. "I tried to put the pressure on me instead of putting it on the team."

"And you know it *was* [pressure on me] because it doesn't take much for me to get all pressured up," Ferguson laughs. "So that's what I was thinking about. How can I screw it up?"

Ferguson had seen the newspaper clippings. Writers statewide predicted Thornridge would be impossible to beat. Those newspaper articles were posted on bulletin boards in locker rooms around the state by coaches hoping to inspire their teams to play their best, especially if given a chance to play the defending champs. Ferguson hoped his players did not pay much attention to the newspaper clippings. He feared what might happen if they started believing the hype.

"I thought, 'How in the world could we live up to that with all the publicity and everyone picking us?'" remembers Ferguson. "How could these 17 and 18 year old kids possibly respond to this? You know, some of them will be out there trying too hard and trying to do it all themselves. I thought the biggest thing we've got to figure out [is] a way that we can convince them that the only way we're gonna do well, over a whole year, is we've got to play as a team. Everybody can't get 20 points every game."

Ferguson worried about making coaching mistakes that might prove costly to his team but was also concerned that a couple of his key players might lose focus. Ferguson remembers Boyd Batts and Greg Rose were players that, especially early in their careers, created headaches for the coaching staff. Rose was habitually late and occasionally failed to show up for school on game days which put his participation in that night's game in jeopardy. Batts was considered a loose cannon. A free spirit, nobody knew what Boyd might do at any given moment. During his varsity years, Batts and Ferguson would occasionally refuse to speak to one another. Point guard Mike Bonczyk liked Batts and Rose, but he admits they tried the patience of the coaching staff. Bonczyk says Ferguson did a fantastic job of making things work for the team with its cast of characters.

"I think he was a great manipulator of personalities," says Bonczyk. "He understood the type of players that he had. He understood the type of individuals that he had. Coach Fergie may have been ahead of his time as far as the manner in which he dealt with players and allowed them input. Most coaches [say] 'This is the way things are. Here's the way we're gonna do it.' Fergie was different from the standpoint [that] he gave us [the chance to offer] input that allowed us the opportunity to grow."

Junior guard Ernie Dunn says he was impressed with Ferguson from the moment he arrived at Thornridge after transferring from Thornton.

"I think he was a great coach because he instilled the fundamentals in us," recalls Dunn. "We had a lot of raw talent, and it could have been all showboating and all that. We had the talent to do that, but Fergie didn't want us to do that."

Dunn says Ferguson knew what it took to keep the team focused and ready to fend off every challenge.

"Fergie explained to us *this* is how we're going to win," says Dunn. "He taught us the defense, the 1-2-2 trap, and he taught us the game. He taught me the game."

When fans saw the Falcons on game night, it was the culmination of a lot of hard work. Despite Thornridge's domination game after game, it wasn't as easy as it looked.

"Most people don't think he coached us, but we had repetitious things to do," recalls Dunn. "We had plays to run. We always knew when to run them and what to do. Like, we score a basket, and we'd throw the press on. We knew when to throw the press on and when not to. We all had to be in sync with that."

Dunn adds that Ferguson was ahead of the times because unlike many coaches in that era, he varied the defenses Thornridge used throughout a game.

"Fergie taught us all that, and that's what threw a lot of teams off," he says. "It wasn't like every play we pressed. We pressed for the first quarter. Then, if we get a good lead, we still may press again in the second quarter. I think he was great at coaching the game. It was fun playing for him. I don't recall him ever having any sit-down talks with us to say, 'Look guys, you're completely out of control.' We always respected him and did what he requested."

Even though he wasn't at Thornridge to be part of the Falcons' first state championship, Dunn knew there were minority players on the team that season that made it difficult for Ferguson. In addition to starter Boyd Batts, Mike Henry and some other reserves were a challenge.

"He had quite a few characters on his team," says Dunn. "Some of the guys that were on the bench with Boyd weren't good influences for him, and that was unfortunate. The guys that grew up with us, while they were on the team, their focus wasn't quite [on] basketball. That's some of the things Coach wrestled with."

Al Holverson had a chance to watch Ferguson while serving as the assistant varsity coach during Thornridge's first championship season and then as a scout for the 1971-72 team. He thinks Ferguson did a remarkable job of balancing the egos.

"You could say Fergie had to be a real psychoanalyst, psychiatrist, [and] diplomat with those kids," says Holverson, "just to hold everything together and keep their heads in line."

In addition to his other responsibilities, Ferguson also had to act as a taxi driver. On occasion, he had to drive some players home to Phoenix.

"Most of the kids lived in the same community," says Ferguson. "After the games a lot of times, I would have to take them home, either myself or one of the assistant coaches. We would take turns taking them home because they had no way to get back and forth."

After dropping off the players, Ferguson would often head to Savoia's, a favorite post-game haunt of the area's high school coaches. They would gather after games to talk about what happened with their respective teams and to hang out with fellow members of the coaching fraternity. During his time at Thornridge, Ferguson lived four years in Calumet City. Then he moved to South Holland. Both locations were close enough for him to make a post-game drive to Chicago Heights to meet with his peers at Savoia's.

"Yes, I was one of the so-called regulars at Savoia's which was owned by the one and only Augie Bamonti," says Ferguson. "Among the regulars were (Bloom's) Wes Mason, (Rich East's) Steve Fisher, (Bloom football coach) Verl Sell, (Thornridge sophomore coach) Frank Nardi, (former La Grange High and Bradley University standout, and future Rich East High coach) Chuck Sedgwick, and a number of other coaches who enjoyed a beer with good friends, as long as they were not [competing] on the court."

"We used to meet every Friday night after the game at Savoia's," recalls Steve Fisher. "Augie Bamonti; and all the Bloom fans, it was like the Italian Mafia over there. We would come from our respective games. About 10 o'clock at night, or 10:30, we'd all show up at Savoia's and close it down. We'd be there long after it closed."

Frank Nardi grew up in Chicago Heights and was a classmate of future NBA executive Jerry Colangelo at Bloom High School. Nardi says Savoia's was a part of the local scene for as long as he can remember.

"When I was growing up as a teenager they had a place on "Hungry Hill" in Chicago Heights," recalls Nardi. "They had a small restaurant there called Savoia's. Then, they moved to the other place on Route 30 in Chicago Heights which was much larger. And yes, that was the meeting place after games."

Nardi says it was important for the coaches to have a place like Savoia's where they could go after a tough night on the bench.

"When you are competing against these other coaches, it gets a little heated some times," laughs Nardi. "But, when you entered Savaoia's all that was done and over with. It was just a great meeting place for the coaches to get over the game they had just played and [to] reminisce a little bit. [There were] no hard feelings or anything like that."

Spending time with fellow coaches at Savoia's gave the tightly-wound Ferguson a chance to decompress after a game. Talking with friends and fellow coaches helped him to calm down after another night in the pressure-cooker. Many of his cohorts would have given anything to have had a chance to coach players as talented as those on the Thornridge team.

However, the better his talent, the more pressure Ferguson put on himself to make sure he did everything possible to help his team win.

"He was just super prepared," says Al Holverson, a former Thornridge assistant. "He was almost over-prepared for everything. I think he probably had a lot of sleepless nights wondering if somebody was going to come up with something he hadn't thought of yet. He would do his weekly plans based on who we were playing. The practice organization and how much time he devoted to things, he was always trying to think of ways that somebody might try to screw things up for him. He would create things to practice just in case somebody came up with those situations."

Ron Bonfiglio assisted in scouting upcoming Thornridge opponents during the Falcons' perfect season.

"Fergie never took anything for granted," says Bonfiglio. "He wanted a thorough scouting report. I'd say, 'Ferg, this is in the bag.' He'd say, 'I don't care. I want it written up.' I would go out on Friday night and scout. Then, I'd come home and touch it up, re-do it and everything. He wanted it [by] ten o'clock Saturday morning at practice. He wanted that scouting report."

"I'm sure every coach is trying to think of some way to counteract something that's gonna happen," says Ferguson. "Oh God, you diagram plays when you sit down on the bus. You go nuts, and you scout and try to do everything [you can to prepare]."

Ferguson also admits to having been superstitious as a coach. One game, he stayed behind to go to the bathroom when his team took the court. After Thornridge won that game, Ferguson was reluctant to leave the locker room with his players. He stayed behind in the bathroom so that he would not jinx his team.

"I just couldn't go out," recalls Ferguson. "I didn't stay there the whole time, but I didn't run out with the team. I don't know. You just get kind of paranoid about different things. People would say, 'Well you'll jinx [the team] if you do this. You gotta do the [same] thing every game.'"

Ferguson adds, with a laugh, "[You mean] I gotta go to the bathroom every game?'"

Whether scouting opponents, diagramming plays on the team bus, or staying in the bathroom to avoid jinxing his team, Ferguson was a worrier. He did not want it to be his fault if his team lost. That led to many sleepless nights.

"I was not a lifetime coach," admits Ferguson. "I couldn't sleep when we won. I couldn't sleep when we lost. I don't think my temperament was good to where I could have just gone on and on and on and had the same enthusiasm for the kids and the program."

By the time Thornridge was winning state championships, Ferguson had calmed down while on the bench. In his first few years at Thornridge, his courtside demeanor was dramatically different.

"When I first started coaching, I was a hollerer and a screamer," remembers Ferguson. "I had some kids that had difficulty keeping up with the game, and I got so frustrated. I knew I was gonna have a heart attack if I didn't get out of that [style of coaching].

"I was an assistant at Thornton, and I thought I'm gonna go over there [to Thornridge] and tear all these teams apart with my great knowledge," laughs the coach. "I was just so frustrated at times that I was screamin' and hollerin'. I could see I wasn't gonna last long. So, I got my life turned around in terms of how I coached, at least in terms of dealing with the kids."

Ferguson alienated some of his players with his intense style during his early years of coaching. They were tired of Ferguson's yelling. It dawned on the coach that they might be more productive if he toned down his act.

"I learned this is a game," says Ferguson four decades after changing his coaching demeanor. "You want to win, and you want to teach the kids. You don't want them mad at you all the time. You want them to enjoy it. So, I had to change my style and take a little different approach to the game. I still let everything bother me, but I didn't take it out on anybody else, [except] maybe my wife. If we won, I couldn't sleep. If we lost, I couldn't sleep. I worried about every game."

Frank Nardi, who left Thornridge to become the head coach of Thornwood High in 1971-72, says he was aware that his friend had many sleepless nights.

"I think Fergie was always that way," remembers Nardi. "There was so much pressure on him to win. I think a lot of that, though, was on the inside of him and not too much from the outside. He was expected to win because they had such great [players]. I think he kept a lot of that to himself."

As the 1971-72 season progressed, the Falcons continued to blow out every opponent. Ferguson and his team made it look easy. Some observers downplayed his impact on the success of the Thornridge team suggesting Ferguson was simply lucky to be coaching great players. The 78-year old Ferguson says he does not waste time thinking about his own place in history.

"I don't worry about that," says Ferguson. "That's never bothered me as far as who gets the credit. I think just to be associated with a great team like that is enough for me."

Ferguson says he understands that he was fortunate to be the head coach at Thornridge when Quinn Buckner arrived at the school.

"Being in the right place at the right time is half of anything you do in life," says Ferguson. "As I say, I was about two years from maybe being canned, or maybe being so frustrated I would say, 'I'm gonna try something else.'"

"Then Buckner came along," the coach continues. "We went to their grade school games and saw some of those players playin', and I said, 'I gotta stay. I gotta stick around for awhile. I better behave myself and not get [fired].' I said to myself, 'That might be my ticket [to success].' And, as it turns out, it was."

"Let's face it. I wouldn't be where I am today," says Ferguson. "I might have been successful in something else, but it wouldn't have been coaching. I've always maintained that. If I hadn't had him [as a player], then [who knows where I would be]. Everything that has happened is an extension [of Buckner] since we won those championships. The different jobs I've had, the honors, the Hall of Fames, and all that, if it wasn't for him, I wouldn't be in any of that stuff. I've always given him all the credit."

When Buckner heard his high school coach was giving him credit for all of his successes in life, Quinn was quick to respond.

"That's an overstatement," says Buckner. "That's really an overstatement. That's Coach Ferguson. He's a good guy. He's a terrific man. He don't owe anything to me. Hell, I was just on a good team."

Buckner continues, "All it was is circumstance and fate. I believe it was supposed to happen to him, as it was supposed to happen to all of us."

"I don't have any illusions, or delusions," laughs Buckner, "about what I [meant to Ferguson and the team]. I understand how I fit into the program."

While Buckner was the most important player in the Thornridge program, Ferguson was the man responsible for guiding the team to consecutive state titles while winning 64 of 65 games over two years. Those in the coaching fraternity understand how Ferguson influenced his championship teams.

"In all the time I've been coaching, there was nobody that I had more respect for the kind of job he did than Ron Ferguson," says Hall of Fame coach Bob Knight. "He did a great job with that team."

Knight became friends with Ferguson while recruiting Buckner to play at Indiana. Knight realized the makeup of the Thornridge team required a coach to have firm control of its cast of characters. Keeping a group of teenagers focused for two full seasons requires great patience and a special gift. Ferguson was that kind of coach. He had the ability to read his team and address its needs.

Gary Cunningham, then a UCLA assistant coach under John Wooden, attended a Thornridge home game while recruiting Buckner and came away very impressed with Ferguson.

"It isn't as easy as people think from the outside," says Cunningham. "You have to get those people to play together, sacrifice for each other. Be a team. I think he did a tremendous job. People that have all the talent don't always win. You have to blend the talent together."

Like Knight and Cunningham, both of whom won NCAA championships, Steve Fisher won a national title after taking over at Michigan. Fisher, who coached his Rich East High School team against Thornridge, appreciates the job Ferguson did during Thornridge's perfect season.

"When you're that good, you [might] overlook what Fergie brought to the table for that team," says Fisher. "He was able to manage those egos and those pieces maybe better than anybody else possibly could. The pressure of expectations of [being] defending state champs, and to be as dominant as they were, he was obviously more than a bit player in the whole process."

Fisher adds, "Fergie was a terrific coach, and a better person. Fergie was never a big ego guy. He was never [about] 'me, me, me.' With him, it was always [about] the players. He did a great, great job."

Ferguson recognizes that he could not have enjoyed success at Thornridge without the sacrifice and support of his assistant coaches through the years. He talks proudly about Frank Nardi, Al Holverson, and Dave Lezeau, all of whom became head coaches and took their respective teams to the state tournament. Ferguson also points out that Ron Bonfiglio, Sam Tortorici, and Bill Hardlannert were very important parts of the Falcon's success. They were freshmen and sophomore coaches who developed the young players while also serving as scouts for the varsity.

Ferguson's last game as a high school coach was the 1972 state championship game. He planned on returning the next season to help his team extend its state record 54-game win streak. But, he was forced to make a choice. He had an opportunity to take over for the retiring Frank

Froschauer as the Athletic Director at Thornridge. However, to get the job, he had to give up coaching the Falcons.

"I had mixed emotions," says Ferguson. "I kind of wanted to stay and coach at least another year because we had the [state record] winning streak going. I tried to get them to let me coach one more year, as both A.D. and coach, and then I would retire from coaching. They thought about it for awhile but then said they couldn't do that. So, I had to make a decision. Those jobs don't come along every year. Once they hand somebody else the A.D. job that job's gone, and I'd have to figure out something else. I thought I better take it right then."

One would think concessions would have been made to allow Ferguson to coach since he had won consecutive state championships. But, it wasn't to be.

"They said, 'You are either going to be the Athletic Director, or you're going to be a basketball coach,'" says Ferguson wistfully. "I decided I wanted to get into administration. I spent three years as A.D. at Thornridge."

Quinn Buckner did not know at the time that his basketball coach was considering an administrative position. Yet, he was not surprised Ferguson used his state championships to secure a better paying job.

"What coach did is what any and all of us could'a, would'a, and should'a done," says Buckner. "All of us that could get to college, got to college. You really just make your next step. Coach clearly had a situation that he maximized. You win [a state championship] twice in a row, you've maximized all you can do at that level. The question is, do you want to stay, or do you want to go on and try to do something else? He wanted to do something else."

Buckner was at Indiana, and Ferguson was the Thornridge A.D. when the 1972-73 season rolled around. Quinn's mother admits she was disappointed when Ferguson gave up coaching. Jessica Buckner felt Ferguson had done a good job dealing with the racist comments from some white parents.

"I hated to see Mister Ferguson leave the area because I thought that he handled the boys and the situation very well," says Jessica Buckner. "You're not just thinking about your own children. You worry about [all of] their safety because people have such strong feelings. It was new territory. These are new kids on the block. They were obviously more talented than the (white) kids that were there, but they just happened to be African-Americans. The other kids, and their families, had to admit, uh, well, it was difficult for them to admit that these kids were better. That was not an easy period for parents. But, we bonded. We bonded."

Ferguson served as the Athletic Director at Thornridge for only three years. He then moved to central Illinois, where he would remain, even in retirement. In 1975, Ferguson was offered a job as an assistant basketball coach at Illinois State University under Gene Smithson who had been hired to replace Will Robinson. Ferguson made sure the job also included an administrative position.

"I said I'm not coming just to be an assistant basketball coach," Ferguson recalls telling Smithson. "'I know how those things go. I'm there for two years, and you go someplace else or get fired.' So he got me in as an Assistant Athletic Director. I had an administrative position which gave me a little more security."

To take the job at Illinois State, Ferguson had to leave his job as A.D. at Thornridge. He might have remained at Thornridge for many years, but in the mid 1970s he had children that would soon be heading off to college. He saw problems ahead unless he took the I.S.U. job and moved to Normal.

"One of the reasons I decided to go was, my kids were all getting not too far away from where I was going to start worrying about where they were going to school," says Ferguson. "I said, 'Well, this could be a big help to me [financially] as far as them going to college.' My daughter, the oldest, graduated from Illinois State, and my two boys both graduated from Bradley [University]. At Illinois State, you don't get free tuition, but the tuition's not anywhere near what it is at a private school. She could stay home, so she didn't have any room and board [costs] until I moved."

Three years later in 1978, Ferguson became the A.D. at Bradley University and benefited from a job perk that allowed children of the private university's employees to receive free tuition.

"My two sons got tuition and books and all the stuff that goes with it," says Ferguson. "They stayed home [to save money] the first two years. I had a little pull. I got them jobs in the [Robertson Memorial] Field House in their off-hours, so they could pick up a few bucks here and there. They'd clean up after the games or set up before the games. Financially, that was a hell of a deal for me. When they were in high school, I tried to imagine how I was going to pay for their college."

Ferguson would have been happy to finish his career as an assistant coach and administrator at Illinois State, but when Gene Smithson left after the 1977-78 season to coach at Wichita State, Ferguson again had to make a difficult career decision.

"I enjoyed the college thing," says Ferguson. "I enjoyed Illinois State, and I would have stayed there when Smithson left, but I didn't want the [head coaching] basketball job. They wanted me to take the head coaching job. I [told them that I] didn't come to the college level to be a coach. So, I went to the A.D. and said, 'What guarantee am I going to have for a job in case the new basketball coach either doesn't want me as an assistant or if it was somebody I didn't want to work with?' He said, 'We can't promise you anything.' So when Bradley came over and asked me to apply for that [A.D.] job, I took it."

Ferguson spent the next 21 years at Bradley, the first 18 as the Director of Athletics, then working out of the President's office as Director of Special Projects. His job those last three years involved fundraising and investigating athletic facilities at private schools similar to Bradley. He considered it the most relaxing job of his career. He believes moving from coaching into administration probably saved his life.

"I wanted to get into college administration," he recalls. "I could not have been a lifetime coach. I would be dead now. I could not handle it. I would have had a heart attack or somethin'. I gave up the hollerin' and screamin' after about the first four years [at Thornridge]. I started enjoying it a little bit more, but I worried about everything all the time. I couldn't sleep half the time stewing about how we were going to get this [Thornridge basketball program] turned around. You can't let that happen to you because you're not fair to your family or anyone else. You get so engrossed in a job that you can't [have quality family time]."

Ferguson was divorced from his first wife Dawn in 1988. He re-married in 1995. He and Linda have been happily married for more than 14 years. Ferguson realizes his preoccupation with trying to turn Thornridge into a winning program put a strain on his first marriage.

"I put so much importance in that," says Ferguson. "I think a lot of it was when I was involved at Thornton we always had such success. I couldn't figure out how in the world I was ever gonna come anywhere close to [doing] what they did at Thornton. It was a long struggle to get there. I wasn't sure I could do it."

Ferguson says he was only able to win big because of the integration of Thornridge.

"You know, you gotta have some players,' he says. "You can help players get better, but better talent is going to win out in the long run, no matter how hard you work. The players worked hard, and they got a lot better. But they just weren't as good as some other players."

The early struggles at Thornridge became distant memories when Quinn Buckner and the other players from Phoenix became Falcons. The consecutive championships and then-record winning streak meant Thornridge would be remembered as one of the nation's best high school basketball teams. Ferguson says it used to annoy him when he would be introduced to someone as Bradley University's Director of Athletics, and in the same breath, as the former Thornridge High School basketball coach.

"It's funny," says Ferguson. "Once in a while I still get it [when being introduced], 'Ron Ferguson is the [former] Athletic Director at Bradley, but he won those state championships [at Thornridge]. He's the former coach.'"

In retirement, Ferguson spends half of the year living near Peoria in Dunlap, Illinois. The winter months he spends in Florida. He is proud of the many things he accomplished while serving as Bradley's A.D. Among the highlights were transferring the women's athletic program from the Association for Intercollegiate Athletics for Women (AIAW) to NCAA Division 1 even though there was no extra money in the budget. He also hired Dick Versace to replace Joe Stowell as men's basketball coach. Versace would eventually run into trouble with the NCAA, but he won three Missouri Valley Championships and twice took Bradley to the NCAA tournament. The Braves also went to the National Invitation Tournament three times during his tenure, winning in 1982.

"We went to some tournament, the NCAA or N.I.T., probably nine or ten times in the 18 years I was A.D. there," says Ferguson proudly. "We won five conference championships. They still haven't won a conference championship since I left in '96, although they went to the "Sweet 16" one year."

While the hardworking Ferguson accomplished a great deal at Bradley, he admits he never found anything quite as exhilarating as winning those state titles with Quinn and company in 1971 and 1972.

"No, because [when] you go into a profession, there are different measures of success in whatever profession you're in," says Ferguson. "If you're a lawyer, do you win a lot of cases? You can be a coach all your life and never have any kind of major success, unless you take pride in doing something good for the kids, you know, [like] developing the kids and their manhood and those kinds of things."

"But, when you start out," he continues, "everyone wants to coach a great team or win a championship of some kind, whether it's a league championship or [state title]. A state championship is obviously a little harder. When you finally do that, you think, 'Well God, I finally accomplished something in my profession.' [After] all the work and stuff you put in all those years, it makes you feel a lot better. That's what you're in it for."

While Ferguson and Thornridge still receive a great deal of recognition from winning the 1972 state championship in undefeated and convincing fashion, the coach admits the 1971 state title probably meant more to him personally.

"Yeah, I think the first [championship] was, in a way, more important," says Ferguson. "You never know what could happen the next year. You gotta take advantage when you get it because you may never get another chance. There's no question that was more important because all of a sudden everything was worth it."

The 1971 state championship might have been more significant to Ferguson since he earned the respect befitting the coach of a state champion. But make no mistake about it. His 1972 team was special. It accomplished things that had never been done. The Falcons thoroughly dominated every opponent, from the opening tip of the season until the final horn sounded at the end of the state championship game.

The team's brash point guard Mike Bonczyk says the 1971 championship was rewarding, but the 1972 championship meant even more because it was validation of Thornridge's greatness.

"Winning the first state title [was fun]," says Bonczyk. "At the time, we didn't realize what we had accomplished. Everything was new. It was great. Then, the work comes in the next year. The second year we validated a lot of things, especially when people talk today about [Thornridge being] the greatest team. We started number one and ended number one. We took names, kicked ass, and everybody says we're on top of the list [of great Illinois teams]."

CHAPTER 6

We Were Gym Rats

As the calendar turned from November to December, *"Theme from Shaft"* was replaced atop the Billboard charts by a song from Sly and the Family Stone. *"It's a Family Affair"* quickly shot up to number one just four short weeks after debuting as the 50th hottest record in America. The funky tune could easily have been the theme song of the Thornridge Falcons. The tight-knit basketball team was indeed "family", and like Sly Stone's latest hit, Thornridge was a clear number one. The only difference was Sly's *"Family Affair"* would fall from number one after three weeks. Coach Ron Ferguson's "family" would remain number one for months to come.

The Thornridge Falcons, champions of the Rockford Guilford Thanksgiving Tournament, were preparing for the only game appearing on their schedule in the first weekend of December against highly-regarded Waukegan. While the team focused on basketball, much of America was talking about a TV-movie that aired for the first time on Tuesday, November 30th on ABC. "Brian's Song" starred James Caan and Billy Dee Williams as Chicago Bears' teammates Brian Piccolo and Gale Sayers, the NFL's first black and white roommates. "Brian's Song" told the true story of the relationship between the two football players and of the death of Piccolo who died young of cancer in 1970.

An advertisement in the new issue of TV Guide that week offered any six Columbia Tape Club stereo tapes for just one dollar. Club members had a choice of tape cassettes, 8-track cartridges, or 7-inch reel-to-reel tapes. The issue was also filled with cigarette ads glamorizing Pall Mall filter tips,

L&M Menthol, Camel Filters, Viceroy, True Filters, and Marlboro. The Marlboro ad pictured a lovely country scene with a simple message "Come to Marlboro Country."

In the communities around Thornridge High School, it was Falcons' country. The season had only just begun but the defending state champs had shown no sign of slippage from the previous season. Even so, it was believed the Falcons might be challenged by the tall and powerful Waukegan Bulldogs. Waukegan was coming off a 64-47 drubbing of Thornton High School. The Thornridge players knew Thornton was a quality team, so they were focused throughout the week of practice as they prepared for the game against the Bulldogs. The Falcons were anxious to get on the court and prove to everyone that they were the class of Illinois high school basketball.

***

GAME 5 (Saturday night, December 4, 1971)
Waukegan

It was touted as a showdown between the two best high school basketball teams in Illinois. On Saturday night, December 4, 1971, Waukegan (2-0) arrived in Dolton to challenge the defending state champs. Thornridge (4-0) was unquestionably the number one team in Illinois. Although no statewide polls had been tabulated, individual newspapers had their own rankings and Waukegan was rated either second or third. Thornridge point guard Mike Bonczyk remembers there was electricity in the air as the Bulldogs came to town.

"Waukegen was ranked [number] two in the state," recalls Bonczyk. "They were loaded. They had [Dave] Bitterman, [Dom] Demkiw, Bill Rucks, [and] they had a couple of guards that were pretty nice [players]. The year before, we barely beat them up at their place. They came down to our place. Our gym sat about 5000, and it was sold out. They piped in TV video into the cafeteria and sold tickets there."

Waukegan was big and powerful, led by six-eleven, 250 pound Bill Rucks who would average 22 points and 13 rebounds during the season and gain recognition as a first-team All-State performer. The Bulldogs had a lineup that also included players standing six-eight and six-five, an incredibly tall high school basketball team for that era. Some wondered whether Thornridge would be able to rebound with the bigger Bulldogs. When Waukegan scored the first four points of the game, there might have been a few in the sold-out Thornridge gym concerned about the home team's 25-game winning streak. The Falcons quickly erased all doubt by taking a 24-8 lead by the end of the first quarter. Buckner scored 7 of his team-high 20 points in that first period. Thornridge pressed Waukegan into 19 first-half turnovers, and the Falcons upped their lead to 45-18 by halftime. The lead reached 70-34 early in the fourth quarter, and Coach Ron Ferguson gave his starters the rest of the night off allowing the reserves finish the 75-50 victory. Bonczyk and Quinn Buckner played tenacious defense and combined for a dozen steals. In addition to Bonczyk's five thefts, he dished out 11 assists. Rucks finished with a game-high 22 points for Waukegan, but four of his eleven field goals came in the final period after the Falcons' starters had gone to the bench. Boyd Batts had 17 points and 9 rebounds and proved he could match up with the big boys. Thornridge answered the question whether it could rebound against a taller team. The Falcons out-boarded the Bulldogs 34-30. Coach Ferguson told reporters after the game it was one of his teams' best efforts ever. He decided to reward his team by implementing a new practice regimen.

"We beat them by 25 points," says Bonczyk. "So Fergie calls the first six guys, the starters and Bill Gatlin, and he says, 'Look, I don't want to wear you out. I want to go to just practicing four days a week. We're not gonna practice on Mondays so some of you guys can work on your grades. If you want, you can come in and work out and shoot on your own. But I want a Tuesday's practice to be a Tuesday's practice. I don't want it to be a Monday's practice.' We said, 'Okay, fine.' So after the Waukegan game, we never practiced on a Monday. We practiced Tuesday and Wednesday. We played hard Tuesday. We played hard Wednesday. Thursday, even though it was a prep day, we still played hard. Friday and Saturday, you play [games]. You gotta understand. We had fun playin'. I'm just tellin' ya. We were gym rats that loved bein' in the gym. All we did was play."

***

GAME 6 (Friday night, December 10, 1971)
Eisenhower (Blue Island)

Six days after beating Waukegan, Thornridge (5-0) again played in front of a sellout crowd in Dolton. This game was important because the Falcons' next six games would be played away from home. The game against Blue Island Eisenhower (4-1) was also significant because it was the South Suburban League opener. Eisenhower had captured the league's football championship just weeks earlier, but Buckner and the Falcons' basketball squad would gain a measure of revenge on a cold December night in Dolton. Thornridge jumped on top early and for the second straight game led 24-8 after one quarter. The lead was 42-21 at intermission after the Falcons shot a school-record 67% (18 of 27) from the field in the first half. Although the quality of play in the second half paled by comparison, Thornridge coasted to a 75-52 victory. The Falcons shot a scorching 60% (32 of 55) from the floor over the course of the game. Junior Greg Rose led the way with 24 points, 10 in the first quarter coming as a result of several fast break layups. Buckner scored 19 and pulled down 14 rebounds to go with 7 assists. Batts added 15 points to help Thornridge win its 27th straight game. Nearly four decades later, Buckner remembers the Falcons were a combination of ability and intelligence.

"We were good basketball players," he says. "I think any time you have the kind of success that we were able to have, you've gotta have smart players. Ernie was exceptionally bright and still is. Greg has very good basketball intelligence, and so does Boyd. Mike was extremely bright. I don't know where Mike got all of his basketball knowledge, but I think he got it from his dad. His dad was a coach, and [Mike] played like a coach's kid. And I understand what I brought to the table athletically as well as intellectually. I think [skill and intelligence] really is what you gotta have in order to have success."

Although his team seemingly had it all, Ron Ferguson felt his Falcons might be tested when they tried to extend their winning streak to 28 games. He was glad he had a full week to prepare his team for a tough road game against chief rival Thornton High School. One thing the Falcons practiced every day was free throw shooting. Ernie Dunn remembers a time he and Buckner squared off from the line.

"I remember in practice Quinn and I had a free throw shooting contest," recalls Dunn. "It was at the end of practice. We were shooting and I'd hit maybe ten or fifteen, and he'd hit ten or fifteen. Everybody stood there watching he and I shoot. We shot like 40 or 50 in a row. I don't even remember who won, but that was one of the most memorable things I remember in practice."

***

GAME 7 (Friday night, December 17, 1971)
Thornton (Harvey)

Only 2.8 miles separate Thornridge High School in Dolton from Thornton High in Harvey, but there had been many miles of separation between the basketball traditions of the two schools prior to the arrival of this group of Falcon players. Thornridge was a relatively new school with limited success in athletics until Quinn Buckner led the football team to the 1970 state championship and the basketball team to the state title in 1971. On the other hand, Thornton had played winning basketball for decades. Many local residents had difficulty deciding which school to root for when the two teams met on the hardwood. Harvey native Lou Boudreau had moved to Dolton and become a Thornridge fan even though the Baseball Hall of Famer had starred for Thornton's first state championship basketball team in 1933.

"Lou Boudreau enjoyed watching our team so much that he came to most of our home games," remembers Thornridge coach Ron Ferguson. "He became a big fan. Lou was a wonderful guy, just the best."

Ferguson understood all about divided loyalties since he had played for Thornton and was an assistant coach at his alma mater before becoming the head basketball coach at Thornridge. Lloyd Batts, Boyd's older brother, was a two-time All-State player at Thornton before the district's boundaries changed and forced the younger Batts to attend Thornridge. The Dunn family also had divided loyalties. Senior Otis Dunn was the star of the 1971-72 Thornton team while junior Ernie Dunn had been forced to leave Thornton and was a starter for Thornridge. Many of the Thornridge and Thornton players were friends off the court, but they always battled one another on the playground courts and in the packed gymnasium on game nights. None of the Falcons or Wildcats wanted to lose to his chief rival. Thornton coach Tom Hanrahan remembers the players' familiarity with one another made for a very intense rivalry.

"Yeah, they played all the time on the playgrounds over there in Phoenix," says Hanrahan. "They grew up with each other. When we'd play away and Thornridge would play at home, there'd be some of that bunch from Thornridge in our gym when we got back from the game. I remember the night when [Quinn and Boyd] were sophomores. They beat Bloom and gave us the [league] title outright. A couple Phoenix kids from that Thornridge team were there and celebrated with the players we had at Thornton that lived in Phoenix. They celebrated [and] then left together.

There was that kind of friendship among the players. It was the type of situation where they'd go on the floor [and] they'd go at each other. But off the floor, they were friends, good friends."

A boundary change during Ernie Dunn's sophomore year at Thornton meant he would be required to transfer to Thornridge as a junior. Ernie was disappointed. He believed if he had remained at Thornton, the Wildcats might have had enough firepower to beat Thornridge even with Buckner, Batts, and Rose starring for the Falcons.

"I honestly thought my junior year, the team we would have had [at Thornton] would have competed pretty well with Thornridge," says Dunn. "Even though we were good friends, I wanted to beat 'em. We had the best sophomore team at Thornton. We won our division as sophomores. We had some good guys. Randy Ramsey was coming up to the varsity. We would have had a decent team. I think I'm the only person that left [Thornton to go to Thornridge] out of the sophomores I played with. I was the only one."

The Thornton coach admits losing Dunn to Thornridge was a crushing blow to his team and a huge boost to the Falcons.

"Oh sure that was a big disappointment," says Tom Hanrahan. "He was the one I think that filled out that [Thornridge] team to give them the success they had."

Hanrahan says it's only conjecture that Thornton would have won numerous state championships if there had been no boundary changes and Dunn, Buckner, Batts, and Rose had all remained in the Thornton school district. But he admits the Wildcats would have been very good.

"Both of those years that Thornridge won the state tournament, we had records that included about twenty wins," says Hanrahan. "That was a lot of wins for that district between the two teams."

Once Dunn transferred to Thornridge, he felt no allegiance to Thornton. He desperately wanted to beat his former school.

"Thornton always gave us trouble because we had played with each other growing up," says Dunn. "We knew everybody, and [we knew] each other's plays. We knew our abilities and what our strong points were. I think that was the game we had the most fear of [losing] every time we played them."

With Christmas just a week away, followers of Thornridge and Thornton basketball were treated to an early present. Fans in Chicago's south suburbs had circled Friday, December 17 on their calendars. Thornridge (6-0) at Thornton (4-1) figured to be an outstanding game. It did not disappoint.

In the Thornton Field House, the noise was deafening during the player introductions. It was then that the Thornton fans made a huge impression on Ernie Dunn who was playing against his former school for the first time.

"They booed me when I got out on the court," remembers Dunn.

As the opening tip approached, the Thornton fans worked themselves into a complete frenzy in the belief that their team might hand the Falcons their first loss in nearly a full year. Thornridge, led by the early scoring of Buckner, quickly quieted the crowd by racing out to a 14-3 lead. However, those fans were again on their feet as the Wildcats stormed back. Junior guard Randy Ramsey burned Bonczyk for 12 points in the second quarter, and his last basket in the period tied the score 29-29 with 1:30 left in the half. A basket by Rose and a 20-footer by Buckner allowed Thornridge to take a 33-29 lead into the dressing room at halftime. Thornridge Coach Ron Ferguson talked no game strategy during the intermission. He simply told his players he was glad this had happened because he wanted to see if his team could play in a tight game in the second half. His players responded. Bonczyk tightened up on defense and did not allow Ramsey to take a shot in the third quarter. Batts and Rose combined to hold Thornton's high-scoring Carl Richardson to just one bucket the entire game. Thornridge used its hustle and overall quickness advantage to methodically pull away in the second half and win 71-54. Buckner led the way with 20 points and 10 rebounds. Batts added 19 points and collected 14 boards. Rose scored 18 points. In the first of three Dunn family showdowns that season, Otis had 19 points and 11 rebounds for Thornton, but Ernie scored 10 points and helped his team get the victory. Ernie fondly recalls his first varsity matchup against his older brother.

"I remember double-teaming him with Boyd," says Dunn, who adds with a laugh, "I remember punching him a couple times. They didn't call a foul on me. Boyd was fronting him, and I was behind him just jabbing him in the back. Every time I double-teamed the guy I'd do it. The referee didn't see it. Boyd fronted him, and I stood behind him and just pounded him in his side. He felt it, and he beat me up when I got home."

The only Thornridge player who was not thrilled with how things went that night was Nee Gatlin. He never got in the game.

"The only game I did not play in my life was against Thornton High School, our biggest rival," says Gatlin. "[After the game I had] tears in my eyes. Here I am with a lot of pride, and I'm sitting over there getting dressed. Ferg walked up to me and said, 'I apologize for not getting you in the game.' I just looked at him with water in my eyes. I know he could see the frustration in my look. That was a downer. Bonczyk was gettin' ate up by Ramsey. I can check Ramsey. I beat Ramsey up all the time throughout our careers. In that game, I'll never forget it. Quinn walked up to [Ferguson] on the bench and said he wanted Coach to put me in. He looked down at me, but never did [send me into the game]. That was the only game I never played in my life."

***

GAME 8 (Saturday night, December 18, 1971)
Proviso East (Maywood)

For the second night in a row, the Falcons would play a former state champion on the road. Exactly one week before Christmas and nine days before they would play in the Carbondale Holiday Tournament, the Falcons were in Maywood to play Proviso East, the school that had won the 1969 state championship behind the stellar play of powerful Jim Brewer. Brewer later starred at the University of Minnesota and had a successful NBA career. But even if he had been playing for the Pirates against Thornridge, it might not have made a difference. The Falcons were simply too good.

In the first minute, Thornridge's full-court press led to fast-break layups for Dunn and Buckner. Shortly thereafter, another steal resulted in a Bonczyk to Rose layup to make the score 10-0 Falcons. It was 14-1 before the host Pirates scored their first field goal midway through the first quarter. Al Holverson, the former Thornridge assistant coach who scouted for the Falcons in the 1971-72 season, recalls that a quick start was nothing unusual for Quinn and company.

"The games were usually over about six minutes into the game," says Holverson. "It would be 28 to 4, something like that. Then they'd just jockey for the final score. But nobody could get the ball past mid-court."

Ron Bonfiglio, the sophomore team's coach that season, says Buckner's football skills translated into success on the basketball court.

"You can imagine how good he was in basketball playing the middle on the press because he did it on the football field playing [as] the safety," says Bonfiglio. "Rose was on the ball. Bonczyk and Dunn were at the 'two' place in the 1-2-1-1 [press]. Quinn had the whole middle. Batts was [playing all the way] back, or he would come up and split the half-court if it was the 1-2-2 [press]."

"We did another thing I think a lot of teams couldn't quite figure out," says Thornridge head coach Ron Ferguson. "When we used our full-court zone press, we dropped into a man-to-man [defense]. What happened many times is you weren't covering the same guy you were supposed to cover. But we had zones [on the court], and if you were in this zone, you picked up whoever the man was in your zone. So once in a while, Batts would be on a guard out front. But that was okay. Most time if you are dropping into a zone they get time to organize, and we didn't want to give them time to get organized. They could not figure out what we were doing or how to adjust to it. Once they struggled [to get] the ball down the floor, they tried to get into their offense. Sure they scored an easy one now and then, but our kids were quick enough that they could recover."

Thornridge was relentless against the Pirates, attacking on defense and offense. Another 10-0 scoring burst made it 24-3. The Proviso East fans sat in stunned silence. The host school scored a pair of baskets in the final ten seconds to cut its deficit to 33-14 after one quarter. The Falcons sank 14 of 19 shots from the field in the first period. They cooled off and made only 3 of 14 in the second quarter but still shot 53% for the game and breezed to an 89-59 win. Buckner finished with 26 points. Batts had an incredible game with 21 points and a career-high 24 rebounds. Rose (14) and Dunn (11) also scored in double figures. With their eighth consecutive win of the season and 29th straight dating back to the previous season, the Falcons were on a roll. Proviso East coach Glenn Whittenberg gave other teams a bit of hope by saying after the game he felt Thornridge was as good as it would ever be. He suggested the Falcons couldn't possibly get any better than they looked against his team. Actually, they did get better. Thornridge averaged 84 points through the first eight games of the season, but the Falcons would average more than 87 points per game by season's end. After scoring more than 90 points twice in the first eight games, the Falcons incredibly scored 90 or more points in more than *half* of their remaining 25 contests.

Coming up right after Christmas would be another test for the Dolton gang. The Carbondale Holiday Tourney and a possible revenge game against the last team to beat Thornridge would add spice to what had already become a very special season.

Around the state, the other top teams continued to win during the first three weeks of December. Unbeaten Lincoln won Big 12 Conference home games over Danville, Champaign Central, and Mattoon and captured road wins over Springfield and non-conference foe Springfield Lanphier.

In the win over Lanphier, deadeye perimeter shooter Mike Swingle scored a game-high 26 points. Six-eight junior center Norman Cook, who would be named All-State at the end of the season, had 23 points and 10 rebounds while six-six forward Tim Bushell contributed mightily with 16 points and 17 boards. Hinsdale Central, La Salle-Peru, Maine South of Park Ridge, North Chicago, and Aurora East also remained undefeated. Quincy won four of five games in December prior to the Christmas tournaments. The Blue Devils posted wins over Rock Island Alleman, Moline, Tilden Tech, and East Moline. Their first loss of the season came on December 10th in a narrow 73-70 defeat on the road against Rock Island. Quincy would quickly right the ship and not lose again for more than a month.

CHAPTER 7

Wasn't Nothin' I Could Do

BOYD BATTS HAS HAD THE most difficult life of all the 1971-72 Thornridge basketball players. His early years were filled with considerable heartache and pain. His mother was unable to care for her many children. His father was shot and killed in a card game when Boyd was only nine years old. Any child would find it difficult to overcome such tragedy. Boyd had a rougher time than most because he had gone with his father and was there to see his father gunned down.

"There wasn't nothin' I could do," says Batts, remembering the moment his life forever changed. "I was with my Dad when he got killed. I was sittin' up under the table."

Boyd is hesitant to talk about the tragedy, but older brother Lloyd fills in the details.

"My dad was shot when my brother was nine years old and I was twelve years old," says Lloyd. "I'll tell you if it wasn't for the grace of God and my aunt [we wouldn't have survived]. My aunt was my father's sister, and we were going to be awarded to the courts because my mother was a deaf-mute and she couldn't take care of us. So on [Dad's] dying day, my aunt promised that she would take us and raise us. She didn't want to see us be out there all alone."

"Yeah, if we did not go live with them, we'd probably [have] been in a foster home," says Boyd. "I was glad that my father's sister took us. It really was my uncle. He said, 'I'm not lettin' my brother-in-law's kids stay in no foster home. They [are] comin' to stay with us.' And they came and got us. They took us [to Phoenix], and the next day we was livin' with them."

The story of the Batts family is filled with sorrow. Lloyd notes that several of his siblings died tragically.

"I had nine brothers and sisters," says Lloyd. "I lost a baby brother. He got accidentally smothered by my father and mother [while] sleeping in-between them. I lost a sister to pneumonia. Then I lost my oldest two sisters and oldest brother when a guy set their building on fire, and they got trapped. All this [happened] when we were young. My [older] sisters and brother died about a year or two after we were awarded to stay with my aunt. If we'd a' been there, we'd a' passed away too."

It's true that had their aunt and uncle not moved Lloyd and Boyd to the south suburbs, the two Batts brothers might not have survived to become two of the state's most celebrated basketball players. And if they had not moved out of the city, they were likely headed for trouble. Before they were even teenagers, Lloyd and Boyd were running the streets of Chicago.

"That was a bad time," says Boyd. "We was doin' a lot of the stupid stuff. I really don't even like to think about the things I used to do. Right now, I don't like people that steal. I don't like people that lie. I'm on the straight and narrow road."

Though siblings, Lloyd and Boyd were not particularly close as youngsters.

"Growin' up we didn't [get along], because we came from a real wild background," says Lloyd. "From bein' in the city where you just ripped and run, rip and run. You didn't do very much of anything, even go to school to tell you the truth. Then when we moved to the suburbs, we had this desire to go back to the city because we knew that's where all our friends was and our family was. But as we got involved in sports, we started to get closer and [began to] adapt to our new surroundings."

Once they moved to Phoenix, the Batts boys no longer ran the streets. They had new responsibilities. Their aunt and uncle had put them both to work.

"We wasn't used to havin' to do chores and work and do things of that nature," says Lloyd. "And [also to] come in at certain hours. We were basically raising ourselves in the city."

Despite their disdain for chores, the Batts brothers were making the transition to life in the suburbs. It was not all work and no play for Lloyd and Boyd. They found they could have a lot of fun playing basketball.

"We made a little wooden basket in the back yard," says Boyd.

"I wasn't really into basketball," says Lloyd. "Then, one of my friends talked me into playin'. We built a basketball court out in the back with a telephone pole. Quinn and [Boyd] was much younger. They wasn't even playin' basketball yet."

Playing on the basket behind their aunt's house and also at Coolidge Elementary, the Batts brothers and their friend Quinn Buckner became proficient at the game. They realized they had real basketball talent. They began to dominate the local playground games, so they started challenging themselves by travelling to compete against players from outside the local area.

"As I grew older and started to play more, they got involved," says Lloyd. "Every time I wanted to play, they wanted to play. So I put a little team together. We used to hear about all the kids in Chicago [and] how good that they thought they were. We used to go down and play against the kids from Dunbar [High School] because they always used to say the kids from the suburbs was afraid to come and play the kids from the city. I knew the city 'cause me and my brother was born and raised in Chicago. We wasn't afraid of Chicago and going to the city to play ball. I had a small reputation at the time because I was voted one of the best players as a junior in high school. Everybody knew who I was. They didn't know who Quinn or my brother was. We would play all the time. We'd drive up to the city and play at Dunbar and different places on the West Side. That's how we got really involved in playing basketball."

Like their friend Quinn, Lloyd and Boyd matured, physically and in terms of their basketball skills. Both Batts brothers were recognized as All-State players once they had become stars of their respective high school teams. Being older, Lloyd was first to garner attention from fans and the media. While starring at Thornton High School, Lloyd made the All-State team in both his junior and senior seasons. His final year at Thornton he received special recognition as the best player in Illinois and one of the best in the nation.

"I was the Chicago Sun-Times [Illinois High School] Player of the Year my senior year," says Lloyd Batts proudly. "They changed it to 'Mister Basketball' after that. I was All-State and All-American as a senior."

The attention Lloyd received made Boyd more determined than ever to improve as a basketball player so that he might receive similar postseason honors. Initially, Boyd had been upset about the redistricting that forced him to attend Thornridge instead of Thornton where he could have played on the same team with his older brother. But Boyd became more enthusiastic about playing for a different school when he realized he would be able to make a name for himself at Thornridge.

"When we was in grade school, it was 'the Batts Boys,'" says Boyd. "Then he went to Thornton, and it was like 'You gonna follow your brother? You gonna do what your brother [is] doing?' I said to myself, 'I'm going for myself now.' When they said I was gonna get bused to Thornridge, I was like, 'I guess here's my chance.'"

"He didn't want to be in his brother's shadow," says Thornridge coach Ron Ferguson. "Lloyd probably was better at handling the ball, but Boyd became a great rebounder and shot blocker. He was about six-seven-and-a-half. He had those long arms and he could block shots like you can't believe. He learned to shoot from the outside. Lloyd was maybe a little more coachable. Boyd was a pouter if things weren't going right, whereas Lloyd had a better head on his shoulders in terms of those kinds of things. But I think [Boyd} got his own identity [at Thornridge], and that's what he wanted."

It was probably a good thing that the Batts brothers did not play on the same high school team. Ernie Dunn, who during his sophomore year was Lloyd's teammate at Thornton before becoming Boyd's teammate at Thornridge the following year, says the Batts brothers always had problems.

"I don't know if it rooted from something when they were young," says Dunn. "But I know they didn't really get along with each other. They still don't. I don't know what the rift was between them. We had a couple all-star legends' games the last four or five years where it was Thornton against Thornridge. Boyd was there. Lloyd was there. And they didn't even talk to each other. I could tell from what Lloyd said that they still didn't get along. You can't make people talk to each other. Obviously something does root between them. Fortunately, they went to two different high schools."

Lloyd suggests Boyd might still be upset about having had to play in his own brother's shadow.

"It could be because he always wanted to try to prove he was better than what he was or trying to prove that he was better than anybody else that was playin'," says Lloyd. "That is okay, but it is how you go about doin' it. It's from your actions and playing. It's not from the newspaper [publicity] standpoint."

Despite whatever personal problems existed between the Batts brothers, Boyd had dreamed of winning a state championship with Lloyd at

Thornton. He admits to some initial disappointment when the boundaries were changed, and he found out he would be bused to Thornridge.

"At first it was like a letdown," says Boyd. "Then when we got over there, and when I met Coach Ferguson, that's what turned my life around. I was a roughneck when I was goin' to school. [I] didn't want to listen. [I was] getting in trouble. [I] got suspended a couple times."

Boyd was indeed a difficult student during his first years at Thornridge. Part of the problem was when he first came to Thornridge in the fall of 1968 he was a part of just the second class of blacks to be integrated into the school. There were white students still resentful about having blacks in their school, and they went out of their way to make the black students feel unwelcome.

"In 1968, it was rough," says Boyd. "[The whites] said they didn't want us there at first. We was bused there, and they used to throw [things] at our bus and everything."

The younger Batts brother thinks there was resentment because white athletes were losing their roster spots on Thornridge athletic teams to more athletically-gifted black players.

"At the beginning there was [resentment], but then it turned different for some reason," remembers Boyd. "I guess [it was] because as a team we [blacks and whites] stuck together. We come to practice together. We walked around the school together. We ate lunch together."

Boyd Batts says blacks were treated differently by the white Thornridge students once the school's athletic teams became more successful due in great part to the infusion of the talented black players.

"Yep, it was a whole lot different," he says. "People used to give us rides and stuff like that. They would come and talk to us, when at the beginning, they wouldn't even say nothin' to us."

While some white Thornridge students were still making it difficult for black students being bused in from Phoenix, Batts was able to make plenty of friends, both black and white.

"You know, I enjoyed my high school years," he says. "I had a lot of friends and a lot of fun. My friends were white. When I started playin' real good for 'em when I moved up [to varsity] my sophomore year and I started playin' ball, people started acceptin' me to their house and invitin' me to parties. Those were good times, man. Those were good times. I miss them days."

As an upperclassman, Boyd played a critical role in helping the Thornridge basketball team reach new heights, but he had earlier tried the patience of the Falcons' coaching staff. Batts did not want to hear that he needed to work on his game in order to improve.

"Boyd didn't take criticism well," says head coach Ron Ferguson. "He would just pout and pout and pout. So [assistant coach] Dave [Lezeau] would put his arm around him [to console him]. Dave was good that way. [Boyd] was very difficult. He was better as a senior, but as a junior he thought he knew everything. He was tough to deal with a little bit. But boy, it was tough [when he was] a sophomore. He was on the varsity as a sophomore, but I had some other [talented] guys so I just sat him down."

Dave Lezeau, Ferguson's right hand man during the 1971-72 season and his eventual successor as head coach at Thornridge, remembers there were times Ferguson and Batts would not speak to each other.

"Batts and Fergie would kind of be on each other's case," recalls Lezeau. "There were some times during the season Fergie wouldn't want to talk to Batts. He would say, 'Hey Dave, go tell Batts he better get his buns in gear defensively.' Fergie didn't want to talk to Batts, and Batts didn't want to hear from Fergie either. I became kind of the liaison or whatever you want to call it."

Frank Nardi, the Ferguson assistant who became Thornwood's head coach in the 1971-72 season, says Batts was not a bad kid, but a young man that needed some direction.

"I got along well with him," says Nardi. "And he was always funny. He always had that little smile on his face. Boy, could he shoot the ball. He had unlimited range. He also played defense. But he was not a leader at all. In my opinion, Quinn kept him in line a lot, which kept Boyd from going off where Fergie had to deal with him."

Nardi gives Ferguson credit for keeping things together when Batts could easily have created a major distraction.

"Boyd was probably the biggest challenge," says Nardi. "And Mike Henry was also a challenge [in earlier seasons]. Fergie did a great job in handling all of that. When they had to be disciplined, he disciplined them. He was not a weak coach. When they needed discipline, he did a nice job. But he did it within the team. There was not too much that people knew about outside of the team."

Ron Bonfiglio, the sophomore coach at Thornridge during the 1971-72 season, coached Batts as a freshman in 1968-69.

"He was a *handful*," says Bonfiglio. "There were times Batts would really test you. I remember [when Boyd was on the varsity] Fergie one time making a statement to Lezeau, 'I'll coach eleven guys. You coach Batts.'"

With a laugh, Bonfiglio adds, "Thank God [Batts] had Buckner and Bonczyk to keep him straight. I remember going into the locker room, and it was a close game. Bonczyk just turned around and grabbed him. Batts was pouting, and Bonczyk said, 'Hey, we're not gonna lose this game. You forget about not scoring your points.'"

Bonfiglio says scoring the basketball was one of the most important things in the world to Batts. His desire to score was not limited to Thornridge varsity games. Bonfiglio remembers Boyd's desire to get his touches once led to a confrontation with his brother during a pickup game on the playground.

"His brother Lloyd threw the ball and hit him right in the middle of the chest with the basketball," says Bonfiglio. "Batts was complaining [that] he wasn't getting the ball. Lloyd just took the ball, threw it, and hit [Boyd] right in the chest. He said, 'Here. You want the ball.' Bang. He just banged the ball off his chest. [Lloyd] said, 'Get in there and rebound. You'll get the ball.' But, [Boyd] had to be scoring. He had to go through that stage. It finally got knocked into him that you don't have to be a great scorer to play well. You can still rebound, block shots, and be an intimidator."

Batts finally began to understand how to be a complete player during his senior season. He had many games in which he scored in double figures and also pulled down ten or more rebounds. His defense and shot-blocking ability was one reason Thornridge dominated its opponents. Batts loved game nights. It was his time to shine. Practice was another matter. Boyd was never a fan of running wind sprints at the end of practice. Point guard Mike Bonczyk says there was one time during his team's perfect season that the players had a good laugh at Boyd's expense.

"Practice would be winding down, and we always ended up with sprints," says Bonczyk. "Boyd knew when practice was starting to wind down, when we had only five or ten minutes left. He would come up with some ailment. He got hurt going up for a rebound, or he came down and banged knees with somebody. He'd limp, and he'd limp, so he wouldn't have to run. So one day in practice, he pulled this [stuff]. I looked at Quinn, and I said, 'Quinn, pass the word. When Fergie says, "Sprint", everybody fall down.' Sure as hell, Boyd pulls his deal where he gets hurt. We get on the line, and I looked at Fergie and said, 'Coach, how fast do we have to go to get this one done?' Fergie said some [amount of] time. [Getting ready to start running sprints], I said, 'Okay, one, two, three.' And everybody fell down."

"Boyd got pissed and walked out of the gym," laughs Bonczyk. "It was unbelievable what he used to do. Boyd was a treat."

Bonczyk says it's understandable why so many people might have been a little leery of Boyd. He remembers Batts had a look that was downright scary.

"Boyd had a look, okay?" says Bonczyk. "If you didn't know him, he was kind of intimidating with the look he used to give people. But oh, he was funny. Boyd had some issues, but the one thing I'll tell you about him is when it came time [to play] on the floor, he answered the bell every game."

Boyd respected Bonczyk and listened when the point guard offered advice. Fellow teammate Quinn Buckner also played a key role in keeping Boyd focused on basketball during his Thornridge days. Though Batts liked and respected Buckner, Quinn was challenged trying to keep Boyd in line. Once during a timeout, Buckner noticed Batts watching the cheerleaders and not listening to the coach. Buckner grabbed Batts, shook him by the shoulder and said for him to pay attention to Ferguson.

"You had to do it with Boyd periodically," says Buckner. "Boyd could easily get lost. He was easily distracted, so every now and then, you'd have to shake him up. I was the one person that most likely could do it."

Batts recalls that incident and says he had a good reason for looking at the cheerleaders.

"I used to go [out] with one of them cheerleaders," says Boyd. "Her name was Gayle Lester. [Quinn] say, 'She'll be there after the game man. Now focus over here.'"

The girl was white, Batts black. In the early 1970s that was a controversial issue.

"It was, but we didn't care," says Batts, "because I really cared for her."

Batts drew criticism from some members of the media after the 1971 state championship game when he held hands with the cheerleader during the on-court trophy presentation which was televised on the statewide network. Actually, Ron Ferguson's entire team was criticized for how it celebrated its 1971 championship.

"After the Oak Lawn game [some people] thought our kids were standing [disrespectfully] and that they were goofing around during the trophy presentation," says Coach Ferguson. "A couple of the black players had their arms around the white cheerleaders and stuff like that. We got a little bit of heat from some of the media."

Batts was aware that he risked criticism for holding hands with the white cheerleader because interracial dating was not generally accepted in the early 1970s.

"[Coach] talked about that right after the game,' remembers Boyd. "He let us know people ain't gonna like that you were doin' that. It was like, man, we came down there [to Champaign] as a unit, a team. If they [are] our cheerleaders, they are a part of our team. So [people] shouldn't have been angry, but that's the way they felt back then."

Teammate and long time friend Quinn Buckner says Batts probably knew there would be a strong reaction when he held the cheerleader's hand on the floor of the Assembly Hall.

"Boyd was a radical," laughs Buckner. "I'm telling you he was a rebel with a cause all the time. That's why you always had to watch him because you didn't know what Boyd was gonna get into. Now here's my honest opinion. Boyd probably wasn't seeing the girl, but he was crazy enough to do that because he was going to [try to] tick people off. Because that's what Boyd did. He's going to anger those who were angry at him. Boyd had that kind of streak in him."

Coach Ron Ferguson knew he could count on Buckner to try to keep Batts focused on basketball. Ferguson felt Quinn always thought like a coach on the court.

"It was a good thing," says the Falcons' coach. "A lot of guys would just say, 'It's none of my business. It's not my job.' But he knew [what needed to be done]."

Al Holverson, the varsity assistant in 1971 and part-time scout in 1972, says Buckner was the glue that held the team together.

"Every team's got a few squabbles here and there," says Holverson. "But Quinn was such a strong leader that the squabble was over. It was just, 'Hey. Cut it out.'"

Dave Lezeau, the varsity assistant coach in 1971-72, says during the perfect season the team stayed on the same page pretty much start to finish.

"There were very little internal problems among the players," recalls Lezeau. "I guess that's really due to Quinn [being] such a quality person. His teammates respected him as the team leader. People bought into him and what we were trying to do. They followed him so there were very few personal conflicts within the team. There some things between coaches and players from time to time, but they were a very together group."

While Batts' senior season was relatively blissful, there was an incident at the end of his junior season that may have been the turning point in getting him to understand that the team was more important than any individual.

"I remember Batts stormed off the basketball court in the last game of the '71 season prior to the regional," says Al Holverson. "The team said that he doesn't [get to] play the next game which was the first game of the regional. That's a strong thing for the team to come up and say, 'You have to be *with* us.'"

"Hey listen, it didn't take a lot to upset Boyd," says Buckner. "You had to be delicate with Boyd because you could lose him. It wasn't so much Boyd losing it. It was how long it takes you to get him back. That was really the problem."

Batts can remember what happened when he was suspended for the first regional game in 1971.

"Other people were sayin' that I was doin' [bad] things, and I wasn't," says Boyd. "I called 'em all liars, and then I cussed too. The coach didn't like that. I was disciplined, but you know I deserved it. I didn't dwell on it. [Coach Ferguson] was tellin' me, 'You need to focus on playing, not focus on other things.' Coach made the decision. I wasn't happy about it, but what could I do? He's the coach."

While they did not always see eye to eye, Batts says he can't recall ever being seriously upset with his high school coach. Batts might have frustrated the coaching staff, but Boyd saw in Coach Ron Ferguson a father figure who cared about his players.

"The first time I got a chance to play for him," says Batts, "I saw a difference in the way he talked to us and the way he treated us while we was playin' and everything."

While Batts doesn't remember being upset with Ferguson, he knows there were times the coach was not pleased with him.

"He got pissed off at me when he thought I wasn't reboundin' and tryin' to score and puttin' the ball in [the basket]," says Boyd. "He'd tell me, 'What's your problem? You can score.'"

Though Ferguson wanted him to score, there were times the coach felt Boyd was taking too many shots. Ferguson believed one player should not be able to outscore an entire team. He wanted balanced scoring on offense. That wasn't always easy with Batts looking to get more than his share of touches.

"You know [when] you play you'll say, 'He [is] having a good game so keep getting him the ball. Feed him the ball,' says Batts. "Coach would say, 'No, it ain't about just giving it to him. It's about everybody playing together because there is no *"I"* in *"team"*.' That's something he installed in our heads."

During Thornridge's perfect 1971-72 season, Batts averaged an impressive 19.1 points and 11.9 rebounds per game. He earned first team All-State honors, but was denied the Illinois High School Basketball Player of the Year recognition his brother Lloyd had received at Thornton two years earlier. Boyd might very well have been named the Player of the Year if it were not for one of his own teammates. Quinn Buckner earned that distinction after averaging 22.7 points, 9.2 rebounds, and 5.4 assists. Nearly four decades later, Boyd admits he was jealous of Buckner's notoriety after Quinn was recognized as the 1971-72 Illinois Player of the Year and the National High School Athlete of the Year.

"Yeah, it did bother me a little bit," says Boyd. "But I just pushed it aside because we needed to just focus on winning. But after we won [a second straight state title], I figured I should have been All-Everything too."

Boyd desperately desired recognition but could not get it playing in the shadows of his brother Lloyd and his friend Quinn. His search for validation led him to distant points around the nation. After graduating from Thornridge, Batts played one year at Vincennes Junior College in Indiana. After one year, he transferred to the University of Hawaii where he lettered as a sophomore. Boyd then transferred to the University of Nevada -Las Vegas where he played two seasons for Jerry Tarkanian. It was a match made in heaven.

"He was ineligible to play at Hawaii because something happened with his transcript," says Tarkanian. "But it wasn't Boyd's fault. The NCAA ruled that he couldn't play at Hawaii, but he could play anywhere else. He could play immediately, and he chose [UNLV] which was really good for us because I *loved* him. Everybody knew about him. He played on a great high school team, one of the best high school teams in the country. I just remember how tough he was. He was just so tough."

Batts may have had problems handling authority during his high school days, but he matured into a team leader while playing for Tarkanian.

"Yeah, he was Captain of my team his senior year," says Tarkanian. "He was a great competitor. He played so hard. We didn't have a big man, so he played center for us. He was so quick. He could front the post and you couldn't get the ball by him. He was so quick. He was so intense. And he was so tough. He's as tough a kid as we had here."

Tarkanian had a reputation for recruiting tough characters at UNLV. The team often was made up of Rebels with a cause, so for Tark to say Batts was as tough as any UNLV basketball player he ever coached is truly saying something. The legendary college coach says Batts even put the fear of God into some of his own teammates.

"I never had any trouble with him, but I'll tell you what," says Tarkanian. "We had a big center from L.A. that was seven-foot and about 250 pounds. He would try to intimidate some guys. Well, he was scared to death of Boyd. Boyd would go right after him, and he knew it. Boyd was skinny, but he was tough as nails."

Having had his authority challenged by Batts during their Thornridge days, Coach Ron Ferguson was somewhat surprised to learn Boyd had been named a captain at UNLV. But Tarkanian says he made Batts a captain precisely *because* Batts was willing to challenge authority.

"Well, I like that," says Tarkanian. "He wouldn't back down from anybody. And he had such quick hands. I doubt that anybody could have beaten him in a fight. His hands were so quick. He'd hit you four times before you know what happened."

Ironically, the player whose primary focus in high school was shooting the basketball became a defensive specialist at UNLV. Batts averaged only 9.2 points as a junior. As a senior, he averaged 11.2 points on the 1975-76 UNLV team that averaged an incredible 110.5 points per game. He was the Runnin' Rebels sixth leading scorer that season, and only once did he lead his team in scoring in a game. He was UNLV's fourth leading rebounder that season averaging 7.3 per game. Three of his teammates averaged more than 8.5 boards per game. There were plenty of rebounds to be had. UNLV averaged an incredible 93.5 field goal attempts per game.

At UNLV Batts was a teammate of several players who spent time in the NBA. He played with Ricky Sobers his junior year in 1974-75 and with Reggie Theus the following season. Other teammates included big men Glen Gondrezick, Lewis Brown, and Jackie Robinson who were on the team both years Batts was in Las Vegas. The Runnin' Rebels all-time scoring-leader Eddie Owens (2221 career points) was the team's top scorer both years Batts played in the desert. In college, nobody worried about getting Boyd his touches. Batts had to be content simply being a part of two successful UNLV teams that reached the second round of the NCAA tournament. The 1974-75 squad, the first UNLV team to be called the Runnin' Rebels, went 24-5. In 1975-76 UNLV finished 29-2 and had an amazing 23 games in which it scored more than 100 points. In 1975 postseason play, UNLV beat San Diego State in a first-round game but lost to Arizona State 84-81 in a West Regional semifinal played at the Memorial Coliseum in Portland, Oregon. In the 1976 NCAA Tournament, Batts and the Runnin' Rebels beat Boise State 103-78 in a first-round game played at the University of Oregon's MacArthur Court in Eugene. However, UNLV lost its West Regional semifinal in Los Angeles to Arizona 114-109 in overtime.

Of all the games Batts played at UNLV, one stands out in Tarkanian's mind.

"We played Centenary with Robert Parish," says Tarkanian. "We fronted the post every game. We never varied from that. I remember people said, 'You can't front Parish. They'll just throw it high to him.' I said, 'We front everybody. We don't back off.' Boyd fronted Parish the whole game. Parish didn't have a point at halftime. He got quite a few in the second half, but Boyd shut him out in the first half. He fronted Parish, and they couldn't get the ball to Parish. [Boyd] was so quick and so tenacious."

UNLV won the game 121-92.

Tarkanian had lost track of Batts and did not know that his former player was now working as a cook in a nursing home in Madison, Wisconsin. Batts played pro ball overseas for a number of years and later worked for the United States Postal Service. Batts has had serious financial problems and says he wishes he had gone back to school to get his degree so he could have been a full-time basketball coach. His college coach wants Boyd to know that he still has fond memories of their time together.

"Give my best to Boyd," says Tarkanian. "Tell him I still love him."

Boyd's high school coach also has warm feelings for his former player.

"He was a good kid at heart," says Ron Ferguson. "He just really had a tough time."

Though Batts had a good college career and later made a little money playing pro basketball overseas, he never made the big money stars make today for playing the game. He also never received the recognition he felt he deserved as one of the nation's top high school players. It was always those closest to him who received the accolades.

Batts deserves great respect for what he accomplished at Thornridge. High school players throughout the United States dream of winning a state title. Batts started on back-to-back state championship teams and helped the Falcons win an Illinois record 54 consecutive games over a season-and-a-half. His performance at the Illinois state tournament his senior year was one of the greatest ever. During a one week stretch when "March Madness" was at a fever pitch in Illinois, Boyd Batts was the most dominant player on the most dominant team in the state's history.

CHAPTER 8

Are They For Real?

AFTER COACH RON FERGUSON GAVE his players and coaches a few days off so they could spend Christmas with their families, Boyd Batts and his teammates boarded a train the morning of Monday, December 27, 1971, and headed to southern Illinois. The Falcons were on their way to compete in the 16-team Carbondale Holiday Tournament. It was in Carbondale one year earlier that Thornridge had been stunned by Mounds Meridian, a small school from a small southern town located near the Kentucky state line. The stunning 48-40 upset on December 29, 1970, was the only defeat suffered by the eventual state champions who bounced back from the loss to finish the season 31-1. Nearly a full calendar year had passed, and the loss to Mounds Meridian remained Thornridge's most recent defeat. The Falcons hoped to get a chance to avenge the loss. If both teams won their first two games in Carbondale, Thornridge and Mounds Meridian would meet in the tournament semifinals.

Thornridge head coach Ron Ferguson was not looking past the first game against Marian Catholic, a school that made the long journey from Chicago Heights, a south suburb located only minutes from Dolton. Ferguson wasn't exactly thrilled with the first round pairing.

"We go down there [because] we wanted to play southern Illinois teams," says Ferguson. "And in the first game we get Marian Catholic. We could have scrimmaged [against] them on Saturdays [at home]."

Ferguson wanted his team to shake off any signs of rust, so he scheduled a practice for that Monday afternoon. The Falcons stepped off the Illinois Central train just a few minutes before two o'clock. By 3 p.m. they were on the court at Carbondale Community High School. It was their first team workout in three days. A few minutes after 4 p.m., the team left the high school for the motel. Once there, the players were told to gather in the lobby by 5 o'clock for the 5:30 p.m. tournament banquet.

Television cameras and newspaper reporters closely monitored the Thornridge team. The Falcons were a big story for the southern Illinois media. Since Thornridge had failed to win the Carbondale tournament the previous year, there were some reporters who wondered if Thornridge might again stumble after venturing so far from home. The Falcons planned to prove themselves to the skeptics. They vowed to show everyone in the south that they were worthy of all the hype. Thornridge had a 29-game winning streak and again entered the Carbondale tournament as the top-ranked team in the state. Coach Ron Ferguson believed in his team but thought the Carbondale tournament would provide a true test. He felt that if the Falcons could win their four games in Carbondale it would be a sign that they could fend off any challenge in the months ahead.

"That was where we lost the only game we lost the year before," says Ferguson. "We kind of laid an egg down there. We were picked number one, and God, we lost to a team that nobody ever heard of. They were pretty good really. The next year they had most of those guys back, and they placed [second] in the [Class A] tournament. They turned out to be a lot better [than people thought], but at the time nobody knew who the heck they were at all. So we had a lot to prove at Carbondale. In the paper [writers asked], 'Are they gonna do what they did last year down here? Are they for real this time?' So we were hoping we'd get [Mounds Meridian] again."

Al Holverson, the varsity assistant at the time Thornridge was shocked by Mounds Meridian, remembers the players were getting a little big-headed before they were upset by the small southern Illinois school.

"Guys were signing autographs before the game," says Holverson.

"Yeah, we were big [fan] favorites," says a bemused Ferguson.

"And we got beat 48-40," continues Holverson. "Nobody could buy a basket down there. There was a lot of foul trouble, so it wasn't a pretty picture. Fergie said, 'Okay guys, do what you want tonight, but [tomorrow morning] we're on the train at six [o'clock].' The next few practices were rather rigorous. They figured it out fast."

Boyd Batts acknowledges that he and his teammates pulled together after the loss to Mounds Meridian.

"When we lost that one game, Coach [Ferguson] told us, 'You lost the game because you all didn't play [together],' says Batts. "He said, 'From this day forward, I'll bet you all play [as a team].' Every player on the team talked to each other and said, 'From here on out, we [are] playin' [together]. We [are] gonna win.' And we didn't lose another game."

Ferguson believes the loss to Mounds Meridian actually benefitted his team in the long run. Realizing they were not invincible, the players became more focused which paid immediate dividends.

"The very next game we played was the first game that started the streak of 54 wins in a row," says Ferguson. "That was at [Chicago Heights] Bloom. We went out that night, and I'll tell you what, we played great. Bloom did not know what hit them. The final score wasn't that far apart (80-69). We got a big lead, and they scored a few at the end and made it reasonably close. But it wasn't really ever close. That was the game that really made us that year. We started with that game and, boy, we didn't lose another game."

The Falcons still had not lost since starting the streak against Bloom on January 8, 1971. Could they keep the streak alive and win the Carbondale Holiday Tournament? Indeed they could.

***

GAME 9 (Tuesday afternoon, December 28, 1971)
Marian Catholic (Chicago Heights)

Thornridge (8-0) and Marian Catholic (4-3) tipped off their first round game at 2:30 Tuesday afternoon in the Southern Illinois University Arena. Perhaps it was rust caused by inactivity over the holiday, or maybe the Thornridge players knew they would likely cruise past Marian Catholic, but the Falcons struggled in the first quarter. That was a huge shock to Thornridge fans since in the first eight games of the season, the Falcons had outscored their opponents 188-95 in the opening period. This time there was no quick start. Marian Catholic surprisingly led 14-13 at the end of the first quarter. Coach Ferguson was not happy with his team's performance and let the players know it between the first and second quarters. Quinn Buckner says it was easy to tell when the Falcons head coach was upset.

"Coach Ferguson was pretty calm, but you knew when he was mad because he'd talk real fast and stuff would start flying out of his mouth," laughs Buckner.

Thornridge was out of sync, particularly Buckner who was battling the flu and wound up making only 3 of 16 shots from the field to finish with only 12 points and 3 rebounds. Though Buckner struggled, Marian Catholic was clearly outclassed. The Falcons awakened from their slumber and outscored Marian Catholic 47-19 over the second and third quarters en route to an 86-52 victory. Greg Rose led the winners with 27 points and 10 rebounds. Boyd Batts had 20 points, 16 rebounds, and 6 blocked shots. The game had been a little more difficult than expected, but Ernie Dunn remembers the Falcons knew every team they played had Thornridge in their sights and firmly in the cross hairs.

"It helped keep us focused," says Dunn, "because the year before they had a tarnished record by losing to Mounds Meridian in a game they should have never lost. That was the focus, to make sure that we knew everybody was out to get us, and they were going to pull out every stop they could come up with."

***

GAME 10 (Wednesday, December 29, 1971)
Eisenhower (Decatur)

The following day, Thornridge (9-0) went for its 30th straight win against Decatur Eisenhower, a strong team out of central Illinois that entered the game having won seven of its first nine games. In its first game in the tournament, Eisenhower had overcome a 17-3 deficit to defeat eventual Class A champion Lawrenceville 63-53. The Panthers held Lawrenceville standout Rick Leighty to zero field goals and only 2 points. It looked like a good matchup on paper, but the Dolton gang never gave the Panthers a chance. The Falcons, known for their fast starts, had one of their best starts of the season. Thornridge won the opening tip, and a quick 3-point play by Greg Rose was immediately followed by back-to-back steals and layups by Quinn Buckner. Thornridge led 7-0 only 23 seconds into the game. The Falcons defense had not allowed Eisenhower to get the ball across the half-court stripe.

"Our attempt was to jump on them early and quick," says Ernie Dunn, "and not let them get into their game plan. For the most part that worked. We'd just make sure that at the beginning of the game we started off with our best defense. We knew where everyone was gonna be. If we got out of position, we played another person's position. It wasn't like Boyd had to run back to play the center. If Greg was back there, or Quinn was already back there, Boyd would jump into the middle. Whatever we had to do, we'd always fill in for each other to make sure we had the position covered. We could all play each other's positions on defense and offense if we had to. Defense was where we excelled. Athletic talent on offense, we were pretty good. But I think the defense is what stifled people more than the offense. The defense brought [us] a lot of our points. People didn't think it was organized, but it really was. We had plays to run [on offense]. It was just that we could get so many steals."

When Decatur Eisenhower was able to control the basketball and run its offense, the Panthers were effective. In fact, they shot 61% from the field in the first half. The problem was they could only occasionally get into their offense. Because of turnovers caused by the Thornridge press, Eisenhower had only half as many shot attempts (46-23) in the first half. By game's end, Eisenhower had committed 32 turnovers, and the Falcons had posted their 30th consecutive win 89-63. Buckner bounced back from his poor first game in Carbondale and poured in 31 points. Rose scored 29 giving Thornridge a devastating one-two punch. In the Carbondale tourney semifinals, the Falcons were hoping for a rematch. They got one, but not the one they were anticipating.

***

GAME 11 (Thursday afternoon, December 30, 1971)
Manual (Peoria)

The Thornridge players had been hoping for a chance to avenge their only loss from the previous season. Mounds Meridian was a good basketball team, but the Falcons wanted to show Meridian that the previous year's result had been a fluke. Thornridge held up its end of the deal by winning its first two tournament games. However, Mounds Meridian was surprised by Peoria Manual 44-43 in the tournament quarterfinals. That meant the semifinal would be a rematch between Thornridge and Manual, teams that had met one month earlier in the Rockford Thanksgiving Tournament. As always, Coach Ron Ferguson was concerned. He thought his players might experience an emotional letdown because they had so badly wanted another chance at Mounds Meridian. He also worried about a possible lack of focus since Thornridge had blown out Manual by 47 points in their first meeting. Ferguson knew that Rams' star Mike Davis had been injured and not able to play his best when the two teams had squared off in Rockford. The six-six, 230 pound Davis, who sat out two weeks following the Thanksgiving Tournament because of the injured knee, was now healthy and a real force inside. Manual coach Dick Van Scyoc was optimistic about his team's chances.

"I felt that we had a shot at 'em," says Van Scyoc. "I felt that we had a shot at 'em every time we played them except at Rockford where we were banged up and [had] just come off the football field. I didn't anticipate playing them at Carbondale, but the schedule worked out. The teams just happened to fall in line, and here we are lookin' at 'em again."

The two teams battled throughout the first half. Thornridge led 21-12 after one quarter, but Manual rallied. After outscoring the Falcons 27-17 in the second quarter, the Rams led 39-38 at halftime. It was the only time all season Thornridge would trail at the half. The Falcons remained confident they would win. They bounced back with a superior second half against Manual. The Rams were still dreaming of an upset midway through the third quarter. The scoreboard read, Thornridge-48, Manual-44. However, Thornridge went on a 19-2 scoring run to take control. The Falcons poured through 54 points in the second half and coasted past the Peoria school 92-65 for their 11th win of the season and 31st straight victory overall. Thornridge made 40 of 68 shots from the field (.588). Greg Rose finished with a game-high 29 points. Quinn Buckner added 24, Ernie Dunn 17. Point guard Mike Bonczyk scored 10 points and recorded a school-record 17 assists.

Peoria Manual captain Wayne McClain finished with 20 points, tying Davis for team honors. He says after getting embarrassed in Rockford, the Rams had wanted another shot at the Falcons.

"They'd beaten us so bad, we kind of wanted a measuring stick to see if we could play with them," says McClain. "We were good, but it just seemed like those guys were so good at every position. Our center [Davis] was as good as their center [Batts], but Quinn was so much better than anybody that we had. They had a good point guard in Bonczyk. We felt there was some parity there, but our defense [had] hurt everybody, and he did a great job of handling our defense. That was the whole key. We just couldn't rattle them."

McLain, who was named to the Carbondale All-Tourney Team, says the Falcons played with the maturity of a much older team.

"That's probably the best way to describe them," says McClain. "They played beyond their years. The thing that was the most impressive about them was everybody knew their roles. Everybody could score if they wanted to, but they just were so methodical at the way they approached the game. They never showed emotions on the floor. They were just a team that had a swagger about them back then that was different than anything I had seen."

"We had confidence," says Quinn Buckner. "We knew we could play. Some of us used to go to the West side of Chicago to play. And the guys on the West side [were good]. I used to play against them, so I knew that I could play. I'm sure there was a certain swagger because of it. Not *arrogance*, because arrogance is the wrong word for me. I was never really arrogant, [but] I always believed in what I could do to the *Nth* degree. My dad was like that, and I've always believed in [having confidence]. I do think that permeated our team because I always shared the *confidence* with my teammates, but not in an arrogant way. We knew we could play."

Coach Ferguson always hated it when his team had to play the host school in a holiday tournament. He could not have been thrilled when Carbondale rallied to beat Chicago St. Patrick 61-57 in the second semifinal game. The Terriers would be the Falcons' next opponent.

***

GAME 12 (Thursday night, December 30, 1971)
Carbondale

There wasn't much time for either team to rest. Thornridge (11-0) had the benefit of playing the first afternoon semifinal while Carbondale (7-2) had to endure a hard-fought game later in the afternoon. That evening in the championship game, Ron Ferguson knew the fans at the SIU Arena would be quite vocal in support of the hometown team. He hoped for another quick start to quiet the crowd. His team delivered. Carbondale led 8-7 three minutes into the game, but Thornridge scored 12 straight points over the next 1:48 to take command. Thornridge led 27-14 after one quarter. After a somewhat even second period, the Falcons outscored the Terriers 21-6 in the third. Game over. An 85-47 romp over the host school gave Thornridge its 33rd consecutive victory and the Carbondale Holiday Tournament championship. Mike Bonczyk assisted on nine of his teammates' baskets giving him 43 assists in the four games in Carbondale. Buckner, named All-Tourney and the tournament's Most Outstanding Player, made 13 of 21 shots from the floor and scored a game-high 29 points. Ernie Dunn and Greg Rose scored 20 points apiece in the title game. Rose, who was also named to the All-Tourney Team, made 7 of 10 shots against Carbondale to finish the four tournament games with an incredible shooting percentage of .717 (33 of 46). Ferguson said while Buckner was impressive, Rose probably should have been recognized as the tournament's MVP. The junior, whose affinity for music was well-known, had played his best basketball while providing some beautiful "string-music" for the Falcons.

Coach Ferguson's team had passed its test with flying colors. In four games in Carbondale, no team had come closer than 28 points to knocking off the Falcons. Ferguson now believed his team was up for any challenge. The players knew it too. Ernie Dunn says he was so focused on just winning the next game on the schedule that he wasn't aware that the Falcons were accomplishing something unique in the history of Illinois high school basketball.

"That season I went through half of it not realizing what was happening," says Dunn. "I knew we were winning. At midseason, all the hype started. You try to avoid the newspaper, but you do see it. I think that was when it started sinking in that we were doing something special. To me, it was just us going out doing what we normally do and playing. I think midseason is when it started turning to the point where everybody was watching us. They were already watching us, but it seemed like [the attention] tripled. We got many more people [paying attention to us] after the Christmas tournament."

While Thornridge was winning the Carbondale Holiday Tournament, Aurora East was capturing its own Christmas Tournament in impressive fashion. Coach Ernie Kivisto's team hit the century mark while easily winning all three of its tournament games. Aurora East scored 106 against Sandburg and 106 against Downers Grove South before knocking off previously undefeated Maine South 100-69 in the championship game. In the final, six-six center Greg Smith made 13 of 17 field goal attempts while scoring 30 points for the winners. Kivisto, obviously feeling good about his squad, proclaimed that his team should be ranked number one in the state. Aurora East was very good, but could the Tomcats match up to Thornridge? Could *any* team really compare to the high-flying Falcons?

Following the Holiday Tournaments, the Associated Press conducted its first Class AA basketball poll of the season. Thornridge was a unanimous number one. The Falcons swept all of the first-place votes from the 16-member poll board. Central Illinois power Lincoln was ranked second after improving to 12-0 by winning four games to capture the Edwardsville tournament crown. Aurora East (11-0) was third, a single point behind Lincoln in the poll. Unbeaten Hinsdale Central (11-0), the

DeKalb tourney champ, ranked fourth, two points behind Aurora East. Quincy (11-1) ranked fifth in the first AP poll after winning the Pekin tournament by scoring wins over Peoria Limestone, Toluca, previously undefeated North Chicago, and host Pekin. Pontiac Holiday Tournament champion Rock Island Alleman (8-1) was rated sixth, followed by Lockport (8-1), East St. Louis Lincoln (8-1), Waukegan (9-2), and La Salle-Peru (10-1). Joliet Central's Roger Powell scored 49 points in a win over previously unbeaten Morgan Park in the Danville tournament. Joliet Central (9-2) ranked eleventh in the first AP poll, and Morgan Park (11-1) was rated twelfth. Champaign Central (10-3) ranked thirteenth, followed by Maine South (9-1), Rockford Holiday Tournament champion Chicago Carver (8-2), and Belleville West (8-2).

CHAPTER 9

We've Been On The Big Stage

LIKE HIS THORNRIDGE TEAMMATE BOYD Batts, Greg Rose grew up under very difficult circumstances. When Rose was eleven years old, his father died after being given a transfusion with the wrong type blood following an automobile accident. Rose's mother was sick and had no job. Rose had five brothers and two sisters. There was little money to clothe and feed the family.

"Yeah, we had food stamps," remembers Rose. "My mother wasn't able to work."

Coach Ron Ferguson knew Rose did not always have enough food to eat.

"I had about five or six kids who were just from the poorest families," says Ferguson. "Batts was one and Rose was one. The best meals [Greg] got was when we went to these tournaments and fed the team. He loved that."

Ferguson cared about every one of his players but felt a responsibility to do whatever possible to make sure his poorest players had enough food.

"I used to go to one of the fried chicken places," says Ferguson. "I'd get several orders to give to the kids to take home so they could have a meal. I had a friend that was a manager for a Dominick's grocery store. At Christmas time, I had them fix up these bushel baskets of food. They'd get canned hams and things like that. I'd take those and deliver them to their house on Christmas Eve. It was very much appreciated by the people that got [the food]. But there was the white element in South Holland that found out what I was doing. They said, 'Well I don't know why you can't give [food baskets] to all the other guys on the team too.' They were racism [based] statements. Somebody always takes exception [thinking] you're catering to a certain element. You can't win. Naturally I got a little heat for that, although no one told me to stop doing it. And I didn't [stop]."

Before Rose went to Thornridge and benefited from Ferguson's charity, he often went hungry. There simply were not enough food stamps to feed the large Rose family. Greg says his hunger forced him to steal.

"When I was about twelve or thirteen, I did [go hungry]," says Rose. "I remember stealing a bag of potato chips from the neighborhood store. [The owner] caught me and said, 'Greg, you never did that before. Why did you do it?' I told him, 'Man, I haven't eaten in a couple days.' He said, 'I'm not gonna take it out on you this time. I'm gonna give you a bag of potato chips.' He said, 'If you [are] ever hungry, call me. Let me know.' And he would feed me."

Other people were aware that Rose and his family did not have enough money for food.

"There was a guy that owned a bakery there in Dolton," says Rose. "He would bring some bakery pastries and stuff. I was [also] able to go to school and get breakfast at the cafeteria. They set that up for me. I felt privileged because I was the only one in there in the mornings."

With little food or money, Greg Rose looked for a way to improve his family's financial situation. A talented drummer, Rose and several of his musically-inclined brothers formed a group and began performing. Kenny Rose, a reserve player on the 1971-72 basketball squad, also played in the band. Thornridge teammate Mike Bonczyk says music was always very important to Greg.

"Greg had a lot of issues as a young kid, and his release was his music," says Bonczyk. "He played drums, and I don't think anybody knew it until halfway through his sophomore year. They had his band perform at one of the after-game dances."

"I had to do what I had to do," says Rose. "That was one of my professions, so that's what I did. Music soothed me, and I always wanted to play music when I was a kid. Me and my brothers were self- taught. We got out there and figured one day we're going to have a hit record."

"Greg used to play a basketball game and literally go and sing after basketball games, even if we had Friday and Saturday games," says Quinn Buckner. "This is a guy who is sixteen, seventeen years old who had to be incredibly mature to do that and then [also] stay engaged with his team. We would lose him every now and then, but it was nothing that we couldn't get by. I really look at the sacrifices those guys made in order for us to be better as a team. It's the sacrifices that everybody made [that really stand out]. Greg was better skilled than I was, and Boyd Batts was better skilled than I was for the most part. They were better players, and they all figured out how to sacrifice. But for Greg to do what he did, in retrospect, it was the responsibility that he showed to his family and to the team that allowed us to be good. Again, for a guy in high school at that age to be that responsible to his family and to his passion for basketball and to his teammates, it was, I don't know if *noble* is the word. But it says something about his moral values."

Coach Ron Ferguson does not remember Rose playing many gigs on game nights.

"I don't think that happened often," says Ferguson. "I think it might have happened once or twice. That wasn't a regular thing. A lot of that was done in the offseason. If he *was* out all night, you couldn't tell. I'll tell you what. He could run up and down the floor faster than anybody. He was faster than heck."

To complicate matters for the young man from Phoenix, Rose fathered a pair of children while at Thornridge.

"I had two in high school," says Rose. "I think I was a sophomore when I had my first one. I *had* to work. Quinn told me not too long ago that he had a lot of respect for what I had to do with kids [to care for]."

Greg made sure to remain in contact with his children when he moved to California to pursue a career in music in 1980.

"I moved to California, but I kept in touch with my kids," says Rose. "I'm a grandfather of seven or eight."

While at Thornridge, Rose was very quiet. He rarely said anything on the basketball court. He was similarly reserved off the court. He kept to himself and talked only to his closest friends.

"Greg was one of those quiet types of players," says teammate Mike Bonczyk. "You talk about a silent assassin. He went out and played, and he never said a word. That was just his personality. He never said anything. But with people that he knew, like Quinn and myself, he'd talk up a storm."

Like many former high school classmates, Bonczyk and Rose failed to stay in touch after becoming adults and moving out of state to pursue their careers. But the two former Thornridge stars got reacquainted after Rose was given Bonczyk's telephone number during the time interviews were being conducted for this book. Rose quickly called Bonczyk.

"I hadn't talked with him in I don't know how long," says Bonczyk. "But he called, and we must have talked for about an hour. It was just, 'What have you been doing? How ya been?' It's like we picked up from where we left off in high school."

Not surprisingly, that scenario was played out time and again as former Thornridge teammates were drawn together following an exchange of phone numbers. Friendships were rekindled. Teammates and coaches who had not spoken in years were calling one another and burning up the minutes on their cell phones. In the summer of 2008, Rose called his former coach. Ron Ferguson was clearly touched.

"I'm surprised that he's talking so much because he used to be very quiet." says Ferguson. "You very seldom could get him to volunteer anything in conversation. I hadn't talked to him since high school. If you had told me [he planned to call me], I would have said I would never hear from him. Him calling, that means everything to me."

Despite his difficult home life, Rose was regarded as a good kid by Ferguson and the other coaches. Frank Nardi, one of Ferguson's assistants prior to becoming Thornwood's head coach in 1971-72, remembers Rose as a nice young man who could really play the game.

"Yeah, [he had a] tough life at home," says Nardi. "[Greg was] a tremendous talent, very, very quick, [and] very quiet on the floor. He's one who let his actions on the floor speak for himself. [He was] not a troublemaker whatsoever."

Rose did have one habit that used to irritate the Thornridge coaching staff. He often stayed in bed in the morning rather than drag himself to school. Dave Lezeau, Ferguson's top assistant during the 1971-72 season, repeatedly drove to Phoenix to get Rose out of bed.

"During that season, Greg Rose was not [much of] a student," says Lezeau. "There were times [that was] my job as the assistant coach. I'd hear from Fergie that Rose wasn't in school. So, I'd have to go to his house, pick him up, and get him to class. Let's say we had a game at night. You had to be in school so many hours to be eligible to play that night. Well, Fergie would call me or he would stop by and say, 'Hey Dave. Rose isn't in school. We gotta get him to class.' I would go to Phoenix, wake him up, 'Hey Greg. Wake up. Wake up. Get in the car. We gotta get you to class so you can play tonight.' And I'd drag him to class. That was part of my duties as the assistant."

Lezeau wasn't the only assistant coach who pulled Greg out of bed and hauled him to school. Ron Bonfiglio, the sophomore coach during the Falcons' perfect season, was a frequent visitor to the Rose family home in Phoenix.

"I've been in his home as many times as anybody," says Bonfiglio. "To practice, you had to be in school that day. Many times in the morning I had to stop for Greg. It got to the point where his mother would see me pull up and she would just say, 'You know where his bedroom is.' So, I'd go right in the house and say, 'Greg, get your butt up. You're going to school.'"

"Oh man," laughs Rose. "Sometimes, I had to get a few more hours sleep."

Rose laughs for ten full seconds before continuing. "And you know, sometimes I would miss the game bus. 'Somebody's gotta go get Greg.' [Coach] would have one of the newspaper writers come by and get me. Sometimes they would bring the bus by my house and say, 'Greg, get on!'" Rose again laughs uncontrollably thinking back to those days when he could barely get out of bed.

"It was always somebody [saying] either 'Find Greg.' or 'Where's Greg?'" says teammate Ernie Dunn. "And he always had a nervous stomach so when he did show up he'd be in the washroom forever before the game would start. You all want to run out as a team, and we're all sittin' there waitin' on Greg. He's a good guy. He's just, you know, in his own time zone."

Dunn thinks maintaining watch over on Rose and Batts was part of the reason Coach Ferguson failed to routinely get a full night's sleep.

"He had to do some extra babysitting with Boyd and Greg," says Dunn. "That can weigh on you [wondering] whether these guys are gonna show up. They did, but it was always [an adventure]. Greg may show up a half hour before the game, or we'd have to find out where he is, or he was not at practice. You know a few of those [types of] things, but nothing ever serious where anybody was in trouble. It's just that keeping up with them is what I think sometimes [bothered Coach]. He didn't have to do that for myself, Quinn, and Bonczyk, or the rest of the team. There were just a couple players he had to keep up with."

Occasionally, Rose stayed in bed because of migraine headaches. When a migraine struck, Rose was nearly incapacitated.

"It started very early when I was a kid," says Rose. "I always wanted to go with my dad, and he'd drive his car real fast. I used to get motion sickness. Then I got migraine headaches. I still get them sometimes. Man,

I wouldn't wish migraine headaches on my worst enemy. Not the way I have them because I lose my sight, [and] I throw up."

Rose's problem with chronic migraines was never revealed during his playing days. The coaching staff, however, was aware Greg could suffer one of the debilitating headaches at any time.

"Yeah, the coaches knew that, but we had our team doctor," says coach Ferguson. "Most of the time he travelled with us. He was aware of the whole situation. He was always available if anything came up."

Though Rose had problems with tardiness, his teammates respected Greg's abilities on the court.

"You hear people talk about who would guard who against this team," says point guard Mike Bonczyk. "There is not a matchup for Greg Rose. Greg was six-four. He could shoot the outside shot. He was the front man on the press. He knew how to get to the offensive glass. I know one thing. If I got the ball in the middle on the break, I knew Greg Rose was going to be in a [fast-break] lane. When you start comparing teams, you can match up with me, and you can match up with Buckner, but the X-factor was Greg Rose. I don't think there's a matchup for Greg Rose. He was awfully good."

"Greg was just so talented that any flaws he had didn't even bother us because he'd make up for [his mistakes]," says teammate Ernie Dunn. "I personally think he was the most talented out of our whole group as far as athletic ability. [He had the] ability to just stop on a dime, jump on a dime, [and] do anything he wanted to. I think his head was probably more into the music, but he did play basketball very well. He was just unbelievable. Unfortunately, we couldn't dunk back then. Greg would jump as high as he could and drop it over the rim. We would all do that but Greg seemed to get higher than anybody. He could get up there with Boyd. He was just extremely gifted. But, I think he more so wanted music. He and his brother Kenny both played in the band. Their whole family did music and survived that way. "

Greg says he had a similar passion for basketball and music.

"I loved both of them the same," says Rose. "I would get through playin' basketball, and I'd go home and jump right on my drums. We would rehearse right after I got through [with basketball practice]. Sometimes, we would rehearse even before I went to play basketball."

The Thornridge team was blessed with several great athletes in the 1971-72 season. As mentioned previously, Quinn Buckner was recognized as the nation's top high school athlete. However, in terms of pure athleticism, he was seriously challenged by Rose.

"Oh yeah, he could jump higher than any of them," says Ferguson. "Rose could jump out of the gym, and he was quicker than the devil. He was a great athlete. I think the guy could have gone on and done a lot of stuff in track. He could have played football too. He could have been a wide receiver or a back, but he couldn't because he had to work. We were lucky he got the time off to play basketball. Sometimes, he had to leave [practice] early because he had to play in the band someplace at night. I'm sure he didn't get the kind of sleep he probably needed."

Rose was an explosive offensive player who as a junior averaged 18.1 points per game during the 1971-72 season. His coach says Greg was also a standout defender.

"He was, because he was so quick," says Ferguson. "His quickness made up for being a little bit unsound [fundamentally] at times."

Whether serving as the point man on Thornridge's hellacious 1-2-1-1 full court press or terrorizing teams at the offensive end of the court, Rose was a terrific talent. He believed, rightly so, that he was one of the team's best shooters. Rose enjoyed ripping the nets with rainbow jumpers from the perimeter. He shot 55% from the field to lead the team during the 1971-72 season. That is an impressive number considering Rose was a volume shooter who averaged fifteen field goal attempts per game. The muscular Rose had many positive attributes as a player. However, he and Batts were peas in a pod when it came to wanting to get their points. They wanted the ball early, and they wanted it often. Their coaches and teammates knew the two Falcons' stars needed their touches.

"Quinn could have averaged 35 points a game, but we knew we had two pretty selfish kids in Batts and Rose," says head coach Ron Ferguson. "They wanted to score, and they wanted to get their shots. If you kept them happy early in the game, then they'd play hard both ways. They'd [play] defense, and they rebounded, and they did all the other things. But boy, if they got pouting early in the game, then sometimes they wouldn't perform as well as they should of. If they were in the last quarter or the third quarter and they had only got four or five shots at the basket, then they didn't [play] defense very well. But most of the time they got [their shots]. They both averaged [more than] 18 points a game. If you can average 18 points a game with those eight minute quarters, that was good."

Rose got many points by hustling back on offense after Thornridge pulled down a defensive rebound or stole the ball. Easy layups are one reason Rose had such a good shooting percentage.

"He got a lot of [fast break layups] because he's so fast," says Ferguson. "He was down the floor most of the time before the other team could take a deep breath. Very few times was Buckner one of the ones down the floor on the break. It was usually Rose and Batts."

Ernie Dunn says all of the other players knew it was important for Rose and Batts to get their points.

"Oh yeah, there was no doubt," laughs Dunn. "Playing the game you knew that if you threw the ball in to them the best [thing] for you to do was to go for a rebound or cut to the basket. You may see [the ball] back, but it was rare. The good thing was they would score. They could score."

"Me and Boyd used to play one-on-one together all the time," says Rose. "When I met Boyd, I was just moving to Chicago from Kentucky. I was nine years old when I moved to Chicago. I started playing basketball sort of late. I think I was about fourteen. I couldn't play. I couldn't dribble or anything, but I could shoot. I knew I could shoot. I used to see these guys playin' basketball on the side of Coolidge [Elementary}. I'd say, 'Who are these guys? Man, those boys are *bad*.'"

Bad was a term used by blacks in the late 1960s and early '70s to mean *good*. Rose knew he was watching somebody special, or really *bad,* when Buckner and his friends were playing in a pickup game at Coolidge.

"I was always watching Quinn." continues Rose. "Man, Quinn taught me some things. I went to play against Quinn one time, and he's always been *thick*. I went to dip on him to steal the ball, and he gave me an elbow. I saw stars. I said, 'Okay, I'm learning.'"

Rose did learn the game, but it was not a quick process. He did not get much opportunity to play at Coolidge Elementary because his game was unrefined. Also, there was a little matter of Buckner and Batts getting all the minutes as the stars of the grade school team. When Buckner and Batts eventually moved on to Thornridge High School, Rose finally got his chance to shine. Rose can remember when he realized he had a chance to be a good player.

"When Quinn and Boyd got out of the way and left Coolidge." laughs Rose with a loud cackle reminiscent of the hearty laugh of former Boston Celtics' star Bill Russell. "I was sitting the bench. I was trying to make the team. When they left, I was ready to play. I could jump. I could shoot. I couldn't dribble, but I would score 40 points. People didn't know I couldn't dribble because I would be out at half court and I would shoot it. You know, like a regular jumper. It would hit bottom [of the net]."

It did not take long for Rose to turn heads when he arrived at Thornridge High School. He became a starter as a sophomore on the 1970-71 Falcons' team that went 31-1 and won a state championship. He was even more accomplished as a player by his junior year, by then having overcome any problems dribbling the basketball. He had become a terrific all-around player. Rose still fought to balance basketball with his budding musical career because he desperately needed to earn money. Coach Ron Ferguson recalls Greg did not even own a sports coat which nearly caused Rose to miss the Rockford tournament.

"We were going to Rockford for the [Thanksgiving] tournament one year," says Ferguson. "I'd told [the players] they have [to attend a] dinner so you need to bring a sport coat. The bus was ready to go. We got on the bus, and Rose isn't there. We call him, and he said he didn't think he could go because he didn't have a sport coat. So he didn't show up [for the bus]. We took off and one of our sportswriters went and picked him up and got a sport coat from Mrs. Buckner so he could go."

Even after Buckner, Batts, and Bonczyk graduated Rose continued to star for the Thornridge basketball team. As a senior, Rose was recognized as an All-State player. At the start of his last season at Thornridge, he led the Falcons to four straight victories to extend the school's state-record winning streak before it was finally snapped at 58 games. Despite his skill, Rose did not play college basketball. He gave up the game to concentrate on his musical career. The move paid off as Greg and his brothers, *The Rose Brothers* as they were known, achieved moderate success in the music industry.

"We signed with a record company called Malaco out of Mississippi," says Rose. "We did three albums for Malaco Records. We got a hit in '85. We had a song out called *I Get Off On You*. It did real well for us. Matter of fact, once it hit for us, we opened up for a lot of people like Anita Baker, The Temptations, the O-Jays, and Natalie Cole. Oh man, we've been on the big stage."

I Get Off On You reached number 28 on the rhythm & blues' charts in 1985. The following year, another of the group's songs, *Easy Lover,* made it to number 29. Greg will tell you that *The Rose Brothers* were not an overnight sensation. It had taken years for the brothers to make it to the big stage. Greg was in high school when he and his siblings assembled the group.

"It was so weird," says Greg Rose. "My oldest brother is ten years older than I am. He came to my house, and I hadn't seen him in a while. He put this instrumental record on [and started singing]. I said, 'Oh man, you *sing?*' And he said, 'Yeah man, I've been singing for a while.' I said, 'Well, [Kenny and me] we play, and we can play that [song].' So we took him back in the [practice] room and started jammin'. It's like history, man. We've been working together ever since."

"Bobby Rose, Larry Rose, and Kenny Rose," says Greg, running down the list of the other Rose Brothers. "Kenny also played on the team with me. Kenny passed away about three or four years ago. He was my boy. We used to do a lot of music together. The CD I just finished, I wanted to get through with it before he passed away. I was with him until he took his last breath. He died of colon cancer."

The passing of Kenny Rose was a significant moment in Greg's life. Greg made good on a promise he had made to his dying brother.

"[Kenny] was telling me, 'Greg, go and get yourself checked out,' says Rose. "'Greg, you gotta do it for me.' I went [to be examined], and they found about four polyps in me. It was a blessing that he made me promise that I would go. He saved my life. Otherwise, I would have been in the same situation that he was in."

Kenny's death did not mark the first time Greg had suffered the loss of a loved one to cancer. Greg's mother succumbed to cancer when she was in her fifties.

"[I was] devastated man," says Rose. "It was real tough. My mother was sickly, but she was my best friend. [She] taught me a lot of things about life. Man, when she passed away it was like, 'I don't think I can make it now.'"

Rose says his mother always kept an eye on him. She did not want Greg to fall in with a bad crowd.

"I would sometimes go out and play basketball at one o'clock in the morning," says Rose. "She would say, 'Where you been, boy?' [I'd say] 'Mom, I've been out playin' ball.' She'd say, 'Don't you lie to me.' I said, 'Mom, I'm not lying. When I make it, you're gonna say, "He wasn't lying."' She'd say, 'Son, I trust you.'"

Greg remembers when he was just beginning to receive notoriety for his basketball abilities during his sophomore year. He sat with his mother and predicted that he and his teammates would win the Illinois state championship.

"She was my best friend," says Rose. "We used to sit at the table and talk one-on-one all the time. I'd say, 'Mom, we're gonna win the state {championship]. We're gonna go downstate, and we're gonna win it.' And she said with a laugh, 'Yeah, whatever.' Then she was seeing me get write-ups in the paper.

I'd say, 'That's me, Mom.' She'd say, 'Oh, you been playin' basketball.' Man, she was just my best supporter."

Because of her health problems, Greg's mother was unable to attend many of his games. She also missed the first of the two championship parades that were held to honor her son and his Thornridge teammates.

"When we came home [from Champaign in 1971], she couldn't come to the first parade that we had," says Greg. "She couldn't make it. But she made it the next year. She had to get up out of her bed, but she made it."

The Rose family was never wealthy, but Greg and other family members came into a little bit of money as a result of his father's untimely passing.

"When I turned eighteen, I got a settlement from my father's death," says Greg Rose. "When I got that money, I figured I'm going to get me a reliable car. And back then, most black people liked Cadillacs and Buicks. So I went and got me an El Dorado."

"Good lookin' car, but it was always in the shop," he laughs.

Rose moved to Los Angeles in 1980 hoping to live the dream and hit it big as a musical performer. He never quite reached the top but continues to make a decent living singing smooth R&B in the style of Teddy Pendergrass at clubs in the Los Angeles area. Greg long ago moved out from behind the drums and is now a lead vocalist. He released a new CD in late 2008. Listening to his golden tones, it is clear Rose is just as talented musically as he was on the basketball court. He says the rush of adrenalin he gets from performing on stage is identical to the rush he got sinking 20-foot jumpers in the Illinois state championship games he played for Thornridge.

"It's the same, just the same," says Rose. "Both of them are entertainment. You have to be a good singer [to be out front on the stage]. I used to play drums all the time, and I didn't get [the adrenaline rush]. But when I moved out front and started lead singing, I felt it then."

Rose says he'll never forget the night one of his brothers asked him to step out from behind the drums to sing at the front of the stage.

"It was a scary thing," remembers the drummer-turned-lead-singer. "My brother Bob made me come out front one night. I used to play drums and sing. People was always asking, 'Who's that singing?' My brother said,

'Greg, come on out and let the people see you.' When I did, I was shakin' in my boots. It was a whole different ball game. The reactions of the people, it was like 'Oh man, this is just like when I played ball.' So I kind of liked it. But it was scary because I didn't know how to communicate with the people. I wasn't a showman then. I learned over the years."

One wonders how good Greg Rose might have been as a college basketball player. He surely had the athleticism. He possessed a beautiful jump shot with plenty of range. His high school coach is among those who believe Rose would have had success in the college game.

"He definitely could have played somewhere," says Ron Ferguson. "He was good enough to play. I just don't know whether he could stay eligible. Possibly he couldn't get in a lot of places [because of academic deficiencies]. He would have had to go to a junior college first and try to qualify. And he just couldn't do it because of his financial situation."

Rose still plays the game to stay in good shape. He has slowed considerably since his high school days, but Greg is quick to tell you that he can still shoot the rock. Once a shooter, always a shooter.

CHAPTER 10

They Couldn't Put 100 On The Scoreboard

FOLLOWING THEIR CHAMPIONSHIP IN THE Carbondale Christmas Tournament, the Thornridge Falcons returned home and spent the next week preparing for what figured to be a tough game against conference rival Chicago Heights Bloom. During that first week of 1972, news was being made across America. President Richard Nixon gave final approval for NASA to develop the space shuttle. William Rehnquist and Lewis Powell Jr. were sworn in as Supreme Court Justices. Melanie's *"Brand New Key"* spent its final week as the number one song on the Billboard charts after a three week run as America's hottest record. Don McLean's *"American Pie"* would become the new number one song and remain atop the charts for a month. On January 7, the same night Thornridge returned to action against Bloom, the Los Angeles Lakers won their NBA record 33rd consecutive game. And the following week, NBC aired the debut of a new situation comedy "Sanford & Son" starring standup comedian Redd Foxx as junk dealer Fred Sanford. The Thornridge players would not see the new program that night. They had a game at St. Viator at the same time the program was televised. The players could not simply record the show and watch it when they got home. Beta Max recorders would not be invented for three more years. VHS recorders were unavailable for home use until 1976. DVRs (Digital Video Recorders) were not yet a figment of anyone's wildest imagination.

***

GAME 13 (Friday evening, January 7, 1972)
Bloom (Chicago Heights)

Thornridge (12-0) started 1972 with a Friday night home game against conference rival Bloom of Chicago Heights (8-3). The Falcons again played in front of a sellout crowd. Not every seat in the Dolton gym had a great view, but fans were thrilled just to be there.

"They had a big stage at one end," remembers Coach Ron Ferguson. "There was a big door that opened to a pair of swimming pools. For swim meets they'd reverse the bleachers on the stage so they could watch the swim meet. Then for the basketball games, they'd have to turn around the bleachers [to face the court]. In the upstairs balcony of our gym, everyone was blocked out by a pillar. You could see straight ahead, but if you're looking down at an angle, there was a pillar someplace. But they still sold out every game."

Falcons' sixth man Nee Gatlin recalls that since Thornridge was a primarily white school, there were few black faces in the crowd at Falcons' home games.

"You had to look real hard, but they [were] out there," says Gatlin. "I knew the sections they were sitting in. It was always in particular sections [of the bleachers]. That was almost designated [as] their spots, and everybody respected that. I'm not talkin' about a racial thing. I'm talkin' about comfort for them. They enjoyed that area. I knew a lot of [blacks] that was there. There was minority [fan support] at the games."

The Bloom Trojans made the short trip from Chicago Heights to Dolton fresh off a third place finish in the Pontiac Christmas Classic, considered to be one of Illinois' toughest holiday tournaments. Thornridge center Boyd Batts had been bothered by an aching back during the Carbondale tourney. It was still giving him trouble when the Falcons took the court against Bloom. You would have never guessed he was ailing. Batts scored 14 points and pulled down 13 rebounds. Teammates Greg Rose and Mike Bonczyk each scored 14 points as well, and Quinn Buckner fired in a game-high 27 points to power Thornridge to an easy 99-65 win. It was the worst loss in the coaching career of Bloom's Wes Mason. The game was basically over almost as soon as it began. Thornridge scored the first ten points, and Buckner sank six straight baskets to help the Falcons take a 31-8 lead after one quarter. It was 56-22 when the teams went to their locker rooms at halftime. With another game scheduled for the next night, coach Ferguson pulled his starters earlier than usual. Batts and Bonczyk left the game in the third quarter, and the other starters were pulled in the final period. Buckner left early in the fourth quarter with Thornridge leading a good Bloom team by the incredible score of 85-38. The only question was whether the Falcons would reach the century mark. They had a chance, but seldom-used reserve Sidney Lewis missed a free throw with one second left that would have given Thornridge 100 points on the night. That was the only disappointment as Thornridge won its 13th game of the season and its 34th straight overall. Once again, the Falcons' quick start had paved the way for an easy win. Coach Ferguson says many of his team's fast starts were a result of the offense the Falcons used at the beginning of each game. It was designed to be effective whether the opponent opened in a man-to-man defense or a zone.

"We put together an offense that we didn't worry what the team played defensively," says Ferguson. "We would run it against the zone or the man-to-man. We didn't have to scream, 'They're in a zone!' We never worried. We pretty much did the same thing [regardless of the defense]. The only thing we did was we moved players around in the same offense. If Buckner had a small guy on him, then we would put him inside."

"I think the unique thing about the team was that we didn't have to hide anybody handling the ball," he continues. "When there is a press, most teams say, 'Don't give it to this guy.' We didn't have to hide anybody handling the ball. Batts could bring the ball down the floor if we had to, and he did occasionally. We could move Buckner into the post where he was just too strong for any five-ten or six foot guard trying to cover him in there. Bonczyk was the only one that really wasn't too interchangeable. But the other kids were really kind of interchangeable which made it nice for us."

***

GAME 14 (Saturday evening, January 8, 1972)
Washington Park (Racine, Wisconsin)

The following evening Thornridge (13-0) travelled to Racine, Wisconsin, to play a non-conference game against Washington Park in front of some 3500 fans in the school's beautiful new field house. The home team had won its last four games, but Washington Park could not slow down the Thornridge juggernaut. The host school was held scoreless for the first five and a half minutes of the game. By the time Washington Park finally did score, Thornridge had the game well in hand. The Falcons led 45-9 at halftime and cruised to a lopsided 83-39 win. It was Don Gardner's worst loss in thirteen years as head coach at tradition-rich Washington Park. The only concern for Thornridge came in the third quarter when Greg Rose was injured crashing into the bleachers behind the basket while chasing a long pass from Ernie Dunn. Rose was briefly knocked unconscious. He was carried off on a stretcher and taken to a local hospital. Rose suffered from shock and had bone bruises on his knees, but X-rays were negative. He was allowed to accompany the team on the bus ride home.

Another week ended with Lincoln, Hinsdale Central, and Aurora East still undefeated. But those teams were still chasing Thornridge in the polls. The Falcons again received every first-place vote after extending their overall winning streak to 35 games.

***

GAME 15 (Friday evening, January 14, 1972)
St. Viator (Arlington Heights)

Thornridge (14-0) had to prepare for only one game the following week. The Falcons would play St. Viator Friday night in Arlington Heights. The host school had won its last five games to improve to 8-4, and the Lions were sure to be a little fired up after what happened to them exactly 365 days earlier. In a game played in Dolton, Thornridge had handed the Lions the worst defeat in school history. The Falcons won that game 97-63. Fans debated whether the score could possibly be as lopsided this time around. The gym was filled to capacity, many rooting for an upset. But more than 2000 St. Viator fans were quieted as Thornridge stormed past the Lions 102-64. St. Viator had delighted the crowd by scoring the game's first four points. However, by halftime the Falcons were up 64-35. The outcome was already decided, but fans stuck around to see if Thornridge could reach the century mark in scoring. With just under 1:30 to play, junior guard Dave Anderson swished a 20-footer from the top of the key to give Thornridge 100 points in a game for the second time in the season. That led to a funny moment as the St. Viator students reacted to the numbers they read on the scoreboard. Thornridge held a 100-64 lead after Anderson's basket, but since the scoreboard only had room for two digits for each team, it appeared to those in attendance that St. Viator had a 64-point advantage.

"They couldn't put 100 on the scoreboard," laughs Falcons' coach Ron Ferguson. "So when the score was Thornridge-00, St. Viator-64, the [St. Viator] students all got up and yelled, 'Scoreboard, scoreboard.'"

The five-eight Anderson was one of the reserves that saw limited playing time during the season as coach Ferguson preferred to keep his starting unit on the court a majority of the time. Whether he played or not, Anderson says he enjoyed every Thornridge game because of the many fans that turned out in anticipation of seeing something special.

"It was really amazing," says Anderson. "Every place you went, people lined up along the sides and up in the rafters. It was just really amazing."

Quinn Buckner led the scoring against St. Viator with 32 points on 14 of 18 shooting. Boyd Batts had an impressive 22 points, 11 rebounds, and 7 blocked shots. Greg Rose, shaking off the effects of the previous week's injuries, added 19 points to help Thornridge win its 36th straight.

At week's end, only three Class AA teams remained undefeated. Number one Thornridge (15-0), second-ranked Lincoln (16-0), and third-rated Hinsdale Central (15-0) topped the Associated Press poll. After winning its first twelve games Aurora East (12-2) suffered back-to-back losses and dropped to tenth in the rankings. Rock Island Alleman (13-1), whose only loss was by one at Quincy early in the season, moved up to fourth in the AP poll, and was followed by La Salle-Peru (14-1), Lockport (11-1), Waukegan (12-2), and Quincy (13-2).

CHAPTER 11

Ernie Knew Who He Was

ERNIE DUNN HAD NOT PLANNED on playing for the Thornridge basketball team. He had grown up hoping to play varsity basketball for Harvey's Thornton High School. But, during his sophomore year, a boundary change was announced which required Ernie to change schools the following year. A grandfather clause allowed his older brother Otis to stay at Thornton for his senior year, but Ernie was forced to switch schools.

"I grew up in Phoenix," says Ernie Dunn. "At the end of my eighth grade year we moved to Harvey. My freshman year and my sophomore year I was at Thornton, but then they changed the boundaries. My junior year, I was forced to go to Thornridge. My brother, as a senior, had an option to go to Thornridge or stay at Thornton. He stayed at Thornton."

Ernie says Otis never regretted staying at Thornton, even though he missed a chance to be part of a Thornridge championship.

"No, he had a great year himself," says Ernie. "And he knew he would be struggling to get as much playing time because initially he played the same position Boyd did. He was happy where he was."

At first, Ernie was not terribly happy. He didn't like the idea of being forced to attend a different school.

"It was forced in the sense that the boundaries changed, and I didn't have a choice unless I moved," says Dunn. "They had already made the boundaries during my sophomore year. So the coach at Thornton [Tom] Hanrahan had already told me that he knew my junior year I was not going to be at Thornton. I was going to be at Thornridge. He moved me up to varsity for the [state] tournament, but he told me I was probably not going to get much playing time. He was going to play Randy Ramsey and the other guys who were going to be there the following year."

When Ernie Dunn showed up at Thornridge High School in the fall of 1971, he began thinking how he might best fit in with the Falcons' basketball team. Dunn had played with and against most of the current Thornridge players while attending Coolidge Elementary. He knew the players well.

"I went to grade school with all of 'em," says Dunn. "I ended up at Thornton High School for two years because of where I lived. But I was always in touch with them, playing against them every year, seeing the guys all the time. I was only like three or four miles [away] in Harvey. I was right down the street from them. We stayed in touch with one another and played against each other for two years before I ended up joining the [Thornridge] team my junior year."

Ernie knew Thornridge had a talented team. He had watched his new teammates Quinn Buckner, Boyd Batts, Mike Bonczyk, and Greg Rose win the 1971 Illinois championship. Dunn, a capable scorer, realized he might have to alter his game in order to earn playing time. The Falcons already had scorers in Buckner, Batts, and Rose. Scoring alone wasn't going to earn him the coveted fifth starting position on the team. He decided to concentrate on defense and rebounding. That decision paid off as Dunn became the fifth starter. From the moment Dunn heard Quinn Buckner say in a preseason meeting that the Falcons could accomplish all of their goals if they did not lose a game, Dunn knew this group was serious about repeating as state champion.

"Quinn would always have something to say, something to think about as Captain," recalls Dunn. "At that stage I was still just learning the plays and stuff, so I was kind of in a fog trying to make sure I just did the right thing. I wasn't sure that I was going to start at that stage. I thought Nee Gatlin would start because he had been there the longest. I was still feeling my way around."

While Gatlin was talented enough to start on any other team in the state, Thornridge coach Ron Ferguson realized Dunn was the perfect complement to the four returning starters. Dunn was athletic, intelligent, and willing to give of himself for the betterment of the team.

"The thing that saved us was Ernie Dunn coming in," says Ferguson. "Ernie came to Thornridge, and he just fit in like a glove. He was really quick and really a team player. And for six-one, he could jump out of the gym. We could put him on the best offensive player. He took pride in that.

That was his way to help the team be successful. He knew he wasn't going to get as many shots, but he contributed so much that way."

"I get a lot of the credit [for the team's success]," says Quinn Buckner, "But the one guy who I thought was intellectually brighter than I am, and always has been, was Ernie Dunn. I thought he was emotionally brighter than the group. Ernie knew who he was. [He] could have forced his game at times, but this was a guy who in high school felt it was more important to be a *part* of the team than try to jump out and be in *front* of the team. We had some guys who were a little more geared toward that."

"I didn't think about it," says Dunn. "But whenever I've played, I've always known in my mind it was a team game. We had to play as a team. I knew what my role was. I knew these guys had already been established. Basically, I played defense most of the time. That's what I liked to do, so I played defense."

Although he focused on defense, Ernie could score. He proved it early in his Thornridge career.

"The first two games in the Rockford Tournament I got about 20-something points each game," says Dunn, "because [the opponents] figured 'Well, these [other] guys can score. We're going to make [Dunn] score.' I ended up scoring some points, and I realized maybe I can help the team [offensively] at that stage. But, I knew that wasn't going to be the norm. I just figured do whatever you need to do to win. That's always been the way I played. I don't want the limelight. I don't care about it. It's not anything that I ever wanted. So if it happens, it happens. But there wasn't an ego there."

The willingness to sacrifice his own game for the good of the team made Dunn a critical component of the 1971-72 Falcons. Buckner says Ernie understood that other players on the team desired to be the focus on offense.

"We enjoyed what we were doing and we enjoyed each other," says Buckner. "And what was apparent is that we were concerned about each other. For example, with Boyd [Batts], he was a terrific offensive player. A very talented player, [but] he would sulk if he didn't get the ball enough. Somebody would make an effort to get him the ball. Now, we may be mad because you gotta give it to him, but at least you make the effort to get it to him. It's not like when he got mad you didn't throw it to him and make him madder. So at least there was enough empathy to throw him the basketball. I think over time all of those things became important. We would worry about guys getting [enough] shots. This is another reason why I always think that Ernie Dunn was so important. Ernie was very conscientious of that kind of stuff. He may have an open shot, and Boyd may have one that would be a little bit of a challenge, but Ernie knew [what to do]. He was emotionally intelligent enough to know it was more important to get Boyd the shot than for Ernie to take the shot. This was a sixteen year old guy making that kind of decision. That's what I've always admired about him."

Dunn found satisfaction in becoming a defensive stopper. Don't misunderstand. Dunn enjoyed scoring when given the opportunity in a game or a practice. He remembers when he was asked by the coaches to pretend to be an upcoming opponent's top scoring threat. While acting the part, Dunn found freedom to make offensive moves and shoot the basketball in volume.

"Every now and then, we'd have one of our second string players play the top person on the other side," says Dunn. "The one time I got to play one of the [other] guys it was kind of fun. There were no rules. You just get to shoot whenever you want. Usually there was structure, but this was one of the first times I got to play the [opponent's best] offensive player, and they just let me go crazy. I thought that was fun."

Dunn could easily have been a big scorer. He had the ability to put up much bigger numbers than he posted for the 1971-72 Falcons. He still found ways to contribute despite having a lack of opportunity at the offensive end. Dunn, a guard, finished second on the team in offensive rebounds. Boyd Batts, the team's six-seven center, averaged 5 offensive boards per game. Despite being six inches shorter, Dunn averaged 3 offensive rebounds per game. He finished the season fourth on the team in scoring at 10.4 points per game. Lanny Slevin, an Illinois radio veteran who has seen or broadcast every state tournament game since 1972, believes Dunn would have received more recognition had he played at a different school.

"It's incredible," says Slevin, a Peru, Illinois, resident. "You got guys like Ernie Dunn and Greg Rose that played on that team. They would have been super stars on other teams. They would have been the best player on their team, but they knew their roles on this team. [Mike] Bonczyk was just out there to kind of hold things together and distribute the ball to the scorers. Boyd Batts and Quinn Buckner were the big scorers at the time, but even they knew [their roles]. There was no ego. At least, it wasn't evident."

There were no major problems on or off the court during Thornridge's 1971-72 season. Most of the racism-related incidents had occurred during the first years of integration at the school. By the time Dunn arrived on the scene as a junior, racial tension had diminished.

"By the time I got to Thornridge, I think it was the fourth or fifth year of the integration," says Dunn. "There wasn't as much tension. I think because of the athletics [football and basketball state championships], the tension had died down already. It had run its course. There wasn't as much violence when I got there my junior year. At Thornton, I was witnessing a lot more of the racial tension. It was pretty bad at Thornton. We'd get out [of school] once every two or three weeks from a fight or somebody breaking out [into] a fight in the lunchroom. Then it turns into a mini-riot where the police would come and spray us with tear gas. I would just try to get out of the crowd because I didn't want to fight anybody. I had no reason to. Most of the time, the people fighting weren't even students. They were people that had come back [to Thornton] to start a fight. It was just violence where people were fighting. It wasn't like they were telling us [blacks] at Thornton to go away or black people [were] keeping whites from Thornton. They just had racial tension -- period. That was part of the era. And [if] you ask the people fighting why they were fighting, they would have never known. Somebody started a fight. Then it's a black against a white, and they just starting fighting. Unfortunately, racism goes deep some times."

Dunn still has trouble understanding the violence he saw at Thornton High in his freshman and sophomore years. He avoided personal involvement, but it was still troubling to witness blacks and whites fighting one another for no reason other than the difference in skin color.

"I would always turn, walk away, and go to my house," says Dunn. "[I would] sit on the steps and talk to some people as they walked by and [have them] tell me what happened to them at the riot. I had no place for it. It didn't make any sense. I didn't hate anyone so there was no point in fighting someone. I never got engaged in it. But I did witness it."

Dunn had learned early in life to avoid confrontation. Jessica Buckner, Quinn's mom, was a teacher at Coolidge Elementary when Ernie attended school there. He knew she would not let him get away with causing any trouble.

"I never had her as a teacher, but I knew her very well," says Dunn. "If we were out of line, I would hear from her. She'd tell our mother in a heartbeat, or she would tell us directly that 'You're out of line.'"

Unlike some of his teammates who had difficult family situations, Ernie came from a loving family with a mother and father who expected big things of him.

"Yes, our family was very tight knit, and we still are," says Dunn. "Unfortunately, my mom and dad barely got through high school, so for them, just for us to do better was what they wanted. My father barely had a grade school education, but he worked to make sure we had what we needed."

Dunn's basketball career ended shortly after his graduation from Thornridge. Ernie had suffered an injury in his senior season and was unable to continue to play up to his high standards.

"I played one year at Lake Land Junior College," says Dunn. "But my back went out my senior year in high school. I only played like ten games and, unfortunately, didn't get many [scholarship] offers. My back was still out. In fact, I couldn't even consistently play as a senior. I played the last game that we lost [while] in traction. I had a belt wrapped around my back with metal stays in it. My movement was very limited, and I never got it back."

Dunn realized his ailing back would prevent him from playing college or pro ball. Therefore, he began planning for his life after basketball. Ernie also needed to take care of some family responsibilities.

"I moved back home with the assumption that I was going to get married and raise this young lady's baby that was mine," says Dunn. "After my freshman year of college, she told me she was pregnant, so I thought I'd go home and do the right thing. But it didn't work out that way, so I just started working in the telecom business. I've been in that since '77."

Now a senior technical consultant at AT&T, Dunn has been very successful in his post-basketball career.

"All the companies I support are multi-nationals," he says. "They are based out of Europe or Japan. I provide them all their data services, internet, anything they need to connect their network or any engineering they need to get their application to work. I do the pre-sales on that. I've got about four or five guys, and we all work together. The business is billion dollar sales, so it's quite large. I'm having fun."

Ernie says he was thrilled to have been part of the 1971-72 Thornridge team that went undefeated and unchallenged.

"It was exciting." remembers Dunn. "It was exciting for me because I was not part of the first [Thornridge championship] team. It was exciting the whole season."

Dunn knows people have not forgotten Quinn Buckner and the fabulous Falcons of 1972 though nearly four decades have passed.

"Yeah, we run into people," says Dunn. "Even at work I run into people that have talked about basketball and talked about Quinn. I never brag and say I know him or anything. People say, 'I met Quinn.' I just sit and listen. Then, somebody in the crowd will always say, 'Ernie played ball with Quinn.' Then, we'll rehash it. It's fun, but I don't go out of my way to make a big point about it. When I play in the gym sometimes, some of the guys talk and say, 'You better guard him. He was on that Thornridge team.'"

Without Ernie Dunn, the road to a second straight state championship would have been a little bumpier for the Thornridge Falcons. With Dunn making the necessary sacrifices and defending the other team's best players, Thornridge was rarely challenged and dominated every team on its schedule.

CHAPTER 12

It Wasn't Anything Personal

THE THORNRIDGE PLAYERS WERE INTELLIGENT. They understood when an upcoming opponent might provide a challenge. They also knew when a team they would be facing was completely overmatched. As the Falcons looked ahead to their next game which happened to be against a team with a losing record, they knew they would have no problem extending their winning streak. That did not mean the Thornridge players would be allowed to relax during the week of practice leading up to the game. Coach Ron Ferguson would make sure his team prepared as if the next game was the most important game of the season. In Fergie's mind, the next game was always the most important game on the schedule regardless of the opponent. As the Falcons continued to win, media interest in the team grew. The Thornridge basketball team was a great story, and radio, TV, and newspaper reporters flocked to Dolton.

"We used to get requests from the media," says Coach Ferguson. "They'd want to come watch practice, and there were some days I'd let them come. They were amazed at how serious the kids were and how [hard] they practiced. I had a philosophy that when we run drills and run our offense and we do anything in practice, how long we're gonna practice is gonna be based on you [players]. When we run a drill, whether it's a warm-up drill or a layup drill, any kind of drill, do it right the first time. I'd say, 'Don't go for behind-the-back passes and try to monkey around and fumble [the ball] down the floor because you're going to be here a long time.' I got them in the habit [of doing things the right way], and I let them out of practice early if they did everything right the first time.

They didn't want to practice three hours. They couldn't wait to get out of there, so they'd work their butts off to do things right the first time. I think that paid off too."

The players understood that practice makes perfect, and they wanted to be perfect. Greg Rose remembers the Falcons' practices were just as intense as the games.

"In practice, we were competitive against each other, and when we stepped on the court, man, the other teams were in trouble," laughs Rose. "They were going to be in trouble. If we had you down, we wasn't going to let you up like a lot of teams do now. What comes to mind [about the perfect season] is a bunch of guys coming together and just having the same attitude like, 'Hey, we're gonna step out here, and we're gonna win it all. We're not gonna let anything get in our way.' We had a bunch of guys that respected one another. If one of our guys was hot, it didn't make any difference who it was, we would feed him [the ball]. We just clicked real well together. It was special. It was so, so special."

***

GAME 16 (Friday night, January 21, 1972)
Richards (Oak Lawn)

On Friday, January 21, the Falcons played their third consecutive road game. Thornridge (15-0) travelled to Oak Lawn to play Richards High School. The Bulldogs entered the game with a record of 5-10, 0-3 in the South Suburban league. It didn't figure to be much of a game, and it was not. Thornridge had dominated the first quarter in nearly every game throughout the season. Going into the game against Richards, the Falcons had outscored their opponents 370-186 in the first quarter. In games so far in the season, Thornridge was shooting nearly 50% as a team which was no surprise since four of the five starters were shooting better than 50% from the field. Smart Richards' fans knew their team was outclassed. It didn't take long to prove it. Thornridge applied early pressure and scored the first seven points in the blink of an eye. It was 15-2 before Richards scored its first basket with 2:16 left in the opening period. The Falcons were never threatened and outscored Richards 23-7 in the first quarter, 22-8 in the second, and 32-10 in the third. Thornridge held Richards without a field goal in the third period while pulling out to a 76-25 lead. The Falcon reserves played the entire fourth quarter as Thornridge breezed to a 95-42 victory. Thoroughly dominated by the state's best team, Richards sank only eight baskets the entire game while Thornridge made 43 (of 84 attempts). Quinn Buckner alone had 14 field goals, nearly doubling Richards' total. Buckner led the Falcons with 28 points, though he played less than three full quarters of the game. Boyd Batts scored 12, and Greg Rose had 10. Nee Gatlin scored 8 points off the bench. Fellow reserves Joe King, Fred Knutsen, and Dave Anderson scored 4 points apiece. Anderson says while he watched the Thornridge starters from the bench he never saw any weaknesses.

"Nah, I never did," laughs Anderson. "I mean you could stop Quinn, and then Boyd would throw up 30 [points], or Greg Rose could do it just as well. Ernie grew a lot. Ernie used to be a guard, and then he got bigger and bigger, so he could dominate. They could all score, and except Bonczyk, they could all rebound. When I look back on it now, it's just like 'WOW!' There's so much quickness and height and overall skill. It was just incredible."

The 53-point margin of victory was the Falcons' largest of the season to date. It would not be their most lopsided win of the year.

***

GAME 17 (Saturday night, January 22, 1972)
Rich Central (Olympia Fields)

Sporting a 37-game winning streak, Thornridge (16-0) was home the next night to face what would surely be a much tougher challenge. Southeast Suburban Conference leader Rich Central of Olympia Fields brought an impressive 14-2 record into Dolton. Coach Jerry Leggett's team was unbeaten in conference and hoped to be able to give Thornridge a true test. If it was a test, the Falcons passed with flying colors. The suffocating Thornridge press took the Olympians out of their game right from the opening tip. Thornridge crushed Rich Central's upset hopes by taking a 35-12 first quarter lead. The Falcons smothered the Olympians defensively and forced 33 turnovers while breezing to a 106-68 win. Again, the "Big Three" led the way for Thornridge. Quinn Buckner scored 27 points while Greg Rose (24) and Boyd Batts (17) combined for 41 more. After the game, the Rich Central coach said Thornridge had to be the best high school basketball team Illinois had ever seen. Ironically, nine years later, Leggett would coach a Quincy team that some people believe was perhaps the equal of this Thornridge group.

It was another night, another dominant victory for the Falcons. There were so many blowout wins for Thornridge during the perfect season you might wonder if the players ever felt a little sorry for the other team. Point guard Mike Bonczyk says that never entered their minds.

"I don't know if it was a matter of feeling sorry," says Bonczyk. "We just played. Because we had a bulls-eye on our back from [winning] the year before, everybody wanted to beat us. I don't think we were going to allow that to happen, so when we got done playing it was like, 'Okay who's the next team?' I don't think there was the matter of any sympathy. It wasn't anything personal. It was just a matter of we were going out to play and win. And that was it."

With one week left in January, Thornridge (17-0), Lincoln (17-0), and Hinsdale Central (16-0) remained unbeaten. La Salle-Peru, Lockport, Maine South, North Chicago, Springfield Southeast, and Tilden Tech each had only one loss. Quincy, ranked fifth in the state, was 15-2.

***

GAME 18 (Friday night, January 28, 1972)
Eisenhower (Blue Island)

Thornridge (17-0) prepared to take its show on the road the following week. The Falcons had a Friday night league game at Blue Island Eisenhower (9-6). The Falcons knew they would be greeted by a hostile crowd. That was part of the fun for the Dolton gang.

"It was tremendous," remembers point guard Mike Bonczyk. "It was something we just had a great time with. We were the defending state champs."

The Falcons had already defeated Eisenhower by 23 points during the first round of conference play. The margin of victory would be even greater in round two. Quinn Buckner popped in 10 points and had 4 assists as Thornridge jumped to a 28-11 lead after the first quarter. Buckner and Boyd Batts combined for 17 points in the second period in which the Falcons outscored Eisenhower 39-17. Buckner had 17 points, 7 assists, and 4 steals in a stellar first half. Curiously, he did not attempt a shot in the second half. The second half was a bit sloppily-played, but the Falcons coasted to a 76-42 victory. With 22 points, Buckner led his team in scoring for the thirteenth time in the first eighteen games of the season. Batts contributed 20 points, and Greg Rose scored 15. The win streak had reached 39 games. The Falcons would be back in Dolton the next night looking to extend the streak to 40.

GAME 19 (Saturday night, January 29, 1972)
St. Patrick (Chicago)

"We played Saint Patrick almost every year," says Thornridge coach Ron Ferguson. "I thought Max Kurland was one of the better coaches. He always played zone [defense]. You always knew you were gonna get a zone. They always played a good one. They knew how to play it. They could extend it, or they could drop it back at different levels. They were always extremely well-coached. I liked Max. I thought he was really a class guy."

Chicago St. Patrick (14-5) was a rugged team, and the physical St. Patrick players gave Thornridge (18-0) one of its toughest games of the season. The Shamrocks seemed well-prepared to handle the full court pressure applied by the Falcons. St. Patrick took care of the basketball and committed only 17 turnovers, fewer than most Thornridge opponents. Saint Patrick took an early 6-1 lead in Dolton, but it did not last. Thornridge was on top 16-15 after one quarter. Shamrocks' sharpshooter, Jim Oleksy, drilled 6 of his 7 shots in the first quarter. Thornridge fans were not overly concerned because in the few games the Falcons had failed to dominate in the first quarter, they almost always took control in the second or third quarters. Not this time. The Shamrocks stayed in contention and were still within nine points in the fourth quarter. In the final period with his team being challenged, Coach Ron Ferguson called a time out and ordered his players to run time off the clock and work the ball for a good shot. The strategy worked. After the Falcons ran some clock, Mike Bonczyk zipped a pass to an open Quinn Buckner for a score. Bonczyk added a couple clutch baskets down the stretch, and Thornridge held off St. Patrick to win 70-56. No Thornridge opponent would come as close the entire season.

"I wasn't so worried about the score," says Ferguson. "You go back now and say, 'Jeez, how did we only win by 14?' But at the time, I thought that was great. I'd have taken five points [in a win]. You're concerned about winning. I was not concerned by how much we won by."

Ron Bonfiglio, the Falcons' sophomore coach that season, says the game against St. Patrick really sticks out in his mind.

"It was a Saturday night game at Thornridge," says Bonfiglio. "They just hung in there with us. [It was] just a tough game. They were hard-nosed, a football-type school out of the Catholic League. [They] Just played us tough and played us physical."

The Falcons made only 29 of 73 shots (39.7%) and were somewhat fortunate to win since they had not played their best. Buckner again led the winners with 25 points which offset Oleksy's 24 points. The Shamrocks' Gary Staniec added 21 points. Greg Rose (18) and Boyd Batts (13) were the only other Thornridge players to score in double figures. Bonczyk finished with 8 points and 12 assists. The 40th consecutive win was far from easy, but at least it was in the books. Buckner admits the Saint Patrick game was the one game he thought the Falcons could have lost.

"Yeah, that was the only one," says Buckner. "Honestly, I remember the game because of the closeness of the score probably as much as I remember the [state] championship game. I don't think we were consciously trying to beat everybody by twenty, but I was aware that Saint Patrick was under that mark. They managed to be there [in contention]. In retrospect, nearly 40 years later, it may have been enough of a scare for me, as a kid, to make sure that we stayed on top of our game. Because you start taking it for granted, there are some people that can make some things go differently than you'd like."

Buckner had a good reason for wanting to play well against Saint Patrick.

"This particular game, [UCLA assistant coach] Gary Cunningham was there scouting Buckner," remembers Thornridge coach Ron Ferguson. "The game wasn't great, but Buckner had a good game. He was the high scorer. I think he played well."

"I tried to go there incognito," says Cunningham. "What I remember about that night was it was sold out. I couldn't go up to the ticket window and get a ticket and get a seat."

"The coach helped me out, and I sat with the band," Cunningham adds with a laugh. "That's where I had to sit to get into the game. The atmosphere was really electrifying in the gym. It was crowded. People were enthusiastic and cheering. The game was a real fast-paced game. It was exciting."

Cunningham came away impressed with not only the atmosphere in the Dolton gym, but also the team's star player. He felt Buckner was the kind of player that could help UCLA continue to win national championships.

"He had the complete package," remembers Cunningham. "He was a defensive player, a good offensive player, an unselfish player. He had all the ingredients you would want from a player. Quinn was really the guy who orchestrated the whole thing on his team. I came back [to UCLA], and I remember telling Coach [Wooden] that he's a complete player. He does all the things that we would want at UCLA."

However, Cunningham knew there was an issue that could keep Buckner from signing with the Bruins.

"At that time, he wanted to play football too," says Cunningham. "He played [football] at Indiana. I don't know whether it was a factor or not, but Coach [Wooden] said, 'If you come to UCLA you have to play basketball. You can't play football.' And that might have been a deal-breaker."

It was. Quinn signed with Indiana and played both sports for the Hoosiers.

The same weekend that Thornridge had to work hard to avoid being upset by St. Patrick, second-ranked Lincoln blew an early 21-3 lead and fell at home to Springfield 58-53 for its first loss of the season. Third-ranked Hinsdale Central also dropped from the ranks of the unbeaten by losing to La Grange 54-45. Top-ranked Thornridge, now 19-0, was Illinois' only unbeaten Class AA team.

CHAPTER 13

I Used To Call Him Hippie

SEVERAL OF THE NATION'S MOST athletic and talented black players were on the Thornridge High School basketball team in 1971-72. Even so, a five-ten white kid with long, dark hair and long, thick sideburns also made a lasting impression on opposing coaches.

"Bonczyk had a lot of *moxie* about him," remembers San Diego State coach Steve Fisher whose Rich East High School team lost to Thornridge in the first game of the 1971-72 season.

"That was my senior year," says Mike Bonczyk remembering when he sported the mutton-chop sideburns. "I was going with the Elvis look."

"Mike's hair was always long, and it used to flop in his face," laughs Quinn Buckner. "I used to call him 'Hippie.' He didn't smoke weed or anything like that, but Mike had the long hair and headband, you know, just the whole look. That was Mike. Mike was a character. Not *was*. Mike still *is* a character."

Bonczyk was a little bit of a rebel in his first year on the varsity, at least in terms of the length of his hair. The blacks on the team sported Afro-style cuts of varying lengths. Quinn Buckner and Boyd Batts preferred a short style, but Greg Rose wore his hair long. During the Falcons' first championship season in 1970-71, Rose's long "Fro" was not a major concern for Ron Ferguson, but the coach wanted Bonzyk to get his long, floppy hair out of his eyes.

"I had a problem with Bonczyk as a junior," says Ferguson. "In those days, you could kinda dictate a little bit what kind of haircut a kid had. Bonczyk was wearing his hair long and hangin' down. I said, 'You gotta get a haircut.' He'd come back with an envelope with a little piece of hair in it."

"Back then the long [hair] look was in," says Bonczyk. "I ended up getting a haircut, and I was mad at my old man. It was before we were going down to the Carbondale [Christmas] tournament. I got into an argument with my dad about it. Fergie kept telling me, 'Get a haircut. Get a haircut.' My dad was [telling me], 'You're getting a damn haircut. Let's go. I'm not gonna put up with this.'"

After getting a small trim that he hoped would satisfy his father and his coach, Bonczyk put a few strands of hair in an envelope to prove to Ferguson that he had visited the barber.

"I wanted [Fergie] to know that I did get a haircut, even though it wasn't much of a haircut," laughs Bonczyk. "[I said], 'Here you go Coach. Just so you know, I did get a haircut.' He kind of laughed and thought it was pretty funny. He asked me if I was ready to play, and I said, 'Well, *yeah.*' I think those were things most coaches deal with, the facial hair [and] the long hair."

Bonczyk was the only white player to see consistent playing time during the Falcons' perfect 1971-72 season. There were white players on the bench, but they usually saw action only when a game's outcome had already been determined. Five of the six members in Ron Ferguson's regular playing rotation that year, were black. Therefore, some people got the wrong impression of Thornridge.

"Everybody assumed Thornridge was a black or predominantly black school because of the basketball players," says Bonczyk. "You had a black overtone on the basketball team. Thornridge was a predominantly white institution. It just so happened that a majority of the players on the basketball team were black, and [they] did most of the playing."

Though there were black and white issues in the community, Bonczyk remembers no racial divide within the team.

"I don't really think we ever looked at the color," says Bonczyk. "I don't think it ever became an issue. We just played basketball."

Bonczyk's ability to be color-blind in terms of race paid dividends when he graduated from Thornridge and went to Illinois State University on an athletic scholarship.

"At Illinois State, I played for Will Robinson, the first black Division-One head coach," says Bonczyk. "I never thought of it that way. He was our basketball coach. I played basketball. I played basketball with black guys. I played basketball with white guys. It didn't make any difference to me, and I think that was a carryover from where I played and who I played with at Thornridge High School."

Even as a high school player, the lefty ball-handling whiz played with an understanding of the game that comes from being the son of a coach. His father, Ed Bonczyk, had toiled as a high school assistant coach before becoming the basketball coach at Thornton Community College.

"He coached initially in Kankakee, Illinois," says the former Thornridge point guard. "Back then, it was called Saint Patrick's. They changed the name to Bishop McNamara which is what it is now. Then, he came up and coached at Thornton [High]. He was gonna assist Bill Purden. Then, when we moved up there, Purden went to Valparaiso. Bob Anderson got the [Thornton High School head coaching] job. My dad coached one or two years at Thornton High School as an assistant. He was there [in 1966], the year they won the state. Then, he went to the junior college."

At the time Ed Bonczyk was coaching at Thornton High School, the Bonczyk family lived in Harvey directly across the street from the high school. In the 1960s, both black and white families lived in the community located west of Dolton. Mike Bonczyk attended Bryant Grade School, one of the schools that fed students into Thornton High. On the basketball court, young Mike was not intimidated when playing with or against the blacks from Phoenix. Supremely confident, Bonczyk looked forward to the day he would be able to represent Thornton High School playing alongside Quinn Buckner and Boyd Batts. He envisioned himself joining with the blacks from Phoenix to form a high school team that might bring Thornton another state championship.

"Thornton was good," says Bonczyk. "Me growin' up in Harvey and going to grade school there, and with Quinn and those guys at Coolidge, it was just a foregone conclusion that everybody would be going to Thornton High School."

Bonczyk believed they could win a state title at Thornton, "because of their track record and their history of success in basketball."

Then, while still in elementary school, Bonczyk learned of the boundary change that would send the black players from Phoenix to Thornridge High School. When Bonczyk heard of the boundary change, he felt he would still be part of a good team at Thornton. However, it looked like he would not play high school ball with Buckner and Batts.

"I don't know if I was disappointed," says Bonczyk. "I knew a lot of people that I went to grade school with, and I'd played against a bunch of people in the Harvey grade schools. I knew a lot of players [who would be going to Thornton]. There were some players that were really good over there at Thornton. But then, the word was the kids from Phoenix were being bused over [to Thornridge] for the integration thing. I knew Quinn and all those guys. It was like, 'Damn, I ain't gonna be able to play with them.'"

However, a year later when Bonczyk headed to high school, he was united with Buckner and Batts at Thornridge. For that, he can thank his father. Ed Bonczyk wanted his son to be in the best possible position to have success in sports. He compared the Thornton and Thornridge teams. Coach Ron Ferguson believes the elder Bonczyk was searching for the best fit for his son.

"I think his dad thought Mike had a better chance of playing at Thornridge than at Thornton," says Ferguson. "They had a lot of great players, so I think he thought that Mike would be better off with us."

Like any father who hopes his child will earn an athletic scholarship, Ed Bonczyk surely realized that Buckner was going to attract a great deal of attention from college coaches. That meant there would be college coaches at Thornridge games when Mike was an upperclassman. What better way for his son to showcase his talents than to play alongside Buckner? Whether or not that was Ed Bonczyk's plan, he moved his family from Harvey to South Holland. Because of the move, Mike ended up at Thornridge. Some people suspected the family moved so that Mike could play alongside Buckner. However, the Bonczyks actually moved because Thornton Community College had relocated to an address within the Thornridge High School boundaries. Mike Bonczyk thinks his father simply wanted to live closer to his work. He does not believe the family's move to South Holland was part of a master plan to help him land an athletic scholarship. Getting to team with Buckner and Batts was just a bonus.

"Well, that might have been an underlying side story," laughs Bonczyk. "But no, I think the reason we moved to South Holland, at least initially, was because my dad was teaching and coaching at the junior college, Thornton Community College. That put him close to [his] teaching and coaching. It just so happened that Boyd and all the boys, and myself, all ended up at Thornridge."

Since their coaching paths had crossed, Thornridge's Ron Ferguson knew Ed Bonczyk and was aware that the Bonczyks were moving to South Holland. Ferguson makes clear that there was no recruiting of Mike Bonczyk. In fact, the Falcons' head coach wasn't even certain that the small point guard would ever play a key role on the Thornridge varsity.

"When Mike came, it wasn't a sure thing that he was gonna get to play," says Ferguson. "We had other people, some pretty good players. Although, I have a feeling because of his unselfishness and some of the other things that he could do, [he would have played]. All those other guys wanted to shoot all the time. He worked out the best because you can't have everybody comin' down and shootin' the ball."

Bonczyk did not find himself on a fast track to the varsity like Buckner and Batts. Bonczyk played on the freshmen team, and on the sophomore squad, before finally making it to the varsity his junior year. Frank Nardi, who coached Bonczyk on the sophomore team, says he knew Bonczyk had what it took to be an outstanding point guard.

"He ran the team very, very well," says Nardi. "He knew exactly what to do with the ball. [He] hustled all the time."

Even after Bonczyk made the varsity as a junior, he did not have a clear path to the starting point guard job. Senior Tony Jackson started some games early in the season. But, as the season progressed, it became clear to Coach Ferguson, Bonczyk should start at the point.

"He shared the position with Tony Jackson," recalls Ferguson. "[Mike] was, you know, really quick for a white kid. You have to be careful how you say that, but he was just as quick as anybody. And he was a great passer."

Jackson was black, and some thought Ferguson might have made the switch to appease some of the white fans who were annoyed by the large percentage of black players getting significant court time. Race had nothing to do with Ferguson's decision to start Bonczyk. Greg Rose, who moved into the starting lineup as a sophomore that 1970-71 season, says Ferguson never played favorites based on the color of a player's skin.

"No, if you can play, you can play," says Rose. "That's the way Fergie felt. It was about who can play the game. That's who's gonna start."

The Falcons' coach says the team's chemistry was outstanding once Bonczyk moved into the starting lineup.

"Bonczyk got along really well with those kids," says Ferguson. "They really liked him too. He beat out another black kid. Naturally, there were a few who said, 'Well, you gotta have one white kid on the team.' You had to deal with that stuff. But, there was no comparison. Tony Jackson was a pretty good player. At the start of the year, I think Jackson started sometimes because he was a year older, and I gave him the nod. But, Bonczyk was about twice as quick as he was. [Jackson] wasn't that quick. He got a little chubby. Bonczyk was the better player. He could pass the ball. He was willing to give it up and didn't care whether he scored."

A coach is lucky to have even one player as unselfish as Bonczyk. In his team's perfect 1971-72 season, Ferguson was blessed to coach a squad that had not one, not two, but three players willing to sacrifice their individual stats for the good of the team. Bonczyk and Ernie Dunn surely could have had more impressive statistics but were willing to trade personal stats for team victories.

"Buckner was the same way," says Ferguson. "He'd give the ball up because he knew that if Rose and Batts scored, then they'd play hard, and we wouldn't have to worry about them. He was a big help because you know Buckner could have been real selfish. He could have easily averaged 30 points a game. He sacrificed because of the team situation."

Because of the unselfish play of Buckner, Dunn, and Bonczyk, Thornridge had an unbeatable combination of players. Buckner was able to do anything he wanted on the basketball court. Dunn concentrated on defense and rebounding. Bonczyk was the playmaker, an excellent ball-handler and passer with the speed to lead the team's heralded fast break. Greg Rose and Boyd Batts were scoring and rebounding machines. The Falcons had the perfect collection of talent, and their flashy point guard made sure everything ran smoothly. Game after game, Bonczyk got the basketball into the hands of the bigger, stronger Falcons when they were in perfect position to score. Bonczyk averaged only 5.5 shots per game. He ended the season averaging 6.1 points and 8.2 assists. His head coach fondly recalls Bonczyk's unselfish style of play.

"When he was a senior, he was wonderful," says Coach Ferguson. "He gave up trying to score just to get everybody else the ball."

Despite being smaller in physical stature, Bonczyk had long ago earned the respect of his peers. For years, he had competed with his Thornridge teammates on the Phoenix playgrounds. Some might consider it dangerous for a white kid to show up to play on the predominantly black courts, but Bonczyk believed it was the best place for him to test his skills and to earn respect as a player.

"Mike had to make some terrific sacrifices," says his teammate Quinn Buckner. "We were all products of being moved from one school to the other. Mike would come and play with us. I'm sure he had to take some abuse for that because of the whole integration thing."

"It was tough because you're talking about a country that, you know, [was dealing with issues of] black and white," says Bonczyk, asked why he went to the black suburbs to play when the black players would never play in white towns. "I don't know if they were ready for all that. For them to come over to the white neighborhood and play, especially when we went to Ivanhoe Park in [predominantly white] Riverdale, that was a tough mix. For me to go over to Coolidge [Elementary School in Phoenix], hell, that was fun."

When Bonczyk was competing against other black players, his Thornridge teammates made sure to protect him from trouble.

"Bonczyk used to be in Phoenix every day," says Boyd Batts. "We played ball together all the time. He was just like one of the brothers to us. Nobody could bother him while we [were] playin'. If you gonna want to try to get real physical with him, then you have to deal with us because you're not gonna hurt our guard."

It is interesting to hear Batts vow to stand up for Bonczyk. The point guard often confronted Batts while trying to keep him focused on playing team basketball. Quinn Buckner gets much of the credit for keeping Boyd in line, but Bonczyk also played a critical role. Buckner remembers many times the five-ten guard would get in the face of the six-seven Batts.

"If Boyd got out of line, Mike would say something before anybody else," says Buckner. "He'd tell Boyd, 'If you don't wanna play, sit down. We'll get somebody out here who wants to play.'"

"He used to call me Scooby-Doo," continues Buckner, "There was a cartoon character [by that name], and I used to watch it a lot. [Mike would say], 'Scoob, Boyd don't wanna play.' And I'd say, 'Well, go tell *him* [to start playing]. Don't tell *me!*'"

Despite his small size, Mike Bonczyk was clearly a team leader. You often see that quality in a coach's kid. Ed Bonczyk was understandably proud of his son. Still, Mike learned that life as the son of a basketball coach can be difficult during the season.

Ron Ferguson explains, "[Mike] said, 'I hated going home whether we won or lost. I got to listen to my dad all night.'"

Even if the point guard did not always enjoy being critiqued by his father, Coach Ferguson found that he enjoyed talking hoops with Ed Bonczyk on the eve of a game.

"His dad and I, and usually our wives, would go out to dinner on Thursday, the night before a game," says Ferguson. "We'd go out to some place and have dinner. It was nice because I could talk basketball with the dad."

You rarely hear of a head coach socializing with parents of a high school player. A coach knows that sooner or later the conversation could turn into a discussion about playing time or how their son might play a bigger role in the offense. Ferguson was glad that did not happen when he got together with Mike's dad.

"He was good," says Ferguson. "He wouldn't try to over-coach me. He was very congenial. He didn't say, 'Change the offense, or do all that stuff'. We just talked. It was kind of relaxing to go out. At home, I'd be walking around like a *nut* the night before a game."

With Thornridge attracting a lot of media attention during its perfect season, Ferguson would occasionally take two of his players into Chicago to be interviewed by sportscasters and sportswriters.

"Quinn and Boncyzk had to do a lot of radio shows and stuff that year," says Ferguson. "Most of the time, those were the guys that went because they were seniors, and they could talk. Batts had a little trouble with the English language. I didn't want to embarrass him and get him on too many shows."

Ferguson always enjoyed when Buckner and Bonczyk accompanied him on a media tour. The three could talk over any problems confronting the team. In addition, black and white issues sometimes crept into the conversation.

"I would go downtown for a TV shot, and we got a chance to really talk about those kinds of things," remembers Ferguson. "Those two guys, they got along really great. I could talk to them about the [race] relations and different things like that. If they had some problems, they'd bring them up, and I'd try to figure out a way to deal with them."

While all of the Thornridge players got along well, Bonczyk and Buckner were probably the closest friends among the five starters. Bonczyk enjoyed Quinn's company off the court, and he certainly appreciated the opportunity to play on the same team as Buckner.

"Oh, he was a man among boys," says Bonczyk. "He was six-three, two-twenty. I watched him play football, and he just manhandled people. Then, on a basketball court, Quinn could go one side of the floor to the other on the full court press. You knew that if you messed up, you had backup. He was tremendous in what he could do as an athlete."

As Ed Bonczyk likely anticipated several years earlier, college coaches flocked to gyms to watch Buckner play. That meant the other Falcons' players received college scholarship consideration.

"You played with the guy that was the number one high school player in America," says Mike Bonczyk. "[Despite] all the attention he received, he was still the same old guy throughout the time we were playing. John Wooden, Bobby Knight, you name the people. They were all looking at him. Just he alone, along with our success [as a team], brought other people the opportunity to be seen to possibly go to college and play. That's what happened."

Bonczyk received an athletic scholarship to Illinois State University in Normal, Illinois, where he played basketball and baseball. He had success on the diamond and on the court. However, after his junior season on the hardwood, he entertained the idea of playing only baseball because of a personality conflict with basketball head coach Will Robinson. Bonczyk's unhappiness had nothing to do with the fact that Robinson was his first black coach. Remember, Bonczyk never saw any black and white in basketball. He and Robinson simply did not see eye-to-eye on basketball matters. The point guard decided to play his senior season after Robinson was replaced by ISU assistant and former Rich East High coach Gene Smithson, who had recruited Bonczyk to play at Illinois State. Bonczyk also stuck around because Smithson hired Ron Ferguson as an assistant coach, thus reuniting Bonczyk with his former high school coach. The Redbirds certainly benefitted from Bonczyk's decision to play his senior season. He had 188 assists which remains the most assists in a season by a senior guard at the school. He helped Illinois State go 20-7, starting a run of five consecutive 20-win seasons.

As a freshman, one of his ISU teammates was All-American Doug Collins, the school's all-time leading scorer. Bonczyk did not crack the Redbirds' starting lineup until the last five games of his sophomore season. He helped ISU win four of its last five games which gave the Redbirds a 17-9 record, their best in five seasons under Robinson. Bonczyk rarely scored in double figures while at Illinois State. However, he excelled in distributing the basketball just as he had at Thornridge High. As a freshman, Bonczyk set a school record with 20 assists in a game against Northern Iowa. As a sophomore, he tied the record with 20 assists against Northern Illinois. Then as a junior, he broke his own school mark with 23 assists against Northern Illinois. No other player in Illinois State University history has had 20 or more assists in a single game. Boncyzk did it three times. He averaged 7.2 assists as a junior and 7.0 assists as a senior. Those numbers rank in the top five in Illinois State history. His career average of 5.7 assists in 85 games ranks third all-time at ISU.

After Illinois State, Bonczyk went into coaching, first for a year at Thornton Community College where he assisted his father, then at a junior college in Oklahoma for a year. He ended up in Woodstock, Kansas, where he met the woman who would become his wife. Mike won a Kansas state championship at Wichita West High School in 1981-82. The next year, his team was ranked in the Top 25 in the nation before being upset in the Kansas state tournament semifinals, one of the biggest disappointments in his coaching career. After spending twelve years in Kansas, Bonczyk reconnected with Ron Ferguson who had left Illinois State to become the Athletic Director at Bradley University. Bonczyk earned a Masters Degree while serving as a graduate assistant at Bradley. He turned his interest to hockey and was involved for three years with the River Men minor league hockey team in Peoria, Illinois. Continuing to look for the perfect occupational fit, he became a coach with the Fort Wayne CBA team where he worked for two years with Hall of Famer Rick Barry. While he was at Fort Wayne, Bonczyk's family stayed in Peoria. The separation was difficult and eventually led to his decision to leave the pro game.

"We'd had our third son, so I decided it's time to get back and start raising my boys along with my wife," says Bonczyk. "They were at that age. They were growing up. I coached and was an Athletic Director at a small school just outside of Peoria. Then, I went to [coach at Peoria] Notre Dame [High School] for five years. We moved back here to Kansas about six years ago. My wife's mom and dad were in failing health. I coached here for about five years, then got tired of the small-town mentality and said the heck with it. So, I'm just watching my youngest boy play baseball and football."

Although Bonczyk has not coached the last couple years, he has been a teacher at Eby Learning Center in Newton, Kansas. It's a job that provides Bonczyk with daily challenges.

"Eby is a school where the kids have had a lot of issues or problems with the law," says Bonczyk.

Bonczyk would like to return to Illinois to again coach in the state where he first made a name for himself in basketball. Ferguson says Bonczyk has applied for several Illinois coaching jobs in recent years, but none have worked out. Bonczyk knows coaching jobs don't pay as well as teaching positions. He can't afford to take a large pay cut to get back into the game. Bonczyk might still find the perfect fit, a job that could lure him back into coaching, and there are those hoping he will. Though he suffered some growing pains in his earlier coaching jobs, Bonczyk knows the game. Ron Ferguson is among those who believe the man who won two state championships as a player and one as a high school coach would do a good job if given another chance to call the shots from the bench.

"He couldn't get along with some of the fans who were on him," says the former Thornridge coach. "He used a lot of profanity on the bench, and that got some people mad. In high school, that's kind of a no-no. But he was a good coach, and the players loved him. They just loved his enthusiasm for the game."

It would be nice to see Bonczyk get another chance to serve the game he has loved his entire life. He still feels intense passion for basketball. It's clear that he misses being involved in the sport.

"Yeah, I'm tryin' to get back," says Bonczyk. "But with the way things are… Hell, I've got a Masters [degree] plus thirty [years' teaching experience]. Sometimes you price yourself out of a job."

Bonczyk enjoyed playing for Ferguson. He knew the coach cared about him off the court as well as when he was wearing the Thornridge jersey on game night. As a high school coach, Bonczyk always kept in mind how Ferguson handled the 1971-72 Falcons during their perfect season.

"Fergie was a tremendous manipulator of personalities," says Bonczyk. "He knew how to rub the ego the right way, or massage it, so that guys came and played. We had some different personalities. I don't mean it in a negative way, [but] you're talking sixteen, seventeen, eighteen year old kids. He was a great manipulator of personalities. That's why everybody loved playing for him."

Without hesitation, Bonczyk says his high school days were the best time of his life.

"Oh, I wouldn't trade high school for the world," he says. "College was a lot of fun. But those two years of playing basketball at Thornridge High School were tremendous."

Bonczyk says he'll never forget the thrill of winning a pair of state championships in high school. But, he has experienced a few things in life that have equaled the thrill of what he and his teammates accomplished at Thornridge.

"Yeah, I think the day I got married, and the days we had the three boys," says Bonczyk. "The three boys have been very special to watch. Two of them now are going out being good productive citizens, and I've got one more [in school]. But from an athletic standpoint, winning the state title both years was tremendous. I don't think you can take one without the other. You win it when you're not supposed to. Then, the year you're *supposed* to win it, you do it convincingly. They say you can't have your cake and eat it. Well, I had both. I had the cake, and I was able to eat it."

CHAPTER 14

You Could Have Beat Me By 200

As Thornridge headed into the final month of the regular season, there were a number of newsworthy events happening around the world. The first scientific hand-held calculator, the HP-35, was introduced with a retail price of $395. The Eleventh Winter Olympic games opened in Sapporo, Japan, marking the first Winter Games held in Asia. It wasn't newsworthy at the time, but future NFL stars Drew Bledsoe and Jerome Bettis were born in February as were future pro tennis standout Michael Chang and future NHL star Jaromir Jagr. Josh Gibson and Buck Leonard were selected to join the Baseball Hall of Fame becoming just the second and third former Negro League stars to be recognized in Cooperstown; Satchel Paige entered the Hall the previous year. A little more than two weeks after Gibson and Leonard became Hall of Famers, future Hall of Fame pitcher Steve Carlton was traded by the St. Louis Cardinals to the Philadelphia Phillies for pitcher Rick Wise. Also, in February, Richard Nixon became the first United States President to visit China. *"Grease"* opened on Broadway. And in a bizarre programming move, former Beatle John Lennon and his wife, Yoko Ono, served as co-hosts on "The Mike Douglas Show" for one full week. Most agreed John and Yoko were no threat to "The Tonight Show's" Johnny Carson, the undisputed king of TV talk. In mid-February, Al Green's *"Let's Stay Together"* became the number one song in America. The same week, Santana's *"No One to Depend On"* made its first appearance in the Top 100. Other songs debuting in February included Neil Young's *"Heart of Gold"*, Paul Simon's *"Mother and Child*

Reunion", America's *"Horse With No Name"*, The Stylistics' *"Betcha By Golly Wow"*, and *"Puppy Love"* by young Donny Osmond.

Meantime, the Thornridge basketball players and coaches worked diligently in hopes of completing an unbeaten regular season. The Falcons had six games left before the start of the postseason tournament. After the close call against St. Patrick, the players were refocused and determined to claim their place in history. Few high school teams make it through a regular season undefeated. Even fewer finish the year undefeated and with a state title. For the 1971-72 Thornridge Falcons, destiny was calling.

***

GAME 20 (Friday night, February 4, 1972)
Thornton (Harvey)

Heading into the last month of the regular season, Thornridge (19-0) was ranked number one. La Salle-Peru (17-1) was second and Quincy (17-2) third. Thornridge began the February portion of its schedule with back-to-back home games against Thornton (12-4) and Homewood-Flossmoor (8-2). Since Saint Patrick had provided such a stiff challenge for the Falcons, there were suddenly Illinois teams who felt Thornridge may be vulnerable.

In mid-January, Thornton coach Tom Hanrahan had apparently felt a little giddy after his Wildcats upset Quincy. Feeling good about his team, Hanrahan hinted that he thought Thornridge was beatable and said he looked forward to getting another shot at the Falcons. Hanrahan made the mistake of telling reporters how he planned to upset Thornridge. His game plan made it into the newspapers and became the talk of sports fans in the area. Hanrahan said the three keys to defeating Thornridge were to control the basketball, slow down point guard Mike Bonczyk, and put offensive pressure on Quinn Buckner. Yes, the Wildcats intended to go right at the All-American. Nearly four decades later, Hanrahan still recalls his rationale.

"From the experience we had playing against Thornridge and scouting them," says Hanrahan, "I had four guards ready to go at Buckner, and [we wanted] to put him on the ball. Whoever he was guarding took the ball in a 1-2-2 offense. We tried to keep him on the ball because off of the ball he was so destructive defensively. We'd had a player like that in Lloyd Batts. We played him off the ball and just let him roam. Buckner was the same way. He was just that good

152

at anticipating what the other players were doing. So we forced him to play the ball. Then also, he was foul prone. He was afraid of picking up fouls, especially early in the game. That was another one of the objectives of doing that. {We wanted] to get him in foul trouble."

"Other things we did," he continued, "[with] the first pass, we would leave the passer. If the ball went to Buckner, we would double-team him. One [Thornton player] would play his right hand. One would play his left. We did things like this gambling that the ball would not go back to that original entry passer. We did a variety of things like this. Nothing worked. We tried pressing them half-court [and used] just a variety of different defenses on them. There wasn't much we could do."

With much of Thornton's strategy finding its way into the newspapers, the Falcons knew details of how the Wildcats hoped to pull off the upset as the two rivals took the court. An overflow crowd, estimated at 5000 fans, was jammed inside the Dolton gym. Another 350 people viewed the game via closed circuit television in the Thornridge High School auditorium. The high-energy atmosphere inside the gymnasium seemed to energize the Falcons. Senior center Boyd Batts scored 14 points in the first quarter to help Thornridge muscle its way to a 26-14 lead. Batts and Buckner each scored 17 points by halftime, and the Falcons led 42-28 at the break. The Wildcats had seemed on the verge of being blown out before ending the half on an 8-2 scoring run. Things went badly for Thornton once star Otis Dunn went to the bench with four personal fouls midway through the third quarter. Thornridge was able to maintain a comfortable margin the rest of the way. The Falcons coasted past the Wildcats 73-52 to raise their record to 20-0. The plan to slow down Buckner failed miserably. The mighty Quinn scored 28 points and pulled down 14 rebounds. During the game, he went over the 1700 point mark for his career. Batts finished with 21 points and 9 boards. Mike Bonczyk again reached double figures in assists with 10.

The Thornton coach has great admiration for the job Ron Ferguson did coaching the 1971-72 Falcons. Having been around to watch Buckner, Batts, and the other Phoenix kids as they grew up before reaching high school, Tom Hanrahan is aware that Ferguson had his hands full. He knows Ferguson did much more than just roll out the basketballs and tell his guys to go play.

"I was familiar with the players," says Hanrahan. "I knew them a little bit and what [Ferguson] was doing. It was a lot of not only coaching the basketball but just keeping them together as a group and a team. I think Buckner probably did a lot of that also. I think Bonczyk did a good job of that too. But yeah, he had some free spirits there."

Hanrahan adds that he feels somewhat privileged to have played Thornridge that season.

"They were just a joy to play against," he says. "The gym was full. The fans were there to see some good basketball, and they got their money's worth."

Hanrahan also believes Ferguson had to deal with more racially-charged comments at Thornridge than he did at Thornton, though both schools had black and white students trying to co-exist.

"Comments from fans, I didn't get much of that," says Hanrahan. "He might have gotten it a little bit more because this was a newly integrated school situation that Ron was in. When Thornton split in '59-'60, Thornridge was an all white school. And they were that way for a number of years. Then, the district was split. You had people that moved out of Harvey into South Holland. That situation was going on. The blacks were coming out of the city [and] going into Harvey. The whites [in Harvey] were selling and moving over to South Holland thinking that that [area] would not be integrated. And then, it did [become integrated]. So, I think there were some hard feelings there."

Since Thornton had dominated Thornridge for a decade, payback was sweet for the Falcons. Ron Bonfiglio, the sophomore coach at the time, remembers how great it felt to finally have Thornton's number after all those years of frustration against Wildcats' teams.

"That's what we always used to fight when we played Thornton," says Bonfiglio. "You had to have an offense to get the ball inbounds. Then, you had to have an offense to get the ball from inbounds to half-court and then down the floor. Finally, *we* became that kind of team."

With the victory, the Falcons had clinched at least a tie for the South Suburban league championship. There was no doubt they would win the league title outright in the days ahead. First, they had to play a non-conference game the next night against Southwest Suburban League co-leader Homewood-Flossmoor, a good team, with a front-line standing six-nine, six-nine, six-eight.

***

GAME 21 (Saturday Night, February 5, 1972)
Homewood-Flossmoor

The Thornridge express continued to roll. The super-quick Falcons (20-0) used their suffocating full-court press to force the visiting Homewood-Flossmoor Vikings into 15 turnovers in the first quarter! The Falcons enjoyed their biggest first quarter in a season full of big first quarters. Thornridge scored the first 13 points. After only six minutes, the scoreboard read Thornridge-32, Visitors-3. It was 36-7 after the first quarter, and Homewood-Flossmoor never recovered. Thornridge cruised to an 89-53 win for its 42nd consecutive victory. Boyd Batts led the Falcons with 24 points, 11 rebounds, and 5 blocked shots. Quinn Buckner and Greg Rose added 18 points apiece.

After the victory, and with only a few weeks left in the regular season, the top five teams in the AP rankings were Thornridge (21-0), La Salle-Peru (19-1), Hinsdale Central (18-1), Lincoln (19-1), and Quincy (19-2). No one knew it, but one of those teams would face Thornridge in the state championship game.

***

GAME 22 (Friday Night, February 11, 1972)
Bloom (Chicago Heights)

Thornridge (21-0) had only one game on the schedule the following week, but it was a big one. Three days before Valentine's Day, the Falcons had the opportunity to clinch the South Suburban League title with a victory over Bloom (15-6) in McCann Gymnasium in Chicago Heights. Concerned that his players might experience mental and physical fatigue in the dog days of the regular season, Thornridge coach Ron Ferguson lightened the load in practice. He still demanded crisp execution and hard work, but Ferguson shortened the length of practice and interrupted the sessions with milk and water breaks. Ferguson would consider increasing the length of practices once the state tournament began, but at this point in the season, he did not feel it was productive to force the players to endure long workouts.

Wes Mason had his team prepared to play the Falcons. Although Bloom had lost by 34 to Thornridge in their first meeting, Mason believed his team would give the Falcons a much better game. His optimism was understandable. The Trojans had scored a total of 199 points in their last two games, lopsided wins over Thornwood and Racine (Wisconsin) Herlick.

In a switch from the norm, Thornridge did not start the game in its devastating full-court press. Ferguson believed his team was becoming too predictable, so the Falcons used only a half-court trap in the first half. The Trojans seemed a bit nervous at the start of the game and were held to only three shots in the first four minutes. But after falling behind 16-6, Bloom scored the next six points to pull within four with three minutes left in the first quarter. Thornridge then went on an 11-4 scoring run and led 27-16 at the end of the period. Thornridge was up 50-37 at halftime. At intermission, Quinn Buckner and Greg Rose were leading a balanced attack with 12 points apiece. Boyd Batts had scored 10 points. Ernie Dunn and Mike Bonczyk had each scored 8. The Falcons dusted off their full-court press to begin the second half, and the switch in strategy paid immediate dividends. Bonczyk found Rose for a basket to open the second half. Dunn stole the inbounds pass and scored. Buckner then stole the ball and drove in for a basket. Just 27 seconds into the second half, Thornridge was firmly in command 56-37. Buckner went to the bench with four fouls two minutes into the second half, and three of his teammates, Batts, Rose, and Dunn all fouled out in the fourth quarter. Not to worry, the Falcons crushed Bloom 90-62. Thornridge shot 52% from the field in the victory. Rose scored a game-high 26 points. Buckner added 24 points and had 6 steals. Dunn contributed 17 points and 7 rebounds while Batts scored 10 points with a game-high 9 rebounds. Falcons' point guard Mike Bonczyk was outstanding. He scored 11 points and assisted on 13 of his teammates' baskets.

With the victory, Thornridge clinched the South Suburban League championship. The winning streak stood at 43 games, just five short of the record set by Taylorville in the 1944 and 1945 seasons. Ron Ferguson and Wes Mason knew this was probably not the last time their teams would be seeing one another. Both expected to be regional champions which meant they could again meet in March at McCann gymnasium in the Chicago Heights sectional tournament. The Bloom coach was already trying to figure out a way to slow down the Falcons in case they squared off again.

For the seventh consecutive week, Thornridge was a unanimous choice as Illinois' number one team in the Associated Press rankings. La Salle-Peru (21-1) remained number two and Hinsdale Central (19-1) number three. Lincoln and Quincy dropped from the top five after each suffered a defeat. Lincoln lost 65-62 at home to Jacksonville. Quincy fell 68-55 at

Moline. Rock Island Alleman (16-3) and Maine South (17-1) moved up to numbers four and five, respectively.

***

GAME 23 (Friday night, February 18, 1972)
Thornwood (South Holland)

February 18, 1972, marked the first-ever meeting of Thornridge (22-0) and Thornwood (5-14). The new high school in Thornridge's district, Thornwood was coached by Frank Nardi, a Ferguson assistant from 1960 to 1968. During the time he was the Falcons' sophomore coach, Nardi had, at one time or another, coached every player now on the Thornridge varsity with the exception of Ernie Dunn and reserve Joe King. Nardi knew the players. He knew Ferguson. He also knew his team was in for a long night playing the defending state champions in the packed Dolton gym.

"I always wanted to be a head coach, and I was [an assistant] at Thornridge for about ten years," says Nardi. "I knew this [Thornridge] team was going to go on to great, great things, and they did. [That first year at Thornwood], we only had freshmen, sophomores and juniors so my [varsity] team was only sophomores and juniors. I told my kids, 'Look, I know these guys, and if you pass the ball more than once, you're going to lose it. So, shoot it. Go ahead and shoot it. Don't pass it more than once.'"

Consecutive win number 44 came easily for Thornridge. The game could have been called after the first quarter with the Falcons leading 35-11 even though Ferguson never had his team use its suffocating full-court press. By halftime, Greg Rose had made all eight of his field goal attempts, and Thornridge led 59-24. Ferguson, uncharacteristically, went to his bench in the second quarter, giving the reserves a rare opportunity to play in the first half. Thornridge shot 63% in the first half and 59% for the game while cruising to a 103-57 victory. Every Falcon played and scored. Sidney Lewis scored 6 points and made a late free throw to give Thornridge its fourth 100-point game of the season. Rose and Boyd Batts scored 19 points apiece, tops in the game. Quinn Buckner and Nee Gatlin each added 13 points. Gatlin also pulled down 8 rebounds to tie Rose for team honors. Ernie Dunn was the fifth Falcon in double figure scoring with 11 points.

"We got beat *a-hundred-and-three* to *57*," laughs Nardi. "Of course, Fergie came up to me, and we shook hands. Fergie says, 'Frank. I hope you're not mad. I know we beat you by a lot.' I said, 'Look, if you wanted to beat me by <u>*200*</u> points, you could have beat me by 200 points. Don't worry about it.'"

"That was a tough game to go against somebody that's been [coaching] with you," recalls Ferguson. "Frank was with me probably longer than anybody, but he had dreams of being a head coach and doing his own thing."

The Thornwood players told Nardi they were just glad to have had a chance to play Thornridge because it meant they could shoot a lot of shots without worrying about the consequences.

"I knew what was gonna happen," says Coach Nardi. "Everybody knew what was gonna happen. But, my kids told me that was the best week of practice they ever had because they were doing a lot of shooting. Unfortunately, not enough of them went in [during the game]."

***

GAME 24 (Saturday night, February 19, 1972)
Saint Ignatius (Chicago)

Thornridge (23-0) had a Saturday night date at Saint Ignatius of Chicago, the South Central Catholic League champion. If the Falcons hoped to match the state record for consecutive victories, they had to beat the Wolves, win the regular season finale against Oak Lawn Richards, and win both games they would play in the Dolton Regional. Thornridge got off to its traditional quick start against Saint Ignatius and outscored the Wolves 25-13 in the first quarter and 45-30 in the first half. Saint Ignatius hung around and trailed only 50-35 midway through the third quarter. Then, the Falcons pulled away, going on a 15-4 scoring run to go up by 25 entering the fourth quarter. Thornridge outscored the Wolves 25-12 after that to win 90-52. Reserve Bill Redman scored 7 points in the final period to help Thornridge reach the 90-point mark for the tenth time in the season. Quinn Buckner led the winners with 27 points and 15 rebounds while improving his scoring average to 23.5 points per game. For the season, Buckner was shooting an impressive 56% from the field. Boyd Batts scored 19 points and pulled down 13 rebounds. Mike Bonczyk's 9 assists pushed him over the 400 mark for his career. He also broke his own single-season school record of 192 assists which he had set the previous season.

Thornridge (24-0) again received all sixteen first-place votes in the Associated Press Illinois Class AA high school basketball poll. La Salle-Peru (23-1) was still ranked second. Hinsdale Central (20-1) was third. Lincoln (22-2) and Quincy (21-3) shared the number four spot in the poll.

***

GAME 25 (Friday night, February 25, 1972)
Richards (Oak Lawn)

Thornridge (24-0) headed into its February 25th home game against Oak Lawn Richards (9-15) needing a win to end the regular season and the South Suburban League schedule without a loss. It was the last regular season home game for the seniors, including starters Quinn Buckner, Mike Bonczyk, and Boyd Batts. Junior forward Greg Rose began the game on the bench because of a bruised thigh suffered the previous week. Junior Nee Gatlin started in place of Rose, the usual point man on the 1-2-1-1 full court press. Even though the starting lineup was changed, Thornridge had no trouble assuming command. The Falcons led 21-13 after the first quarter and 43-25 at halftime. Though the Thornridge players seemed somewhat uninspired, Batts sank seven baskets in the second quarter. Two minutes into the second half, Rose came off the bench to provide a spark. Before the Richards' players knew what hit them, Thornridge was heading into the fourth quarter with a 73-32 lead. Buckner and Bonczyk put on a dazzling display of basketball in the third quarter. Buckner made three consecutive steals and set up Bonczyk for scores. An imaginative behind-the-back bounce pass from Buckner to Bonczyk led to a two minute standing ovation. At the conclusion of the Quinn Buckner show, the reserves entered the game in the fourth quarter to finish off a 90-53 victory. Six-six senior Keith Hutchinson came off the bench and capped the senior night performance by sinking a 12-foot jumper late in the game. Though the Falcons hadn't played their best, their individual numbers were outstanding. Batts finished with 26 points, 16 rebounds, and 7 blocks. Buckner had 17 points, 11 rebounds, and 5 assists. True to form, Buckner passed up a chance to score more points and possibly claim the league's scoring title. Instead, he kept his teammates happy by distributing the basketball, often in dazzling style. Dunn scored 14 points, and Gatlin scored 13 in his rare start. Rose scored only 3 points in limited duty.

The Falcons had gone through the entire 25-game regular season without stumbling and without ever being seriously challenged. Along the way, the Falcons defeated eight conference champions. None of them even came close. Thornridge certainly seemed to be in a league of its own.

***

When the final Associated Press Illinois Class AA high school basketball rankings were released, no one was surprised to see Thornridge a unanimous choice at number one. The undefeated Falcons received every first place vote the entire season which was unprecedented. The Falcons knew eight more victories in the postseason would give them a second straight Illinois championship. While no team had yet been able to match up to Thornridge, there were outstanding squads throughout Illinois that still believed on a given night they might be able to challenge the high-flying Falcons. La Salle-Peru (24-1) ranked second in the final AP poll. Hinsdale Central (21-1) was third in the balloting followed by Lincoln (23-2), Maine South of Park Ridge (20-1), North Chicago (22-1), and Waukegan (19-3). Eighth-rated Quincy (21-4) ended its regular season in disappointing fashion with an 80-75 loss at Collinsville. Rock Island Alleman (19-4) ranked ninth in the final AP poll. Lockport (19-3) was tenth. Ernie Kivisto's 11th-ranked Aurora East (21-3) team believed it was good enough to win the state championship. East St. Louis Lincoln (19-3) was also solid and was ranked 12th in the final regular season poll. Aurora West (17-4) headed into the postseason tournament rated 13th. Moline was 14th in the final poll. Peoria Manual (19-6) which had to play without the injured Mike Davis early in the year lost five of its first nine games but won fifteen of its last sixteen. Dick Van Scyoc's Rams were clearly on a roll. Kankakee Eastridge (20-4) rounded out the top 16 in the final regular season AP poll. The voters did a fairly good job of determining which teams might do well in the state tournament. Four of the rated teams would reach the state semifinals. They would put on a show that would long be remembered.

Frank McCully photo

Students camp out for tickets during 1971 title run

Frank McCully photo

Fans support Thornridge in 1971 tournament

Quinn Buckner smiles after
a 1971 tournament win

Frank McCully photo

Boyd Batts celebrates during
1971 championship season

Frank McCully photo

Frank McCully photo

Quinn Buckner and Mike Henry, 1971 heroes

Frank McCully photo

Boyd Batts during 1971 trophy presentation

Point guard Mike Bonczyk

Center Boyd Batts

Guard Ernie Dunn

Forward Greg Rose

(Above) Greg Rose (44) in action vs. Collinsville in 1972 IHSA tournament
(Below) Ernie Dunn (24) guarded by Quincy's Kel Gott
(45) and Larry Moore (right) in 1972 IHSA final

Boyd Batts (31) scores in 1972 IHSA final. Watching: Quinn Buckner (25),
Quincy's Larry Moore (33), Jim Wisman (11), Kel Gott (45)

Glenn Dreesen photo

Boyd Batts (31) scores over Jim Wisman (11) in 1972 IHSA final.
Quincy's Rick Ely (13) and Larry Moore (glasses) look on

Ron Ferguson photo

Coach Ron Ferguson during 1972 IHSA trophy presentation.
Boyd Batts (with towel), Quinn Buckner (25), Nee Gatlin (42),
Mike Bonczyk (23), and Joe King (41)

Frank McCully photo

Quinn Buckner with 1972 championship trophy

Boyd Batts, Mike Bonczyk, and Quinn Buckner with game ball
and 1972 championship trophy on Thornridge HS football field

Coaches Sherrill Hanks of Quincy and Ron Ferguson of Thornridge

Coach Ron Ferguson at home 2008

CHAPTER 15

We Made Everybody Look Good

MANY LONGTIME BASKETBALL FANS IN Illinois can remember the names of the 1971-72 Thornridge starting five, but even the most avid fan would be unable to name many of the players who came off the bench during the Falcons' perfect season. They might remember Nee Gatlin, an integral part of Ron Ferguson's playing rotation. But most of the reserves saw action only in the closing minutes of a game after the starters had given the Falcons an insurmountable lead. Other than Gatlin, who averaged 4.5 points, no bench player averaged more than 2 points per game. Even so, those players can proudly say they were an important part of the team that veteran observers believe is one of the nation's best ever. They were at practice every day working to make the starters better. They sacrificed sweat and blood, though they knew their minutes on game nights would be few.

"We weren't the deepest team in the world," says Coach Ron Ferguson. "We only really played six guys, and there was a real drop off in talent after that. [It's] tough for me to talk about that too much because it's kind of a negative thing about the other kids on the team, so I don't really like to emphasize that. We actually had some other guys that were pretty good players, but the distance between them and the [first] six guys [was sizable]. Gatlin was our sixth man. We had no [set] positions. If Gatlin came in for Batts, who was the tallest guy, we just moved the next tallest guy in to center. Everyone moved around. Our offense was adjustable where everybody could play any position. We just rotated [those] six guys."

Ferguson's coaching philosophy was different than many coaches of the era. He based his substitutions on talent rather than position. Since Gatlin was the most talented of the reserves, the junior was always the first player off the bench.

"Gatlin was a good player," recalls Ferguson. "He could play any position. I never believed in a substitute at guard or center. I had a sixth man. Whoever was the best player, the sixth man, he comes in. The other guys adjust. If the center gets in foul trouble, I don't look for the next biggest guy and bring him in. I bring in the next best player, and then the seventh man, and the eighth man. Those are going to be the first substitutes no matter who comes out. It made guys get ready. They had to learn more than one position. That's why our offense wasn't too complicated so we could do that."

Ferguson's substitution philosophy created matchup problems for opponents. They never knew where the man they were defending would be at the offensive end.

"I was big enough I could play in the post," says Quinn Buckner. "If you could settle Boyd down, he could play guard as good as anybody. Ernie could play anywhere because he was just that gifted. And that's what coach Ferguson used to do with us. He could interchange us. But listen, when you think about that [being done] in high school, that's a pretty high basketball IQ to be able to do that. It really is. It's hard for [opponents] to be able to practice for something like that. The guy guarding me may expect me to be in the center, but the guy guarding Ernie may not expect him to be there. Now, they've gotta play him, and Ernie was as capable as anybody if you put him in the middle of a zone."

"When Bill [Gatlin] came in, we didn't miss a beat because he was flexible," recalls guard Mike Bonczyk. "He could play off guard. He could play small forward. He could play a little bit of point [guard]. We were so interchangeable, and as coach Ferguson has said, we could all handle the ball. We all could pass the ball. We all could shoot the ball. And the one thing that he got us to do collectively is, he got us to play defense. We knew that if we stopped people, we were going to the races because we got out and ran."

Although he did not receive the same level of publicity as the five starters, the six-one Gatlin was critical to Thornridge's success during the perfect season.

"I kind of feel sorry for him," says Coach Ferguson. "He could have been bitter that he was kind of left out. He had just as much to do [with our success] as the first five did. He was always the first [player off the bench] no matter who came out. Consequently, he played probably as many minutes as some of the starters. Batts was in foul trouble a lot, and he was [sitting] out a lot because of that. I feel a little sorry about Gatlin and his role. I think of the picture I took with the five starters. It should have included Gatlin."

Nobody could blame Ferguson for wanting a personal photo with the Thornridge starters. After all, Buckner, Batts, Bonczyk, Rose, and Dunn would long be recognized as the best starting five in Illinois high school basketball. Yet it seems Ferguson, on more than one occasion, failed to include everyone in a team photograph. One such oversight haunts him to this day.

"I made a horrible mistake in 1971," recalls Ferguson. "At that time in the Illinois High School Association [state tournament], you could only dress ten players. We had like fifteen on the team. Even though I couldn't dress them, when I took the team picture, I forgot to include the other five guys. I had a couple parents, they weren't nasty, but they said, 'My kids are hurt. We were part of the team.' That was probably the biggest mistake of my life. I took some heat for it, and I deserved every minute of it. I felt bad. It was a horrible mistake, and it's bothered me ever since. It really has. As much as I apologized, it never seemed to do the trick. I've always felt bad about that."

Ferguson believes his failure to include all of the players in the picture was a result of his inexperience.

"I hadn't faced anything like that," says Ferguson. "I didn't know what the hell I was doing."

Though Ferguson expresses concern about Gatlin's feelings, the former Falcons' player holds no grudge. Gatlin is proud to have contributed to the success of the team.

"We won the state championship, and I was in there as part of that squad," says Gatlin. "[I was] the sixth man. I really enjoyed that. We [were regarded] as one of the greatest teams in Illinois history, and people still recognize that. That class with Quinn when they were seniors, it was a phenomenal year. The [offensive] execution was real easy because any of those three senior starters could have easily averaged 25 [points]. Mike Bonczyk can shoot. He can go to the rack. He can handle the ball better than anybody. Boyd Batts can shoot the lights out [and] take it to the rack. Quinn can just do anything he wants to do. Any of those guys could have scored, but they weren't selfish."

Since each starter was so gifted, Gatlin did not mind coming off the bench to contribute to the team. He understood his role.

"Just to blend in," says Gatlin. "Don't try to do too much. Instincts just started to take over. As a player with those guys, [when] you play with them so long, you know what they can do, and they know what you can do. As long as they trust you, everything was good. You wasn't gonna play if they didn't trust you."

The Thornridge starters trusted Gatlin. They considered him an integral part of the team. Gatlin had earned their trust because he always delivered, even in a tight game. He played without fear.

"I always felt that I could play with anybody," says Gatlin. "I never had any feeling in my heart that I was scared. I never went in with the attitude that I would play scared. When I entered the game with those guys, I could do what I was supposed to do. I knew the plays. I knew where I was supposed to be. I could improvise. I could handle the ball. When you win, you just fit into that mold. You don't mess up the flow. And everything was cool. Everybody got along. When you win, everything comes together. I remember a lot of the racial dissension at that time. That was really memorable. The sports brought us together. I mean, *winning* really did."

Gatlin says black athletes were also responsible for Thornridge's success in other sports.

"We wrestled. We played football. We ran track. I played baseball for a couple games," says Gatlin. "Basketball was a natural, along with football and track, for a lot of the black athletes at that time."

Gatlin was not the first in his family to attend Thornridge High School. Older brother Otelious was in the very first class to integrate the school in 1967-68. Nee is proud that his brother was one of those first black students from Phoenix to attend Thornridge as freshmen.

"1971 was the first [integrated] graduating class," remembers Gatlin. "So the four years prior, my brother and those guys integrated the school. When they were freshmen, I would say the maximum number of African-American students [at Thornridge] might have been 50 to 70. My brother and that class were really kind of physical. They were big guys who wrestled and played football. They didn't let nobody bother nobody. They were tough. That was the right class to integrate Thornridge because they were like protectors for anybody else [younger than] them. Our class was more, 'Let's go to school. Let's play some ball.' *They* were the leaders. I'll never forget them because of what they did as far as leading the way [as] pioneers."

Gatlin observed changes in attitude between blacks and whites at Thornridge during his time at the school. Despite their early struggles to coexist, blacks gained acceptance from whites on and off the basketball court and playing fields.

"We learned from racism," he says. "Then, winning in sports brought us all together. You never knew Thornridge would be like that in three or four years. It was like night and day. [In the beginning], you wouldn't see any interracial dating. You wouldn't see any white and black friends. You wouldn't see them sittin' in the lunchroom [together]. But sports did [change] that."

Gatlin was known to a few Thornridge students as Bill, but while still in grade school his closest friends began calling him Nee. Some of his high school teammates never knew how he got the nickname.

"My middle name is Cor-NEE-lius, so the nickname came out of that," explains Gatlin. "It just stuck. People didn't even know my name was Bill."

When the Falcons won their first state championship in 1970-71, Gatlin was playing on a very good Thornridge sophomore team.

"I was on the sophomore squad with Sidney [Lewis] and Greg's brother, Ken [Rose]," says Gatlin. "[Ken] was a pretty good player. Greg got moved up [to varsity] that year. We had a pretty nice nucleus, a decent team. We probably won 20-plus games. We was lookin' forward to bouncin' up [to the varsity] the next year. [We were] just waitin' our turn."

Gatlin says when he became part of the Thornridge varsity in 1971-72, he felt proud and protective of the Falcons' number one state ranking. He recalls that having the top rating served as motivation for the players whose ultimate goal was another state championship.

"The rankings made you want to stay where you were at or get to the mountaintop," remembers Gatlin. "Everybody knows that it's cool to be ranked high, but at the end of the day, you want the trophy. That's the bottom line. You could be number one up to the end and don't win it. It would be disappointing. So, when you're expected to win it, and you win it, it's really rewarding for real. Winning, that's why you played."

Gatlin will never forget the feeling of being part of an undefeated state championship team.

"It was packed [in the gyms]," says Gatlin. "We had a bulls-eye on our backs. We're playing on one of the best high school teams. Was it the most exhilarating thing that ever happened to me? Sports wise, of course. No question about it. Just seeing everybody happy, man, that's a trip. We had fun out there. That's what it was all about in high school. Everybody knew about Lincoln and Quincy. They had great programs in Collinsville as well. Everybody knew about that [even] up north. Winners know who winners are. We watched other teams and other players. You wondered what they did this week. Even though you played and did your own thing, you wondered what everybody else did."

The season provided great memories for Gatlin, memories he can share with his grandchildren.

"I'm fifty-three years old, married, with a wonderful wife and seven grandkids," says Gatlin. "I'm employed with Hanes International, a highly corrosive and resistant steel manufacturer in Kokomo, Indiana. I've been on the job now about fifteen years, lookin' to get out at sixty-two [years of age]."

In 1971-72, 80% of Thornridge's starting lineup was black, but a majority of the Falcons' reserves were white. Of the players coming off the bench, only Gatlin, five-ten junior Ken Rose, and six-foot junior Sidney Lewis were black. The other six reserves were white. Six-six senior Keith Hutchinson would have been talented enough to play major minutes on Ferguson's early Thornridge teams but saw limited playing time during the perfect season. With five-ten junior Bill Redman, five-ten junior Joe King, five-eight junior Dave Anderson, five-nine junior Fred Knutson, and six-six sophomore Ken Kremer, the Thornridge team photo had an even blend of black and white faces. Seven blacks and seven whites played for Thornridge during the perfect season. Most of the blacks played significant minutes. Most of the whites spent much of the time on the bench. Even so, Head Coach Ron Ferguson never based playing time on the color of a player's skin. Longtime Ferguson assistant Frank Nardi, Thornwood's head coach in 1971-72, says if anybody questioned why blacks were getting most of the playing time, they simply did not understand basketball.

"If they were basketball fans, they knew who should start," says Nardi. "Those guys, they were just tremendous guys. I give Fergie a whole lot of credit. He got those guys to play their positions, to mesh in, to work together. If there was any jealousy on the court, I have no idea where it came from."

At least one of the white players understood that Ferguson was putting his best players on the court. Junior guard Dave Anderson does not remember any reserve player being resentful of the starters.

"There was no real resentment," says Anderson, son of 1966 Thornton state championship coach Bob Anderson. "Those guys were just so good that you just watched and hoped they were beating somebody by enough points that you could get in. That was really about it, at least for myself. I mean they were *good*."

"It wasn't like, 'Jeez, I think I can do as good as him,'" laughs Anderson. "That never really came up, you know."

In 1972, a few people believed Coach Ron Ferguson occasionally ran up the score by leaving his starters in for most of the game and rarely playing the substitutes. The insinuation that Ferguson was pouring it on still bothers him today. He points out that opponents outscored his team in the fourth quarter that season.

"We were actually outscored (594-578) in the last quarter," says Ferguson with a hint of irritation. "Now, not in every game, but if you look at the points, quarter by quarter, people couldn't say we were running up the score in the last quarter. We got to play a lot of kids [although] most of them were not in at key times."

Though playing time wasn't shared equally, Anderson says there were no cliques on the team. The starters, the reserves, the blacks, and the whites, they all got along.

"Before the black kids went to Thornridge," says Anderson, "most of us, me and Billy Redman, Fred Knutson, we [white kids] got bused to Phoenix to go to grade school. So, we played grade school ball with these guys as well. And then, with my dad coaching Thornton, they all knew who I was because I was always on the bench with the Thornton guys. So, I knew all the black guys long before I went to high school with them. But, you know, there's no color in athletics. If you can play ball, [skin color] doesn't matter. I can't really think of anybody that didn't get along. Ernie Dunn, Greg [Rose], Nee Gatlin, myself, we all played grade school together. I grew up with those guys. All of us juniors, we came up together."

Anderson played in 27 games and scored a total of 40 points during the 1971-72 season. He says his personal stats were far less important than being part of the state championship team. Though his contributions were small on game nights, Anderson enjoyed being part of the Thornridge show.

"Being on the bench, you don't really get involved too much," says Anderson. "But, the biggest thing that I always remember is the sold out gyms. Every place we went, it was just packed and standing room only.

That always stood out to me. Probably the coolest thing was just the aura of the whole team. Everybody wanted to see the team."

Anderson was among the interested spectators as he watched from his front row seat. He played when called upon but was quite content to watch his friends put on a dazzling display of basketball night after night. Some players admit to being in awe of Quinn Buckner and the other Falcons' stars, but Anderson says his teammates were friends, not basketball gods.

"No, I don't remember anything like that," says Anderson. "Like I say, we played together for so long that you never really looked at them like that. You knew they were really good, but it was still, 'I've known Quinn since he was twelve years old. That's just Quinn.'"

On the rare occasions Thornridge was involved in a close game in the second half, Anderson never worried about losing.

"No. Those guys just had it all," Anderson says. "It was hard to watch and think somebody could come close to them. It was a good solid five [or] six man team. Nee [Gatlin] wasn't much of a drop down [in talent]. He wasn't quite as athletic as the rest of them, but that first five [was great]. A lot of teams had two guys or three guys, but all *five* of them at the same time like that? You knew eventually they would wear somebody down. [Opponents] just couldn't keep up with the [Falcons'] speed. When we would throw that full-court press on them, people just couldn't get through that thing."

During the Falcons' perfect season, a number of teams got the chance to play Illinois' top-ranked team. Some teams played Thornridge twice. A few had the misfortune of having to play the Falcons three times. Anderson and his fellow reserves had the most daunting task. They had to go up against Quinn and company every day in practice.

"It was always us against them in practice," recalls Anderson. "If you look at the roster, on the bench there were like four of us that weren't even over six foot [tall]. We had Ken Hutchinson. He was a big guy, but other than that, we didn't have much as far as height. So, we got our lunch handed to us pretty often. In practice, [the starters] didn't really goof around or anything. They were serious. Just like when we played on the playgrounds, they all played aggressively. They were just as good in practice as they were in the games. Obviously, in the games you get a little bit more adrenalin."

Anderson had adrenalin flowing when he made the biggest play of his career during the televised quarterfinal round game against Collinsville during the state tournament at the Assembly Hall.

"I stole an inbounds pass and went the length of the court and scored," says Anderson. "That was kind of cool for me. I'd been to Champaign with my dad [when Thornton played there]. I'd been on the floor and all that kind of stuff, but to actually get in the game, and then steal a pass and go the length of the floor and score. That was pretty cool for me. I did it on TV. And like I said, the biggest thing for me was just [seeing] the packed gyms. When you first came out onto the court for warm-ups, the whole place was going crazy. That was always really a cool feeling."

Anderson has worked as a plant manager the last 17 years. He worked at a steel facility in South Holland before becoming the plant manager at Brown Paper Goods in Waukegan, Illinois. Anderson is proud, and more than a little thankful, to have contributed in some small way to Thornridge's perfect season. He believes his basketball resume may have played a part in him landing his current job.

"Where I'm working right now, the owner of the company, his grandfather was [Coach] Phog Allen from Kansas," says Anderson. "When I interviewed here seven years ago, he was asking about me and what I did in high school. I said I played some high school basketball. That's when he told me about Phog Allen being his grandfather. He goes, 'Where did you go?' I go, 'Thornridge.' He goes, 'Oh, they had a really *great* team.' And he was going on and on. I said, 'Yeah, I was on that team.' He said, 'Oh my God.' Seven years, and they still talk [about it] every time we get together and basketball comes up. They start talking to me about, 'That must have been great, and this and that.' When that [Thornridge] name comes up and people recognize it, it definitely sparks interest. They kind of look at you a little differently."

Anderson was unable to play basketball his senior year at Thornridge. He tore ligaments in his ankle just prior to the season and did not make the team. So, his final game as a high school basketball player was the 1972 Illinois state championship game.

"For years after the championship, every March a picture would come out in the paper of Quinn holding the trophy," says Anderson, with a laugh, "It just so happened I was standing next to Quinn, so my picture was in the paper for twenty years. You know, me and Quinn."

While Anderson laughs about being getting a constant reminder of his involvement with Thornridge in the Illinois state tournament, another player, Sidney Lewis, watched the Falcons play from a seat high above the court in the Assembly Hall. In the '72 Illinois state tournament, teams could dress only twelve players. Lewis was not one of the lucky dozen chosen to be in uniform during Thornridge's state tournament run.

"No, I got kind of canned off the team when they went downstate," says Lewis. "They gave me some tickets, and I just came on my own. It was kind of tough. It was kind of difficult just watching them instead of bein' down there on the floor with them. I was disappointed."

Even so, Lewis considers the time he spent as a Thornridge basketball player as one of the best times of his life.

"That's probably about the best, just bein' part of that championship team," says Lewis. "I'm just happy that I was on that team with Quinn and all the other guys. We was probably the best team in the nation. A lot of people said we probably could'a beat some small college teams back then."

Coach Ron Ferguson rarely played Sidney Lewis that season but appreciated his effort in practice. Lewis, who has now returned to Phoenix, Illinois, to work in construction, played in only 15 games that season. He scored 13 points, making 5 of 24 shots from the field and 3 of 7 from the charity stripe. Ferguson recalls Lewis lacked offensive skills but contributed in other ways.

"He hardly played, but he was a good guy in practice," says Ferguson. "He couldn't shoot worth a lick, but boy, he was tough. [He] could rebound and play defense. He was hard-nosed. You know, we had a lot of guys that would have played on a normal team. We wouldn't have won the state championship, but we would have had a good team. If I'd had those kids my first three or four years at Thornridge, we'd have been a lot better."

Lewis is proud of his role which was to help the Falcons' starters be better prepared on game nights.

"Just helping them out in practice a lot and making them better players," recalls Lewis when asked about his contribution to Thornridge's perfect season. "We practiced hard. We made everybody look good. In practice, we mostly had to run the other team's plays. We knew most of the [Thornridge] press, so we made it much harder on them. Then, when they got in the game and played against the [other team's] players, it was all benefiting them."

It would have been natural for Lewis and the other reserves to be frustrated because of their lack of playing time, but he never resented having to spend most of his time on the bench watching Quinn and the other starters.

Sidney says, "No, not really because they was the best."

CHAPTER 16

March Madness

LONG BEFORE "MARCH MADNESS" BECAME synonymous with the NCAA college basketball tournament, the phrase had been used for decades in Illinois to describe the excitement surrounding the state's annual high school basketball tourney. "March Madness" first appeared in print when Henry V. Porter, an Assistant Executive Secretary of the Illinois High School Association, wrote an essay that was published in a 1939 issue of the organization's magazine *Illinois Interscholastic*. Illinois sportswriters then began using "March Madness" to describe the hysteria surrounding the state tournament. In the 1940s and '50s people began referring to the state tournament itself as "March Madness."

In late February and early March of 1972, "March Madness" was again revving up throughout the state of Illinois. Teams were looking forward to the first Class AA state tournament for enrollments of 751 and higher. As the start of the state tournament approached, newspapers were filled with accounts of Thornridge's remarkable regular season. In every corner of the state, sportswriters asked whether Thornridge was the best Illinois high school basketball team of all time. A United Press International story comparing Thornridge and great Illinois teams of the past was printed in many of the newspapers throughout the state. Most observers considered Thornridge the best the state had ever seen.

Thornridge would begin the single-elimination tournament at home because the Falcons were hosting the Dolton regional. In previous years, every Illinois team competed in district or regional play which meant a team had to win at least three games to advance out of the regional tournament. Since Illinois had split into two classes, fewer teams were plugged into the tournament brackets to compete for the Class AA title. Only two wins were now necessary to advance out of the regional and into a sectional tournament. As Thornridge approached the state record for consecutive wins, and with everyone targeting the defending state champions, some newspaper writers suggested the Falcons might be subject to increased pressure while trying to live up to the high expectations. Coach Ron Ferguson admits he was feeling the heat, but the players contend they were oblivious.

"I don't know if there was any pressure," says Mike Bonczyk. "We just played. We didn't understand history at that time. We were just playing basketball and trying to win. Then all of a sudden, they start talking about the streak, winning so many in a row, and dah-dee-dah-dee-dah. I don't remember us ever saying, 'Oh man, if we don't win what's going to happen?' We just played basketball. We were just so driven our senior year, Quinn, Boyd, and myself, that I don't think there was going to be a way in which we wouldn't win the state title. Somebody was going to have to play awfully good, and we were going to have to play awful bad."

***

DOLTON REGIONAL OPENER (Tuesday night, February 29, 1972) St. Francis de Sales (Chicago)

Posters and banners lined the winding corridors of Thornridge High School as the Falcons (25-0) prepared to tip off the state tournament with a game against lightly-regarded St. Francis de Sales (9-15). One of the posters showing support for the state's top-ranked basketball team read "Nothing Like Us Ever Was." Few would argue.

The Thornridge players and coaches understood it was now the second season. It was tournament time. There could be no letdowns even against an inferior team like St. Francis de Sales. The Falcons took the lead just seconds into the game. Boyd Batts sent the opening tip to point guard Mike Bonczyk who dribbled to within 20 feet of the basket and swished a left-handed jumper. Usually Bonczyk was a pass-first, shoot-second type of player, but on this night, he and his teammates knew there was little possibility of an upset. They could play free and loose. Bonczyk had an open look and quickly took the shot. The unselfish Falcons then returned to form. Their next eight baskets came from point-blank range with each score set up by a nifty pass from a teammate. The Thornridge offense was spectacular and the defense suffocating. Greg Rose, showing no adverse effects from the injury that had limited his playing time the previous week, poured in 22 first-half points. The Falcons led 31-15 after one quarter and 64-29 at the break. When the third quarter ended, Thornridge had scored an incredible 89 points in just 24 minutes, and the Falcons led by 44. The starters left the game at that point, and the reserves played the remainder of the night. The Thornridge bench was productive. Six-six sophomore Ken Kremer, who had been promoted to the varsity just four days prior to the game, had 12 points and 10 rebounds in the 4th quarter in an impressive debut. Nee Gatlin, one of five Falcons in double figures, came off the bench to score 14 points. Rose finished with a game-high 26. Batts scored 19, and Buckner added 18. Ernie Dunn and Mike Bonczyk scored 8 points apiece, and Bonczyk added 12 assists and 4 steals. When the final buzzer sounded, Thornridge had established a new school record by scoring 113 points in a 113-59 romp. The Falcons also set a school mark by shooting 62.7% from the field. With the victory, Thornridge moved on to the regional final to play the winner of the next night's game between Thornton Fractional North and Thornton Fractional South.

There were games played at 56 regional sites statewide, and the other highly-rated teams all posted victories on the opening night of the postseason. Second-ranked La Salle-Peru edged Ottawa 63-58. Third-ranked Hinsdale Central got a school-record 50 points from Jim Flynn in a 115-69 win over Addison Trail. Flynn scored exactly half of his team's first-half points as the Red Devils scored a whopping 72 points in the first two quarters. Fourth-ranked Lincoln beat Springfield Lanphier 70-56. Most of the other ranked teams posted blowout victories. Maine South pounded Luther North 116-40. Lockport walloped Romeoville 95-64. Greg Smith scored 30 as Aurora East pounded Oswego 91-48. Other winners included Waukegan, Rock Island Alleman, East St. Louis Lincoln, Peoria Manual, and Kankakee Eastridge. Quincy edged Springfield Griffin 65-52. The winners moved on to play Friday night in regional championship games.

***

DOLTON REGIONAL FINAL (Friday night, March 3, 1972)
Thornton Fractional North (Calumet City)

The Dolton regional final pitted Thornridge (26-0) against Thornton Fractional North (19-4), the Southeast Suburban conference champion. The Meteors were enjoying their best season in a quarter of a century and featured three players capable of having big games offensively. Brian Summers was averaging 17 points per game. George Demopolous was averaging more than 16 points, Bob Gregolunas just under 15 a game. Having heard so many times that his team had no chance to beat Thornridge, North coach Dick Daugherty boldly predicted that his team could upset the Falcons. He understood his comments would become bulletin board material in the Thornridge locker room but felt his players needed to know that he believed in them.

There was almost certainly no way Thornridge would lose to Daugherty's team. A victory over the Calumet City school would give Thornridge a share of the state record for longest winning streak and propel the Falcons into the Chicago Heights sectional. In addition, the Friday night game would be the last game for Quinn Buckner, Boyd Batts, and Mike Bonczyk in Dolton. Surprisingly, Thornridge came out flat and trailed most of the first quarter. The Falcons had trouble putting the ball in the basket until Boyd Batts got rolling. Batts scored 13 points in the period to give Thornridge a 23-18 lead after the first quarter. Coach Daugherty believed if his Meteors could handle the Thornridge press, match the Falcons on the boards, and have their best shooting night, they could make things interesting. In the first half, the Meteors scored a few layups after beating Thornridge's press. The rebounding battle was almost dead even. And North shot 60%, Thornridge, a woeful 32%. Daugherty got everything he asked for, yet his team still trailed 49-31 at the intermission. Thornridge stopped using its press and went to a man-to-man defense. The Falcons then pulled away in the second half. The bench players were on the floor in the final minutes of the 101-68 rout. Fred Knutson drained a 20-footer with 21 seconds left to put his team in triple figures for the sixth time. Even as the Falcons recorded one blowout win after another, Thornridge coach Ron Ferguson never warned them about being overconfident. He knew that his players had the right mindset. He was more concerned about a key player sustaining an injury. That was especially true in the game against Thornton Fractional North.

"Their coach said some stuff in the paper," remembers Ferguson. "He says, 'We're not in awe. We think we can play with them.' They won their conference. They had football players, big [guys] six-two, six-three, six-four. They were all football players and just stronger than hell. On the boards, I'll tell you what. For awhile there, they just knocked us down. We made a lot of free throws. I think Batts and Buckner had about 30 points apiece. [T-F] North did play pretty good. They were physical. That was a good game to have in terms of a team getting physical with us. But, I was scared we were gonna get somebody hurt. It was that rough under the basket which scared me to death because one kid out for the season could have made a big difference."

In their final game in Dolton, Batts and Buckner posted impressive numbers. Batts ended the night with 33 points, 17 rebounds, and 7 blocked shots. Buckner added 32 points, 12 boards, and 6 assists. No other Thornridge players scored in double figures. With the victory, Thornridge tied the Illinois high school record for consecutive wins. The 48 straight victories, dating back to December of 1970, equaled the state mark set by Taylorville which went 45-0 in 1944 and won the first three games the following season. The Thornridge players and coaches liked having a piece of the record, but more importantly, the Falcons were moving on to the sectional tournament for the second straight year and just the second time in school history.

There was a major surprise in central Illinois as fourth-ranked Lincoln squandered a 16-point third quarter lead and lost on its home court to Springfield Southeast 66-64. Mark Haynes scored 35 points as Southeast improved to 23-3 while ending the Railsplitters' season at 24-3. In other regional finals, second-ranked La Salle-Peru won its 18th straight while raising its record to 26-1 with a 75-58 win over Streator. Gary Hopps led the winners with 25 points. Third-rated Hinsdale Central avoided a huge upset with a narrow 62-59 win over Willowbrook. Fifth-ranked Maine South won its own regional by downing Ridgewood 80-51 in the final. Sixth-rated North Chicago improved to 24-1 by beating seventh-ranked Waukegan 49-47 in a showdown between two of the top teams in the state. Number eight Quincy barely survived its game against Jacksonville 74-73. In another thrilling regional final, ninth-ranked Rock Island Alleman eliminated 14th-rated Moline 66-63. Andy Sottos led Alleman with 27 points. 10th-ranked Lockport advanced into sectional play with a 79-64 win over Lincoln-Way. 11th-rated Aurora East got 36 points from center Greg Smith in a narrow 73-69 win over 13th-rated Aurora West. Rated teams East St. Louis Lincoln, Peoria Manual, and Kankakee Eastridge all won their regional finals as well. Fifteen sectional tournaments would begin the following week with 70 teams battling for the right to play in one of the seven super-sectional games to be played around the state. In addition, the Chicago Public League playoffs would continue with the champion, for the first time, automatically earning a berth in the state quarterfinals in Champaign. Some ranked teams had fallen by the wayside, but many of the premier high school teams in Illinois still could dream of catching Thornridge on an off night. Unranked, but dangerous South Suburban rivals, Bloom and Thornton were both regional champions and would be waiting to take their shots at Thornridge in the sectional tournament.

***

CHICAGO HEIGHTS SECTIONAL OPENER
(Tuesday night, March 7, 1972) Bloom (Chicago Heights)

"March Madness" was reaching a fever pitch as play began in the 1972 Illinois Class AA sectional tournaments. Thornridge (27-0) would set a new state record for consecutive wins if the Falcons could beat conference rival Bloom (20-7) on the Trojans' home court. The Falcons had already defeated Bloom twice, and neither game was close. Few people gave Bloom much of a chance, although Thornridge coach Ron Ferguson always believed it was difficult to beat a good team three times in a season. Bloom coach, Wes Mason, devised a plan that he hoped would give his team an opportunity for an upset. He told his team to hold the ball in order to prevent Thornridge from running its high-octane fast-break. No team had attempted to stall against the Falcons. Mason thought it was worth a try. He figured if the Falcons did not have the ball, there was no way they could again dominate his team.

A capacity crowd of 3100 had jammed into the gymnasium but could hardly believe what was happening. After Thornridge won the opening tip and missed its first shot, Bloom held the basketball for nearly four minutes before taking its first attempt at the basket. The stalling tactic was clearly frustrating the Falcons. Bloom successfully maintained possession of the ball for most of the first quarter and took only four field goal tries. The annoyed Falcons made only 1 of 10 from the field in the first quarter and had trouble working the ball inside against the Trojans' diamond (1-2-1) zone. Bloom standout Harold Goodson defended Quinn Buckner man-to-man while the other Trojans set up in a zone. The Falcons scored their only points of the first quarter with 2:05 left in the period. Greg Rose tipped in a miss and cut a 4-0 deficit in half. A Mark Barwig basket gave Bloom a 6-2 lead after one quarter.

"They held the ball," remembers Thornridge coach Ron Ferguson. "We were behind the first quarter. When they started holding it, we got a time out. I said, 'The one thing they want us to do is start trying to steal the ball, trying to get us in foul trouble. So play really tough, sound defense, but don't be gambling so we pick up a bunch of fouls.' [I thought], 'Eventually we'll win out over that. Play great defense so they don't score too much. If we just keep it close, then I'm not worried.'"

"They'd gotten up six to two. They stalled the whole first half," says Ernie Dunn. "I was chasing Harold Goodson. But then, they took me out of the box-and-one [defense], and we let them stall until halftime."

Even though Bloom continued to slow down its offense in the second quarter, Thornridge began to turn the momentum. The Falcons turned up the heat by going to their full-court press. The three seniors Bonczyk, Buckner, and Batts, all scored on layups following steals. And Rose hit from the corner as Thornridge ripped off nine straight points to take an 11-6 lead. Though Bloom continued its slow-down tactics, a Bonczyk jumper from the top of the key with 3 seconds left in the period gave Thornridge a 16-12 halftime advantage.

"They held the ball," says the Thornridge point guard. "We were reluctant to shoot. Boyd was getting pissed because he couldn't get any touches [because of] the way the game was [being played]. We were pissin' and moanin' at halftime. Then, Bloom decided they were gonna run in the second half. Bad move. It wasn't even close."

Despite Bonczyk's assertion that the game was soon over, Bloom actually kept it close for much of the third quarter. Bloom was only down eight, 30-22, until Thornridge exploded for eight straight points in the final 70 seconds of the period. The Falcons had control entering the fourth quarter up 38-22.

"We went into a press a little bit in the second half," says Falcons' coach Ron Ferguson. "And as soon as we got a ten point lead, they started to play [up-tempo]."

Once Bloom was forced to play catch-up, it was clear Thornridge was going to win. Bloom coach, Wes Mason, realizing his team's season was about to end, picked up a pair of technical fouls in the fourth quarter. Ron Ferguson sat quietly on the Thornridge bench while his Trojans' counterpart imploded in frustration.

"I didn't get any technical fouls that year," laughs Ferguson. "It's hard to yell at the officials if you're winning by 20 points. They'd look at you like, 'What in the world? Are you nuts?'"

Ferguson, keeping his starters in the entire game even though Buckner, Bonczyk, Rose, and Dunn each had four fouls, watched the Falcons score seven straight points in a 27-second span in the final minute to wrap up a 65-42 victory.

"When I look back, that was probably our toughest game because the score at halftime was close, four points up, 16-12," says Ferguson. "That was the only time [when] I walked in at the half that I had some concerns [about winning] because of the way Bloom was playing."

It was now official. No team in Illinois high school basketball history had won as many games in a row as Thornridge. The Falcons' streak had reached 49 games. In the record-setting win over Bloom, Batts led Thornridge with 20 points and 10 rebounds. Rose finished with 19 points, Buckner 14. Dunn and Bonczyk each scored 6 points. Even though Thornridge had struggled to score against Bloom, no other team tried to slow down the pace against the Falcons that season. Bonczyk believes coaches realized it would be futile to try to stall.

"I guess maybe because a lot of teams didn't have three or four ball-handlers that they felt comfortable with," explains the Falcons' point guard. "We could half-court-trap you. We could man-to-man-trap you. We full-court pressed. Fergie had an array of weapons defensively that whatever teams tried to do to us with the ball, we could counteract it. Bloom held the ball, but in the second half Fergie said the hell with man-to-man and pressin'. We weren't scoring, so you couldn't put the [full-court] press on. We went to a half-court trap. I think teams [could not stall against Thornridge] unless they had three solid ball-handlers where they could hold the ball, penetrate [on the] drive, and lay it up."

"Although," he adds, with a laugh, "you *still* had to get past Boyd in the middle."

Quinn Buckner says he's not surprised no other teams tried to slow it down against Thornridge.

"No, not really," says Buckner. "One of the things I learned is if you press a team, you force them to speed it up. I mean, you really do. But, everybody had to be in that mind set. If somebody tried to slow the game up, you [press]. You gotta remember, you got athletes out here [on the Thornridge team] that can make plays that a lot [of players] can't. You got three or four of them that are making plays that high school kids probably have no business making. At that point, you start to fluster the [opponent's] coach and some of the players."

Coach Ron Ferguson told a newspaper columnist after the game that he had anticipated a slowdown from Bloom since the Trojans had already been trounced twice by Thornridge that season. But, he admits it was unusual for Wes Mason to have his team hold the ball.

"The last guy I would have thought would [try it would] be Wes Mason," says Ferguson. "That's what surprised me. But Wes was one of my dearest, dearest friends. Wes Mason was the only coach that I'd ever known that could beat you by 30 points, and you didn't mind going out and having a beer with him after the game."

Ferguson, who served as one of Mason's pallbearers when the Bloom coach passed away years later, had no time to share a beer with his friend after this game. The Thornridge coach had to start preparing for his team's next challenge. The Falcons would be facing another familiar foe for the third time in the season. In the sectional final, with a trip to the "Sweet 16" on the line, Thornridge would have to face chief rival, Thornton High School.

At other sectional tournaments throughout the state, fans turned out in huge numbers to support their favorite team. Some drove home that night still dreaming of winning a state championship. Others drove home bitterly disappointed because their teams' seasons had come to an abrupt end. There are no second chances in the Illinois state tournament. Like the NCAA tournament, it is one and done.

Among the teams advancing to sectional finals were second-ranked La Salle-Peru and third-ranked Hinsdale Central. Hinsdale Central, playing the sectional on its home court, edged Proviso East 68-65. In Elk Grove, fifth-ranked Maine South of Park Ridge won 74-66 to eliminate Saint Patrick, the team that had come the closest to Thornridge during the regular season. In Waukegan, number six North Chicago beat Mundelein 57-52 to improve to 26-1. At the Springfield sectional, eighth-rated Quincy took care of Mattoon 81-63. Ninth-ranked Rock Island Alleman shot an astounding 70% from the field in a 78-65 win over Rockford Auburn in Moline. Tenth-rated Lockport, playing in the sectional at Joliet Central, edged 1971 finalist Oak Lawn 49-45. Among the other opening round sectional winners were ranked teams Aurora East, East St. Louis Lincoln, Peoria Manual, and Kankakee Eastridge. Unranked teams Collinsville, Conant of Hoffman Estates, Washington, and Evanston were also among the winners in first round sectional play. Each of those schools needed to win one more game to get to the "Sweet 16".

***

CHICAGO HEIGHTS SECTIONAL FINAL
(Friday, March 10, 1972) Thornton (Harvey)

Thornridge (28-0) and Thornton (19-6) renewed their rivalry in a game that was different than any other in the series. For the first time, they met after each had won a regional championship. Some people wondered if the Wildcats might slow the pace as Bloom had effectively done three nights earlier. But Thornton coach Tom Hanrahan never considered it.

"No, not really," says Hanrahan. "It was just hard to do because they were so good at that man-to-man defense."

The Wildcats, playing a more conventional style, looked like they might be capable of pulling off the upset. The Falcons seemed out of sync all night, and Thornton's 1-3-1 zone looked effective early in the game. Thornridge passed on perimeter shots while trying to get higher percentage shots close to the basket. At the end of the first quarter, Thornton was down by only five, 15-10. The Falcons increased their lead to 30-19 at intermission. Thornridge then outscored the Wildcats 17-8 in the third period to take command. In the fourth quarter, with Boyd Batts and Greg Rose in foul trouble, Quinn Buckner took over the game. Buckner scored half of his game-high 28 points in the final stanza. Batts scored 13 points before fouling out with 2:21 to play. Upset about the call, Batts was whistled for a technical foul. As he left the court, the Thornton fans peppered him with onions, a reference to the fact that Thornridge High School was built on land that was once an onion field. The Falcons coasted to a 71-43 victory over Thornton, and in the process, Thornridge became the first team in Illinois history to win 50 consecutive games. The Falcons played one of their worst games of the season that night and still won by 28. Thornridge, just four wins away from a second straight state championship, had reached the "Sweet 16" for the second year in a row.

To return to Champaign, the Falcons would have to defeat an excellent Lockport team that had raised its record to 23-3 by beating Joliet Central in the sectional final in Joliet. Second-ranked La Salle-Peru saw its magnificent season come to an end when it was upset 68-67 by Kankakee Eastridge. The Kankakee school would next face eighth-ranked Quincy. Quincy had to overcome an eleven point deficit in the last six minutes to edge Decatur Eisenhower 87-85. Eisenhower had surprised Springfield Southeast in its first sectional game in Springfield and very nearly eliminated another quality team in Quincy. Third-rated Hinsdale Central won its own sectional tournament by beating Cicero-

Morton East. Fifth-rated Maine South was upset by La Grange in the Elk Grove sectional, but sixth-ranked North Chicago improved to 26-1 by beating Mundelein-Carmel in the sectional final at Waukegan. In other sectional finals, number nine Rock Island Alleman beat Sterling in Moline. Number eleven Aurora East took care of Wheaton Central in Aurora. At Edwardsville, located just a few miles across the Mississippi River from St. Louis, Collinsville surprised number twelve East St. Louis Lincoln. At the Peoria sectional, Peoria Manual handed Washington just its fourth loss in 27 games. At West Frankfort in southern Illinois, Mascoutah improved to 28-1 with a win over Benton, Doug Collin's alma mater. Evanston got past Skokie-Niles West in the Arlington Heights sectional, and Conant of Hoffman Estates beat Rochelle at Barrington. The two state tournament teams from the Chicago Public League were determined when Crane beat Harlan and Marshall defeated Carver. Crane and Carver would meet for the Public League championship and the automatic berth into the state quarterfinals in Champaign. The dream of a state championship was still alive for sixteen teams. Interestingly, of the sixteen teams that had reached the "Sweet 16" the previous year, only Thornridge had managed to make a return trip. The Falcons were one win away from Champaign. Only Lockport stood in the way.

CHAPTER 17

No Laughing Matter

AS THE THORNRIDGE BASKETBALL TEAM played its way through the 1971-72 campaign, it seemed everyone wanted to see for themselves what the buzz was all about. The undefeated team was the subject of many newspaper articles and was shown on Chicago television stations. The Falcons' record-setting season was one of the biggest sports stories of the year in the Chicago area. Thornridge games were such a hot ticket that it wasn't easy to get into the gym wherever Thornridge played.

One of the fans who saw the Falcons in action was comedian Tom Dreesen. The Harvey native had attended Thornton High School and was a Thornton fan. However, in 1972, Dreesen, still living in the area, wanted to see the Thornridge team with his own eyes. Long before he became a regular guest on The Tonight Show with Johnny Carson, Dreesen partnered with Tim Reid who later played Venus Flytrap on the TV comedy *WKRP in Cincinnati*. The two young men were standup comedians, and they worked comedy clubs throughout the Chicago area.

"At that time, I was part of a comedy team, Tim & Tom, America's first black and white comedy team," says Dreesen. "We started in 1969. I had a wife and three kids, and Tim had a wife and two kids. I was doing odd jobs and side jobs and what have you. One of those was shooting pictures with my brother Glenn. Glenn owned Dreesen Photography in Harvey, and he was the official photographer for the Star-Tribune. I would sometimes cover [Thornridge] games with him. I had a Rolleiflex camera, and he had a little more sophisticated equipment. I think he used a Nikon.

There was a great deal of interest [in the Thornridge Falcons]. They were always sold out, so I would get in on a press pass."

Dreesen felt a kinship with the black players from Phoenix who had transformed Thornridge into a winning team. Like several of the Falcons, Dreesen was part of a large family that hardly had enough money to survive.

"I grew up in Harvey," says Dreesen. "I had eight brothers and sisters. We lived in a shack, and five of us slept in one bed. We had no bathtub, and no shower, and no hot water. We had to boil water. We were raggedy-ass poor. I grew up around blacks in West Harvey and established friendships that I still have to this day. Maybe they identified with me. I played basketball, you know, street ball, against blacks and with blacks, all my life. I think their identification with me probably was because I was poor. I've got an album I recorded in Harvey in front of an all-black audience called 'That White Boy's Crazy.' Richard Pryor wanted me to call my album 'That Honkie's Crazy' because he had an album called 'That Nigger's Crazy.' The reason I didn't do it, no black guy ever called me a honkie in my life. They always called me 'White Boy.' I was eleven years old when I found out my name wasn't White Boy. Even now in Harvey, if they were arguing about something, they'd say, 'Oh man, he scored three touchdowns in that game.' 'Don't lie to me, I remember.' 'Hey, wait a minute. White Boy! White Boy! Come here! You tell us [if he scored three touchdowns in the game].'"

Though Dreesen felt absolutely no animosity towards minorities, he was unable to avoid racial confrontations after he and Reid formed the black and white comedy team. Not everyone was thrilled with the idea of a black man and a white man working together. For those with racist attitudes, it was no laughing matter.

"I'm sure [this kind of thing] happened to these kids on the basketball team," says Dreesen. "With Tim and me on stage, if there was a black guy who hated white people with a passion, *hated* white people, he wasn't mad at *me*. He was mad at *Tim* for being with me. See, Tim would be an Uncle Tom. If there was a white guy, a redneck, who hated black people with a passion, and he saw us together, he wasn't mad at *Tim*. He was mad at *me* [because in his opinion] I'm a nigger-lover. And he didn't mind calling me that either."

Dreesen and Reid occasionally experienced more than just name-calling.

"The fourth time Tim Reid and I ever appeared on stage in Chicago Heights, Illinois, a guy put a lit cigarette out on [Tim's] face," recalls

Dreesen. "[The guy] smashed it in his face. It turned into a donnybrook. I boxed when I was in the service, and I had a lot of street fights as a boy in Harvey. I jumped up and threw a punch that would have knocked out Muhammad Ali. I threw as hard of a punch as I could. He moved, and I went straight over his shoulders. He pulled me across the table and almost crushed the life out of me. He outweighed me by about a hundred pounds. He picked me up and smashed my legs onto the table. He crushed my ribs. Two of the guys from behind the bar jumped over the bar and tried to help me. It was a madhouse. That was [what it was like in] that era."

"There were a lot of tolerant people, and there were a lot of people who accepted what Tim and I did," he continues. "But, there were others on both sides of that fence. Amidst all the turmoil of that time, here were these kids bringing [home] a state championship, not with an average basketball team, but with a dominating team that might be considered the best basketball team in the history of the state of Illinois."

Since he had attended Thornton, Dreesen probably would have preferred if the blacks from Phoenix had played at Thornton High School rather than at Thornridge. He remembers that the desegregation demonstrations and the changing of the school district's boundaries created quite a stir in Phoenix, Harvey, South Holland, and Dolton.

"I remember it really caused a lot of controversy in the area," says Dreesen. "You gotta remember. The Vietnam War was raging. Students were burning their draft cards and flags all across the land. [There was] a lot of civil unrest. Then, on the other side of town, blacks were burning cities down all over America. One of the largest riots was right there in Harvey. At that time, I was a Deputy Marshall. I worked for the city of Harvey. Because the riots took place in the neighborhood that I grew up in, I used to drive the Mayor in and out of the riot zone in my private car, a '57 Chevy, so it was inconspicuous."

"In the midst of all that, here Tim and I became a comedy team," he continues. "We were trying to make people laugh. We went to Thornridge, and we went to Thornton. We had drug education programs. So, I do know what they were going through. There was a great deal of civil unrest."

Although the unrest had quieted down somewhat by 1972, racist attitudes still existed in many white communities in Chicago and throughout Illinois. Dreesen knows Thornridge coach Ron Ferguson upset some white fans by starting four black players.

"Can you imagine the flack [he got], the *pressure* that was on Ron Ferguson?" Dreesen wonders aloud. "The interesting thing is how we learn from children. All the prejudices that the parents could have brought to those games, and yet those kids, they brought the community together. If nothing else, for the one hour or so that the community would get together to watch them, all prejudices went out the window. You go back to the children of the community trying to show the adults how to behave."

Ron Bonfiglio served as one of Ron Ferguson's assistant coaches at Thornridge in the 1960s and early '70s. He says the first years of integration at the school were tempestuous and that the problems between blacks and whites were simply a sign of the times.

"Oh, it was a tough era," says Bonfiglio. "There were a lot of white kids there who didn't accept it. That's just the way they grew up. At that time, [there was] a lot of white flight coming out of the city to the suburbs. Yeah, it was a tough time. It was a tough time teaching. It was a tough time coaching. But, we didn't feel it as much [at Thornridge]. The greatest thing was the basketball team. As soon as we integrated, four years later we won a state championship. That really brought the school together."

Current Phoenix, Illinois, Mayor Terry Wells grew up in the community he now serves. As a small child in 1972 Phoenix, Wells worshipped the Thornridge players. Other youngsters rooted for the Cubs, White Sox, Bears, or Bulls. Wells idolized the hometown high school basketball team's players. The Thornridge players were not athletes only seen on television or read about in the newspapers. Quinn Buckner and the other black players were neighbors in Phoenix.

"As a kid, you had your sports heroes," says Wells. "But, my heroes were guys that I could put my hands on. I could run around the corner and see Quinn. I could see Quinn play basketball at the village courts. And all these guys, they were all right here in the community. They were my heroes. They were nothing mythical. And the community felt the same way [about them]."

Wells says it is disappointing that the small community has not received more credit for producing the players who became the stars for Thornridge.

"When people talk about Thornridge they always say Dolton," says Wells. "People always assume these guys all came from Dolton. Phoenix never got the credit for it. It's just unfortunate. [The school] was in Dolton, so that's the assumption that people have."

Wells says there was initially strong resistance to the desegregation of the community's grade schools and high schools. He now realizes it was the best thing that ever happened to him.

"I think it's a fairy tale story," says Mayor Wells. "You have to go from the race issue. It was forced busing. It was something that a lot of people did not like, both black and white. I was part of that busing. They were doing the same thing at the junior high school. I'll tell you, it was the best experience of my life. It set me up. It put me in a better school. It put me in a situation where I was around white kids after fifth grade. I got a better education. There were better resources."

Wells says parents had a more difficult time dealing with integration of the schools than the students.

"The parents were angry, and [they were] yelling and screaming," says Wells. "I had my issues going in. I didn't want to go to that school. I didn't want to hang around with white kids. I got there and found out that kids are kids. Color is nothing. The kids adjusted. The parents still had problems, but we were running around just being kids. It really set me up for the success I've had in life. I had a better education, and it all worked out in the long run. That whole issue about race, it was a problem. It was an issue in the beginning. But in the end it became a non-issue. And, I truly believe sports turned it around."

The Thornridge players today feel pride in having changed people's attitudes in the early days of integration at the school.

"That was the common thing that we all did," says Ernie Dunn. "We all had sports in common. That's how we stuck together. Sports, not just the basketball, I'd say the football too. A lot of good friends from Phoenix had also played football, and they won the mythical state championship in football. They were great. Most of the guys that were a couple years ahead of us that kind of pioneered going to Thornridge, they were the ones that started the football dynasty."

The black athletes were accepted by most Thornridge students because of their success in sports, but there remained white students who disapproved of having dark-skinned students in their classrooms.

"I think there were a few classes, in acting and stuff like that, where we were able to flourish, get along, and not have any fights," remembers Dunn. "But metal shop, I'd say it was a bit contentious there. It was unnecessary prodding of people with those hot pokers. It was like, 'Jeez, what is the point of *that*?' For the most part, sports kept us together in the community. Even in Phoenix, it kept us all together. Everybody in Phoenix knew just about everybody. You knew the families, not like it is today where in communities you only know a couple neighbors."

Tom Dreesen remembers the impact that the Thornridge basketball team had on the nearby communities, both black and white.

"What brought the community together was this team," says Dreesen. "Think about that. With all of the social unrest that was going on in the school, here Quinn Buckner and these kids, Bonczyk and all those guys, [they brought people together]. When you would go to see a game, all of a sudden all of that [racial bias] went out the window when you saw these black kids and white kids, not only playing together, but winning and dominating."

Every basketball fan in Phoenix and Harvey, as well as South Holland and Dolton, knew the Buckner family. Both parents were teachers. The Buckner children were serious students. Quinn also just happened to be regarded as the best high school athlete in the nation. He was a hometown hero. Everybody loved watching Buckner lead his team to another Thornridge victory. Dreesen believes Buckner was the key to the Falcons' success on the basketball court.

"Quinn Buckner wasn't flashy," recalls Dreesen. "Quinn Buckner wasn't Michael Jordan. Quinn Buckner wasn't even a Lloyd Batts like they had at Thornton [two years earlier]. He reminds me of Larry Bird. When I first heard about Larry Bird, I couldn't figure out [what made him special]. Larry Bird wasn't flashy, but he was always where the action was. He was always there. I would make the same analogy to Buckner. Buckner would get the defensive rebound. He would bring the ball down court and set up the play. He would pass off, and if one of his teammates would shoot, he would get the offensive rebound and get [the ball] right back to the guy that missed to encourage him to shoot again. He was so everywhere. He was so in control of the game. He was so aware of not only where they were points-wise in the game, but [also understood] the emotion of the game, if you know what I mean. If his teammates were getting flustered or frustrated, he knew how to almost automatically bring them back into focus simply by his playmaking ability. In a game that I was covering, Greg Rose missed an easy layup in the fourth quarter. He was frustrated and angry with himself. The other team rebounded and went back and scored. Quinn brought the ball down court and had a wide open shot just left of the key. Instead, he passed off to Rose so Rose could make the shot. Rose came back and hit like four in a row right afterward. No one noticed that [sacrifice made by Buckner]. They all credited Rose's ability to come back [from the blown layup]. They didn't notice what Quinn had done. That was his true value to that team."

When told that Buckner always tried to get Rose and Boyd Batts their touches early in games, Dreesen says it just shows how intellectually superior Quinn was in terms of basketball savvy.

"Buckner knew [basketball] better than anybody," says Dreesen. "He just had total control of that team. Ron Ferguson has said for years that people have given him a lot of credit [for Thornridge's success]. He says, 'I was just lucky to be the coach of Quinn Buckner.' I'm sure Ron helped develop him, but Quinn was a leader, a floor leader, at a very young age."

Dreesen became a close friend of Ferguson.

"Ron and I ended up on the same softball team," says Dreesen, who has lived in southern California since leaving Illinois years ago. "We played 16-inch softball which is real popular back there. Ron was always just a class guy. He was intelligent. He was mature. He was a good teacher. You could tell he cared about those kids. I think he wanted to teach them fundamental basketball and teamwork more than anything. He was a teacher as much as he was a coach."

Dreesen also became quite close with Hollywood star Frank Sinatra. He served as Sinatra's opening act for the last 14 years of Frank's career. In addition to their business relationship, the two men developed a long-lasting friendship. Dreesen spent many a Sunday at Sinatra's home playing a friendly game of poker with other celebrities such as Gregory Peck, Kirk Douglas, Robert Wagner, Dom DeLuise, Jill St. John, and Angie Dickenson. Dreesen says Sinatra would never play, though he hosted the Sunday poker game for more than 20 years. Dreesen still considers it somewhat amazing that a former dirt-poor kid was invited to be in the company of Hollywood legends. He and Sinatra were still close at the time of the former Rat Pack star's death. Dreesen was one of the pallbearers at Sinatra's funeral.

In the early 1970s, Dreesen saw firsthand what might well be the greatest high school basketball team in Illinois history. Later, he saw greatness while touring with Sinatra. Dreesen, like Quinn Buckner, always seemed to be right in the middle of the action.

CHAPTER 18

We Had Our Game Face On

THE 16 TEAMS STILL IN the hunt for the first Illinois Class AA basketball championship did not have much time to prepare for the super-sectional games scheduled for Tuesday, March 14, 1972. Only four days had passed since the sectional finals. Basketball fans around the state analyzed the matchups trying to determine which of the teams might provide a challenge for the defending state champions from Dolton Thornridge. Some believed Peoria Manual might be able to give Thornridge problems. Manual had lost six of its first ten games while star Mike Davis recovered from a knee injury, but the Rams had won nineteen straight games to reach the "Sweet 16". Fans also remembered that when Thornridge handed Manual its most recent loss in the Carbondale Christmas tournament, the Falcons had trailed at halftime. If they were to meet a third time this season, might the Rams pull off an upset? Manual (23-6) would face Rock Island Alleman (24-4) Tuesday night in the Peoria super-sectional at Bradley University. The winner would move on and become one of the eight teams that would play in the Assembly Hall in Champaign.

In other games Tuesday night, Hinsdale Central (25-1) would play La Grange (22-4) in the Aurora super-sectional at Aurora East High School. Kankakee Eastridge (24-4) would play Quincy (25-4) in the Normal super-sectional at Illinois State University. Mascoutah (28-1) would take on Virgil Fletcher's Collinsville Kahoks (19-9) on the campus of Southern Illinois University in the Carbondale super-sectional.

In Tuesday afternoon games, Crane (26-4) would face Marshall (13-12) for the Chicago Public League Championship in Chicago's International

Amphitheater. Also, once-beaten North Chicago (26-1) would go against the Evanston Wildkits (16-8) in what amounted to a home game for Coach Jack Burmaster's Wildkits since it would be played at Northwestern University in Evanston. Aurora East (25-3) would play Conant of Hoffman Estates (19-6) on the campus of Northern Illinois University in DeKalb. And in the most enticing of the super-sectional matchups, unbeaten Thornridge (29-0) would take on Lockport (23-3) at Crete-Monee High School.

Lockport coach Bob Basarich had been riding an emotional roller coaster during the state tournament. Regional wins over Romeoville and Lincoln-Way came with relative ease. However, Lockport had to survive fierce sectional challenges from Oak Lawn and Joliet Central to reach the "Sweet 16". It appeared for a time that Lockport's playoff run would end in the sectional final.

"We were playing Joliet Central at Joliet Central," says Basarich. "And with 35 seconds to go in that game, we're down four points and [Joliet Central's] Roger Powell is taking the ball out of bounds. The PA system announces that the J-C fans should pick up their tickets for the [super-sectional] game at Crete-Monee. We intercept two passes in a row and score on layups. Then, they miss a shot. We rebound it, and they fouled us. We made the free throw. They came down and shot and missed, and we won the game."

"There's always somebody that has fun with us, right?" continues Basarich. "We get to the locker room, and somebody runs in [yelling], 'Thornridge got beat! Thornridge got beat! You're on your way to the state!' Well, the locker room goes crazy. But about a minute later, somebody comes in and says, 'They didn't get beat.' Oh no. Now we gotta play 'em."

Modern day scouting involves coaches going to high school games armed with digital cameras that record video of the teams being scouted. The video is then used to help prepare a game plan for an upcoming opponent. In March of 1972, video tape recorders were bulky and expensive which meant few schools owned one. Most high school coaches had to settle for grainy black and white film that might have been shot in one of their games a year or two earlier. In 1972, most scouting reports were compiled by assistant coaches who sat in the bleachers at games, frantically scribbling notes and diagramming plays. The varsity coach would then decipher the notes and come up with a game plan for his team.

The Lockport coach did not really need film or a scouting report on Thornridge. Basarich was hoping for Divine intervention.

"We had the priest, the ministers, and rabbis come in, and we all prayed together a lot," jokes Basarich. "No, the truth is that I'm not one of these coaches who say, 'Okay, I think we can upset them.' We only played one way that season, and we weren't going to change anything. What made the difference? I mean if we stalled, they would have beat us. If we ran faster, they would have beat us by more. The thing is, you weren't going to outfox that particular team."

Lockport was averaging 80 points a game, so there was almost no chance the Porters would slow the pace as Bloom had done in its sectional loss to Thornridge. Basarich says he never considered attempting a stall to hold down the score.

"Moral victories don't mean much," says Basarich. "So you slow the ball down, and you lose 30-20. Everybody goes, 'Hey, you held them to 30 points! You did a great job!' Well, you *lost*. You weren't going to beat Thornridge that year. It just wasn't going to happen no matter what you did. There were a lot of good teams in the state, but nobody could match them."

***

CRETE-MONEE SUPER-SECTIONAL
(Late Tuesday afternoon, March 14) LOCKPORT

Lockport coach Bob Basarich felt horrible. He spent hour after hour in bed battling pneumonia as his team prepared to face Dolton Thornridge in the super-sectional. Already ill, Basarich felt even worse knowing in his heart that his team's season was about to end. He wanted to believe his young team had a chance to upset Thornridge. However, he was realistic. His team was talented but no match for the Falcons. On the day of the super-sectional game, doctors allowed Basarich to climb out of bed to coach his team. He should have stayed in bed.

"Okay, so we're headed to Crete-Monee [to play Thornridge]," says Basarich. "Our bus breaks down on the way there. We had to hitch-hike our players and our equipment [getting rides] from fans going to the game. We're standing on the side of the road hitch-hiking. So we get to the game. We go through that whole mess, and then we gotta play Thornridge. Of course, it was no game."

The game was played in the Warrior Dome at Crete-Monee High School. A sellout crowd watched as Thornridge took advantage of its devastating full-court press to bolt to a 10-0 lead in the first three minutes.

Greg Rose scored the Falcons' first eight points before Mike Bonczyk nailed a 20-foot jumper to put his team up by ten. Isaiah Harper, Lockport's only senior, finally got the Porters on the scoreboard with 4:05 left in the first quarter. But shortly thereafter, Rose found Quinn Buckner with a 15-foot behind-the-back pass for a layup. Thornridge led 18-6 after one quarter and 35-17 at halftime. Lockport scored four quick baskets early in the second half to climb to within twelve at 37-25, but Thornridge quickly regained control. Buckner sank a spinning jumper from near the midcourt stripe to end the third quarter with the Falcons firmly in command leading 56-30. Thornridge coasted to a 74-46 win despite an 18-point, 9-rebound game from Lockport's super sophomore Ellis Files. Thornridge had balanced scoring in the win. Boyd Batts led the way with 18 points and 12 rebounds. Rose scored 17, Buckner 15. Bonczyk and Ernie Dunn scored 10 points apiece. The Falcons made only 4 of 13 from the charity stripe but shot a blistering 58% (35 of 60) from the field. The Lockport coach had expected to come up short against the defending state champions, but still found himself growing more and more frustrated as Buckner stole the basketball from the Porters six times.

"I had five technicals in 29 years, and I got one that day," says Basarich. "The thing about it is that there's no doubt about Quinn Buckner's ability. He was just fantastic. But they allowed him to semi-[attack] people. When Quinn Buckner stole the ball, it couldn't be a foul. It's Quinn Buckner! Besides having a great reputation, he's a great player. I got up and complained to the official, and he gave me a technical."

Though disappointed, Basarich shook the hand of Ron Ferguson and thanked the Falcons' coach for not thoroughly embarrassing his team.

"When that game ended, I thanked him because he held [the score] down," says Basarich. "We were old friends, and we got along just great. We liked each other."

Nearly four decades later, Basarich knows the better team won that day in the Crete-Monee Dome.

"That's one of my losses that doesn't bother me because I knew I was going to lose before I got there," says Basarich.

Ferguson is quick to point out that Basarich had a good squad in 1972 and even better teams in the years to follow.

"Lockport had an excellent team that year," recalls the former Thornridge coach. "The next year they did go down [to the state tourney in Champaign]. Then, years later [in 1978], they won it. Bob Basarich was an excellent coach. I think the only game Thornridge ever beat Lockport was that game."

Since exactly one-fifth of the Falcons' 30 wins had come against two schools, conference rivals Bloom and Thornton, Thornridge star Boyd Batts had been unsure that his team was capable of beating other good teams from around the state. After beating Lockport, Batts realized he and his teammates were the real deal.

"At the beginning when we was winnin' all them games, we was playin' the same teams we'd been playin' for years," says Batts. "Then, we got to play different teams, and we found out that we could play with anybody. When we won the super-sectional, it was like heaven. Everybody started talkin' about 'We [are] gonna win it again this year.'"

The victory over Lockport gave Thornridge its 51st straight win and sent the Falcons back to Champaign with continued hopes of defending their state title. Thornridge immediately started looking ahead to its Class AA quarterfinal game with Collinsville. The Kahoks had picked up their 20th win of the season by beating Mascoutah 78-69. Rich Knarr scored 29 points to lead his team to victory and give Collinsville a shot at Thornridge.

Elsewhere, red-hot Peoria Manual advanced to the state quarterfinals by beating Rock Island Alleman 61-41. Paul Maras scored 20 points, and Mike Davis added 19 to lead the Rams to their 20th consecutive win. Joe Wharton scored 22 points as Evanston surprised North Chicago 62-60. Jim Flynn scored 23 to lead Hinsdale Central past La Grange 66-59. Greg Smith scored 23 and five of his teammates scored in double figures as Aurora East cruised to an easy 93-53 win over Conant of Hoffman Estates. Larry Moore scored 27 points to help Quincy advance with a 76-70 win over Eastridge, snapping the Kankakee school's 16-game winning streak. Crane won the Chicago Public League championship by beating Marshall 75-63. Future University of Illinois player Nate Williams scored 26 to help Crane nail down the Public League's automatic berth in the Class AA quarterfinals.

After the win over Lockport, rumors began surfacing that Thornridge coach Ron Ferguson might step down after the season to become the school's Athletic Director. Newspaper reports discussed the strain on Ferguson as his team continued its pursuit of a second straight state title. If the rumors were a distraction to the Falcons' players, it did not show. They seemed to be entirely focused on winning the next game and extending their winning streak. No matter what Ferguson decided after the season, the players just wanted to win another state championship. The Falcons had achieved another of the team goals Ferguson had written on the blackboard prior to the season. They were heading back to Champaign.

***

Thornridge and the seven other "Elite Eight" teams had only two full days to prepare for their first games in the Assembly Hall. All four of the Friday, March 17th quarterfinal round matchups would be televised statewide through the sponsorship of Illinois Bell, a subsidiary of AT&T. Two years before the U.S. Department of Justice filed a civil antitrust suit accusing AT&T of being a monopoly and twelve years before AT&T was broken up into the "Baby Bells", the game announcers referred to the broadcast's sponsor as "the phone company."

Thornridge (30-0) and Collinsville (20-9) were to play in the first game of the day scheduled for 12:15 p.m. The second afternoon game pitted Peoria Manual (24-6) versus Evanston (17-8). At 7 p.m., Aurora East (26-3) and Hinsdale Central (26-1) would battle before Crane (26-4) and Quincy (26-4) would meet in the last of the quarterfinal round matchups. Each game would feature at least one Illinois high school coaching legend. Thornridge's Ron Ferguson, looking for his second straight state championship, would be matching wits with Collinsville's Virgil Fletcher who eventually finished his coaching career with 792 wins. Manual's Dick Van Scyoc retired in 1994 after 44 high school seasons and 826 victories which at the time was the most victories in Illinois history. Evanston's Jack Burmaster wound up with a career record of 362-145 as coach of the Wildkits. Hinsdale Central's Ken Johnson had to go up against Aurora East coaching legend Ernie Kivisto who won 544 games in his career. And Crane's Dan Davis had his hands full knowing he had to coach against Quincy's Sherrill Hanks who won 446 games before leaving high school basketball to coach at Quincy College. It was a class field of coaches, each of whom hoped to win it all in Champaign.

***

CLASS AA QUARTERFINALS ASSEMBLY HALL IN CHAMPAIGN (Friday, March 17, 1972) COLLINSVILLE

When the state's top-ranked team left Dolton and headed south towards Champaign, the players and coaches were riding in style.

"We had cars from Bauer Buick," remembers Ernie Dunn. "I know that because I worked there in the summer. We drove those cars down to the state tournament, you know, like three or four of us in a car. We didn't take one big bus together. There was a coach driving with three or four of us [players in the car]."

While travelling to Champaign, some players talked quietly among themselves. Others listened to the AM radio. As they left the Chicago suburbs for the drive south, WLS played one of the hottest songs in America. Michael Jackson's Motown hit, *"Rockin' Robin",* was flying up the charts. It was only the second solo release for the 13-year-old Jackson, but it was one of the hits that helped him become a major star.

After arriving in Champaign on Thursday, March 16, the day before their first game in the Assembly Hall, the Falcons players read in the Champaign News-Gazette that Collinsville coach Virgil Fletcher was telling his players they were capable of pulling off an upset of Thornridge. Fletcher, the dean of Illinois high school coaches at the time, certainly could not have entertained any thoughts of ever beating Thornridge when his team struggled to a 2-6 start. However, Fletcher's team was on a roll after winning 18 of its last 21 games. The Kahoks had not lost in more than a month and had defeated another "Elite Eight" team, the Quincy Blue Devils, in the final game of the regular season. Fletcher knew this Collinsville team was not the best of the 11 teams he had guided into the state tournament in his 26 years at Collinsville, but the Kahoks were very much improved from the previous season when they went an uncharacteristic 3-19. Collinsville was dangerous, and the Falcons knew it.

Some high school basketball teams were allowed by their coaches to play music in the locker room prior to their games. Lincoln coach Duncan Reid had played the Staple Singers' *"Respect Yourself"* to remind his players to respect the game and their own abilities. The Thornridge players needed no such reminder. Prior to the Collinsville game at the Assembly Hall, the Thornridge locker room was quiet just as it had been all season. No music played. There was no joking or playing around. The Falcons were focused on one thing. They had to beat Collinsville.

"Oh man, we had our game face on," recalls forward Greg Rose. "It was like a job before we got on the floor. When we got a lead, that's when we had fun."

Coach Ron Ferguson points out that the Thornridge players had matured from the previous season when there had been some rowdiness in the locker room.

"It wasn't always that way," says Ferguson. "I think probably the year before we had to get a little discipline in there. But I'll tell you, when we started that [1971-72] season, we got together. There wasn't one guy not on the same page in terms of [staying focused before games]. They took a lot of pride in themselves. They got a taste of [success] their junior year, and they didn't want to let it go [as seniors]."

Ferguson admits he was still having a difficult time enjoying the experience of coaching his team in Champaign. He continued to worry night and day. He worried that he hadn't prepared his players for anything they might come up against in the next game. He worried about his team having one of those nights where, for some reason, things just don't work out. He worried mostly about the team's lack of depth and what might happen if one of his regulars was hurt.

"Injuries to a key player," says Ferguson. "I think if it had been Batts, Buckner, or Bonczyk, it would have really hurt. We might have gotten by without Dunn or without Rose. Gatlin could fill in nicely. He won't score as much, but he does other things pretty good."

Going into the game against Collinsville, he tried not to pay attention to that gnawing thought in the back of his mind.

"You know, you get down to the state tournament," says Ferguson, "and you play the first game. What if Buckner gets hurt or something like that?"

The Thornridge coach was simply incapable of giving himself permission to enjoy the moment. He would, however, enjoy the start of the game against the Kahoks. The Falcons' full-court press led to several Collinsville turnovers and a quick 9-1 Thornridge lead. It was 25-9 before Collinsville's Rich Knarr hit a jumper to make it 25-11 after one quarter. Knarr would sink five buckets in the second quarter en route to a 25-point performance, but Thornridge increased its advantage to 48-32 by halftime. Falcons' center Boyd Batts was very active at both ends of the court. He was blocking shots, dominating the boards, and scoring at will. The young man, who always believed he deserved more recognition then he received, got plenty of acclaim for his performance against the Kahoks. Batts finished the game with 34 points. He made 15 of 20 shots from the field and pulled down a game-high 18 rebounds while leading Thornridge to a 95-66 win. Although the term "double-double" had not yet become part of basketball vernacular, Batts had his second straight state tournament game with double figure totals in points and rebounds. He would have two more monster games the next day in one of the most impressive performances in state tournament history. Batts' impact on the games came as no surprise to Thornridge point guard Mike Bonczyk.

"You knew Boyd was gonna be big," says Bonczyk. "He's six-seven [or] six-eight. He can get the ball off the glass. He can lead the break. At the beginning of the year, he used to get frustrated. We were gone [on the fast-break] layin' it up, and he wasn't a part of it. So, what he'd do was get the rebound, look, check it, make us come back and get [the ball], and then we had to walk it down. We'd get mad and say, 'Boyd, we're trying to run.' He'd say, 'Oh. Okay.' The next phase of Boyd's maturity was he'd get the rebound, wouldn't check it, and [would] start to dribble it up the floor and lead the break. But, he had a tremendous year. The state tournament was just tremendous with all the points he had. A lot of people look as his numbers, but you don't know [from the numbers] what he brought to the table defensively. If somebody beat you [on the dribble], he was there. He'd block it or change a shot, and you're going the other way."

Batts clearly had a major impact on both ends of the court against Collinsville, and he wasn't the only Falcons' player to go off on offense. Greg Rose had a huge game against the Kahoks with 24 points on 12 of 17 shooting. Quinn Buckner made only 6 of 17 from the floor but finished with 19 points. The victory was Thornridge's 31st of the season and extended the Falcons' state-record winning streak to 52 games.

The Falcons moved into the state tournament semifinals where they would meet a team they had already defeated twice during the regular season. Peoria Manual advanced to the semifinals with an impressive 82-53 win over Evanston in the second Friday afternoon game. The Rams, who won their 21st straight, were again led by their big men, Paul Maras (26 points, 14 rebounds) and Mike Davis (19 points, 16 boards). After losing to Thornridge by 47 in the Thanksgiving tournament in Rockford and by 27 in the Carbondale Christmas tourney, Peoria Manual would get one more chance to play Thornridge.

In the first Friday night quarterfinal, Aurora East edged Hinsdale Central 83-81 which ended the Red Devils' outstanding season after they had won 26 of their first 27 games. Hinsdale Central shot 58% from the field but committed 23 turnovers. All five Aurora East starters scored in double figures. Jeff Hollis led the way with 23 points. Greg Smith added 21 points and 11 rebounds.

Quincy earned the last semifinal berth by beating Crane Tech 87-71 in the final game Friday night. Guard Larry Moore scored a team-high 36 points for the Blue Devils. Quincy forward Bob Spear added 18 points and 12 rebounds and helped hold Crane All-State player Nate Williams to only 15 points.

Four teams remained in the hunt for the Illinois Class AA title. All four would be playing two games the next day, but only two would qualify to compete for the state championship. Saturday, March 18, 1972, would be one of the most unforgettable days in Illinois high school basketball history.

CHAPTER 19

We Had A Chance To Beat Them

BOTH STATE TOURNAMENT SEMIFINAL MATCHUPS were intriguing. Thornridge (31-0) versus Peoria Manual (25-6) was scheduled for 12:15 Saturday afternoon. That game would be followed by a showdown between Aurora East (27-3) and Quincy (26-3). All four teams desperately wanted to play in the last game Saturday night because that meant they would be playing for the championship. The losers of the two afternoon contests would play for the third place trophy in the early game Saturday evening. None of the four teams had any interest in being part of the third place game. Their sights were set on playing for, and winning, the first Illinois Class AA title.

Throughout the state, newspapers were filled with recaps of the Friday games. Many previewed the Saturday semifinals. Thornridge was still the favorite having won 31 straight games during the season, 52 straight dating back to the previous campaign. However, Manual was a real concern for Falcons' coach, Ron Ferguson. He remembered that the Rams were the only team to have held a halftime lead over his squad. He also believed in the old adage that it is hard to beat a good team three times in a season. Ferguson considered Manual a very good team.

Manual coach Dick Van Scyoc thought his team had a chance to pull off the upset. The Rams had not lost since falling to Thornridge in Carbondale in late December. His big men, Mike Davis and Paul Maras, were both healthy and playing well. Van Sycoc thought if Davis and Maras had big games, and if a couple Thornridge players got into early foul trouble, the Rams might be able to surprise the Falcons.

Wayne McClain, Peoria Manual's point guard and team captain, remembers thinking the Rams had a team that was capable of winning the state championship.

"Mike Davis, six-six All-Stater," says McClain, starting to name the other Rams' starters. "[He was] big, quick, a big guy [who] could shoot it. [He was] just ahead of his time. We had George Caldwell who was about six-four, an athletic guy. We had Paul Maras, the only white guy on the team, who was six-six. [He] was kind of a lumberjack-type player but could shoot the ball extremely well. Michael Humbles was about five-eight. He was just a beast on defense. He created havoc with teams. He would undress you at half-court. [Humbles was] just a really solid defensive player."

Since the Rams had dropped their first two games to Thornridge by a total of 74 points, there were some who thought the game might be another blowout. The Peoria Manual coach thought otherwise. In his pre-game comments, Van Scyoc convinced his players that they could compete with Thornridge.

"He was very smart as a coach," says McClain. "I just remember it being so positive, you know, [Coach saying], 'The previous times we played them, we hadn't reached our peak as a team. This is probably going to be our best chance to get them.' We played them really well. We probably played them as well as anybody that entire year."

***

CLASS AA SEMIFINAL ASSEMBLY HALL
IN CHAMPAIGN (12:15 p.m. Saturday, March 18, 1972)
MANUAL (PEORIA)

Getting a chance to play at the Assembly Hall, home of the University of Illinois' Fighting Illini, was a thrill for all of the high school players who reached the "Elite Eight." The Thornridge players were somewhat accustomed to playing on the big stage at the state tournament. Players on the other teams, however, were getting their first taste of what it was like to play before 16,000 fans in Champaign. Peoria Manual captain Wayne McClain says his biggest high school thrill was getting to play at the Assembly Hall.

"Oh, no doubt about it," says McClain. "[It was a thrill] just being able to go out on the floor. I had been to games and heard the voice, the guy talking on the [public address] microphone during the games. The introduction and coming out of that tunnel, it was just unbelievable. It just seemed like you was in a whole different world, you know, that you have arrived. Growing up as a kid, the Assembly Hall was the ultimate place to be."

As the Rams prepared to tip off against Thornridge, McClain knew people throughout Illinois were watching on TV.

"You know that you're being showcased," says McClain. "That [broadcast] ran all the way across the state. Your relatives, from the southern part of Illinois to the northern part, are writing or calling your parents saying, 'Hey, I saw so-and-so on TV.' A lot of other people was getting to watch the fruits of your labor by [us] being at the state tournament."

As the two teams walked onto the court for the opening tip, the Rams were intent on keeping Quinn Buckner from taking over the game.

"Buckner was just a great athlete," remembers McClain. "People forget that he was one of the best football players in the state at that time [in addition to being one of the best] basketball players. UCLA was recruiting him. That's when UCLA was winning national championships. Everybody was recruiting him."

Buckner did not dominate against the Rams, but the Falcons had plenty of other weapons. Peoria Manual scored the game's first basket. Thornridge scored the next eight points and held an 18-8 lead after one quarter. Thornridge point guard Mike Bonczyk, playing with a bad cold, picked up three personal fouls in the first quarter and went to the bench. Boncyzk would later return and played the remainder of the game without picking up any more fouls. Boyd Batts, trying to contain Manual's All-State center Mike Davis, also got into first-half foul trouble. He went to the bench in the second quarter. Even so, the Falcons were able to keep their lead. Manual shot only 26% from the field in the first two quarters and scored only seven first-half baskets. Thornridge led 35-19 at halftime. It got a little more interesting in the third quarter. The Rams outscored the Falcons 20-15 in the period. Davis scored 14 points in the third quarter to rally the Rams. However, he did not have enough help from his teammates. Greg Rose put the clamps on Paul Maras, holding the six-six forward to only 4 points on 2 of 9 shooting. Manual coach Dick Van Scyoc even sat the struggling Maras for part of the second half choosing to use a quicker lineup in an attempt to spur a comeback. Trailing by only 11 points Manual was still in the game heading to the fourth quarter. The Rams' players still believed they could come back and upset the Falcons.

"Going into the fourth quarter, I remember thinking that we had a chance to beat them," says Wayne McClain. "I remember in the huddle telling the other players, 'Hey look. Let's just stay with it. We might have a chance to beat them.' But, you know, they were just so good at finishing."

And the Falcons did finish against the Rams. Hoping to slow down the high-scoring Davis, Thornridge coach Ron Ferguson switched from a man-to-man defense to a 1-3-1 zone, a strategy that quickly paid dividends. The Rams' big man had to work harder to get his shots, and Thornridge maintained its double-digit lead. Up by 13 with three minutes to play, Thornridge slowed it down on offense, making sure to take care of the basketball while managing the clock. When the final horn sounded, the Assembly Hall scoreboard high above center court displayed the numbers; Thornridge-71, Manual-52. As promised by the Falcons' players one year earlier, Thornridge had made it all the way back to play for another state championship.

Peoria Manual star Mike Davis had done all he could to prevent it from happening. Davis finished with a game-high 25 points and 15 rebounds. Thornridge, though, got significant contributions from all five starters. Rose led the Falcons with 20 points and pulled down 8 rebounds. Ernie Dunn had a big 16 points and 9 rebounds. Buckner was solid with 14 points and 12 boards. Batts had been hampered by four personal fouls yet still scored 14 points and pulled down 10 rebounds for his third straight double-double of the state tournament. Bonczyk finished with a team-high 8 assists. Coach Ron Ferguson would later say that Peoria Manual was the toughest team Thornridge faced all year. Meaning no disrespect to the other teams the Falcons played that season, Ferguson still believes Manual may have been his team's toughest foe.

"I really felt in my own mind that the best team we played was Peoria Manual," says Ferguson. "They really had a good team. I felt sorry for poor Dick Van Scyoc because he's a good friend."

"We really did have confidence," says Van Scyoc. "We'd played 'em twice. We knew their personnel, and I thought our guys matched up with them pretty well. We did have a chance, but they were just too overpowering for us. When you beat a team three times, that's a tough job, especially [when you beat] a good team. That's what I base my evaluation of [Thornridge] on because we had a good ball club. There's no question about it. We were very physical and strong-willed. Caldwell, Maras, and Davis were all six-four or better. I was very confident, and I felt going into that game in Champaign that we had a chance to beat them. And still we lost by 19."

Van Scyoc was impressed with the Thornridge players' ability to seemingly turn up the intensity when needed. Any time the Falcons were being challenged, they were able to do whatever was necessary and sometimes in spectacular fashion.

"They sure could," says Van Scyoc. "It just shows you what an outstanding team they were. You just can't take a team and do something like that with average players. Average players don't do those things."

The Manual fans were greatly disappointed with the game's outcome. Many of the fans who had made the drive from Peoria to sit in the Manual rooting section were black, but there were also white fans from Peoria at the Assembly Hall. Much like the Thornridge team had galvanized the black and white communities in Chicago's south suburbs the Manual team had drawn together blacks and whites in the heart of Illinois.

"Oh yeah," says Wayne McClain. "Manual is on the south side [of Peoria]. It was the melting pot of the city. It's only black now, but back then it was black and white. That was the poorest part of the city. When I was there, you had some racial tensions. But the thing that helped us so much was we just didn't feel that and [didn't] see it. We were a predominantly black team. We had a really good white player in Paul Maras. That, for us, transcended anything that was going on in our school. It wasn't that bad, not at all, but the basketball made you color blind. That's the best thing about athletics. It does make you color blind."

Like it or not, McClain and his teammates still had one more game to play. They would begin the evening session by playing for the third place trophy. The Thornridge players would try to get some rest for the state championship game that would follow. The only question that remained was which team Thornridge would face in the title game. Both Aurora East and Quincy were capable of putting up big numbers offensively. Aurora East coach Ernie Kivisto had said earlier in the season that he believed his team was the best in the state. Would he get a chance to prove it?

When Aurora East and Quincy took the court for their state semifinal game, the Thornridge players and coaches settled into seats at the Assembly Hall. Coach Ron Ferguson wanted his players to see part of the game to give them an idea of what they would be facing later that night.

"We let the players watch about a quarter, and then they went back [to the hotel] with the assistant coaches," recalls Ferguson. "I stayed and watched the whole game. But, [the players] saw it on TV too, and they saw *107* to *96*. That had to keep 'em awake watching those teams make just shot after shot after shot. Certainly that took away a little bit of [us] maybe being overconfident. You think, 'God, who wants to play either of those teams?' I think [the players] figured, 'Wait a minute now. We better not take them for granted. Whoever wins that game is gonna be a tough team.' Anybody that scouted that game knowing they gotta play one of those teams had to be scared because, by God, they scored at will. And they were shooting it from all over, so it wasn't like they couldn't shoot from outside. I thought, 'What in the world are we gonna do? We'll have to score a hundred points to beat them.' Sometimes, you look at another team and you get scared because they look so good that you don't know if you compete that well with them."

So which team would get the chance to try to deny Thornridge its place in history? Would it be the high-scoring Tomcats of Aurora East or the Quincy Blue Devils, the last remaining team from outside of the Chicago area? Both had been ranked among the state's best teams all season. It promised to be an exciting semifinal. Fans at the Assembly Hall, and around the state, settled in to watch the two teams put on an offensive display that has never been equaled in the Illinois state tournament.

***

The Aurora East – Quincy semifinal featured two All-State players. Aurora East was led by six-six center Greg Smith, a white kid whose toughness around the basket was becoming legendary. Quincy had been led all season by bespectacled five-nine guard Larry Moore, who averaged 28 points during the regular season. Moore had been the key to his team's success all year. Against the Tomcats, Moore got off to a slow start, most of his shots bouncing off the rim. Quincy fans were concerned but remained hopeful because of the inspired play of center Don Sorenson and reserve forward Kelvin Gott. The two big men were helping the Blue Devils stay close. Aurora East had shown it was capable of putting up huge numbers offensively. The Tomcats had scored 100 or more in winning the three games they played in their Christmas tournament in December. Now, in the state semifinals, it appeared Aurora East was again on its way to scoring 100. The scorekeeper at the Assembly Hall could not relax since both teams were scoring nearly every trip down the court. At the half, Aurora East had scored 50 points. Surprisingly, the Tomcats did not have the lead. Quincy had also torched the nets for 50 first-half points. In the second half, the Blue Devils hoped to contain Smith, the Aurora East center who would later play at Bradley University. Despite Quincy's efforts to slow him down,

Smith continued to scorch the nets at the Assembly Hall. By game's end, Smith had made 18 of 25 from the field, many of his shots contested by Blue Devil defenders. He finished with a game-high 44 points. Aurora East scored 96 points, certainly enough to win most any high school game. However, this was no ordinary game. Quincy had its best offensive game of the season and beat Aurora East by 11. Never before had a team scored 96 points in the Illinois state tournament and lost.

After reaching the century mark only one time all season, the Blue Devils set a new state tournament record with 107 points. Moore scored 20 in the second half to finish with 32 points. Fellow senior Don Sorenson had 20 points and 13 rebounds. Despite the huge games by Moore and Sorenson, the Blue Devils would not have defeated Aurora East if junior forward Kelvin Gott had not come off the bench and played the game of his life. When Moore missed, and he *did* miss 24 of 37 shots from the field, Gott was often there to grab the carom. Gott finished with 25 points and 12 rebounds to lead Quincy to the 107-96 victory, a win that put the Blue Devils in the Illinois Class AA state championship game against Thornridge.

"I like to tell people that we played our best game of the year that day," says Bob Spear, who scored 13 points in the victory. "Unfortunately, we played it at about 2:30 in the afternoon against Aurora East [and not against Thornridge that night]."

"That's exactly right," adds Larry Moore. "Those guys were in great shape. They pressed every possession, whether they missed [or] whether they made [their shots]. It just sped up the game. We ended up shooting lots of layups, and we had lots of 3-point plays. It was one of those helter-skelter games. Actually, we were pretty good in those kinds of games."

"Their press was like a 3-1-1," recalls Spear, at that time a rail-thin junior forward. "They were just going to contest the inbounds pass and bring guys way up [the court]. That was the recipe for how we scored 107 points. We didn't dribble the ball down, set it up, and score. We basically said, 'Okay, [if] you want to press us, we'll run it right through you. It'll be two-on-one all day.'"

The 203 total points scored that afternoon by Quincy and Aurora East remains the highest-scoring game in the history of the Illinois Class AA tournament. No losing team in a state tournament "Final Four" contest has ever scored as many points as Aurora East did that day in Champaign. Moore, who launched a remarkable *68* field goal attempts in Quincy's quarterfinal and semifinal wins, remembers a special moment that occurred in the final seconds of the game against Aurora East.

"One thing that really stood out," recalls Moore, "I think Hanks had taken out most of the starters. I remember standing up right in front of our bench, you know, those [players'] chairs. Ernie Kivisto, the coach from Aurora East, right near the very end, walked all the way down the length of the floor in back of the chairs. It really surprised me. He came up and put his arm around me. He said, 'I didn't think anybody could run with us for 32 minutes and beat us. You guys really proved us wrong.'"

The Blue Devils did not have long to savor their victory. Four hours after beating Aurora East, Quincy would be back on the court trying to cap its season with a win over a team that had been perfect over the last 15 months. After the long high school basketball season, it all came down to one game. Larry Moore and the Quincy Blue Devils would play Quinn Buckner and the defending champion Thornridge Falcons. More than 16,000 fans would be inside the Assembly Hall that night to see if the first Illinois Class AA championship trophy would be heading west to Quincy or north to Dolton. The matchup was intriguing because while nearly everyone had expected Thornridge to be in the final, Quincy was somewhat of a surprise.

CHAPTER 20

That's What Illinois Basketball Is

THE SCHOOL THORNRIDGE WOULD MEET in the state final had a great basketball tradition. The Quincy Blue Devils had reached the state tournament's "Sweet 16" in 21 of the last 39 seasons. Quincy won the Illinois championship in 1934, and twice came close, only to lose in the state finals. Under Sherrill Hanks, Quincy finished third in 1962 and second in 1965. The Blue Devils had won at least 20 games in each of the 11 seasons Hanks had coached at the school. Even though Quincy had a winning tradition, there were not very high expectations for the 1971-72 Blue Devils. Quincy had disappointed its fans by failing to advance out of the regional tournament in 1970 and 1971. In addition, this 1971-72 Quincy team was young and inexperienced. Tony Ball, Chuck Heitholt, and Mike Hanks, the coach's son, had all graduated in 1971 leaving only Larry Moore and Don Sorenson as returning starters. It was difficult for any Quincy fan to believe these Blue Devils would play in the state final. Nearly four decades later, Mike Hanks remembers his father's 1971-72 squad far exceeded expectations.

"That was a team that kind of came from nowhere," recalls Mike Hanks. "There were no expectations at the start of the year that that team was going to do anything. They didn't even know who the best player was going to be. It ended up Larry Moore scored a lot of points, and then a lot of guys just rolled."

Starting two seniors (Moore and Sorenson), two juniors (Bob Spear and Rick Ely), and a sophomore point guard (Jim Wisman) a majority of the time, the Blue Devils were thought to be a year away from being a serious state championship contender.

"That team wasn't really supposed to make a big splash that year," says Don Sorenson, the team's center. "We had Larry and myself coming back, and a couple of [juniors] that had gotten maybe a *little* varsity experience. But all of a sudden, we started winning some big games and really started doing well."

"We were not an extremely talented team," remembers Larry Moore, the team's leading scorer. "We didn't really have very many athletes. Probably our best one would have been Wisman. Spear was not a good athlete. Don Sorenson was probably just an average high school athlete who got a lot out of what he had. I was probably a borderline athlete [just] a little above average as far as athletic ability. I was five-nine and maybe about 165 [pounds] soaking wet in high school. But, we did not have good athletes. What we did have was just tremendous chemistry."

Generously listed at five-eleven in game programs, Moore became one of the state's top scorers during the 1971-72 season. He averaged 28 points per game during the regular season and 26 a game during his team's eight-game state tournament run. He was a volume shooter who topped the Blue Devils in scoring nearly every time he laced up his basketball shoes. On the nights he struggled to find the range, he kept shooting. That was okay with his teammates. They understood they would win only if Moore got untracked.

"The guys on that team, they could have cared less whether I shot 4 times or 30 times," says Moore. "If I was open, they would get me the ball, particularly if I'd hit a couple [shots]. I was really a streaky shooter. If I hit a couple, there would be guys that would pass up open 10-footers to throw the ball out 20 feet so that I could shoot."

Moore was a late bloomer. He did not become a varsity starter until midway through his junior season. Even then, he was not regarded as a primary offensive player.

"My junior year I was probably our fourth or fifth option," says Moore, "even though I ended up with pretty good numbers. I got better as the year went on. I didn't even start like the first eight games. [Coach Hanks] threw me in there right after Christmas. I was maybe averaging three or four [points] a game. I ended up [averaging] probably 12.5 points a game. For Quincy High and the schedule we played, that's very respectable. But, I was not one of our top options."

Moore was driven to become a star. He says the motivation came when the Blue Devils lost to cross-town rival Quincy Catholic Boys in the regional tournament his junior year.

"They should have never beat us, but they did," says Moore. "I really felt bad about how we lost. It was kind of that snowball effect. One mistake led to another, and then pretty soon, you're doubting whether you can hit a basket. I remember waking up that next Saturday morning telling myself I was *never* going to be in that position again. I was gonna be prepared to take over a game if I had to."

'I didn't ever expect to do what I did my senior year, but I spent just hours and hours [practicing] by myself," continues Moore. "Coach Hanks opened up our gym every night Monday through Friday, and we played, just the guys who were on the team."

While some players seem to come by their abilities naturally, Moore worked hard to develop his shot and his overall game. A spot-up shooter as a junior, Moore challenged himself to become a more complete player, a player who could handle the ball and shoot off the dribble.

"I would just go up and down the floor trying to shoot shots that I thought I'd be getting in a game," recalls Moore. "I'd walk out of that gym, and the pads of my hands and my fingers would be bleeding. I shot so much and did so much ball-handling up and down the floor, I'd walk out of there, and there would be calluses that were ripped open from shooting [the ball]. I worked at McDonalds that summer. If I worked in the morning, I would get in the gym all afternoon [and stay there] until the open gym [that night]. And vice-versa, if I worked in the afternoons, I would be at the YMCA all morning."

"The first time I thought I had a chance to be a good player was right after we lost to Catholic Boys," continues Moore. "By [IHSA] law, you could still have practices, so Hanks had us in the gym on Monday. He had all the underclassmen playing against the upperclassmen. Most of our stuff was pick-and-rolls. Don Sorenson set me a pick. I came around the pick, pulled up, and shot the ball. After he pivoted and went to the basket, Sorenson stopped and opened up expecting the ball. I don't even know if the shot went in, but I remember Hanks blew his whistle. He walked out to the middle of the floor. He grabbed me by the jersey and walked me over to Sorenson and said, 'Here is gonna be one of the best shooters in the state of Illinois next year. When you open up and go to the basket, you are going to *rebound*. You are not going to expect a *pass* from somebody who is the best shooter in the state of Illinois.' At that time I wasn't even

17 yet. That really struck a chord with me, and I worked really, really hard that spring and summer and fall."

Moore's dedication and hard work paid off. In his senior season, he became the most prolific scorer in Quincy High School history. Without Moore, the Blue Devils would have been just an average high school basketball team. With him leading the offense, Quincy became a team capable of beating almost any team in Illinois.

Six-one sophomore Jim Wisman had to prove himself before earning a spot in the starting lineup. Senior Kimber Gay started three of the first four games and scored 10 crucial points in the season-opening win. However, by the fifth game of the season, Wisman had replaced Gay in the starting lineup. The talented sophomore point guard started every game thereafter. Among the guards, Wisman was the team's best defender. His offensive skills were also impressive for such a young player. While primarily looking to get the basketball to his teammates, Wisman still averaged 10.4 points during the regular season and 12.7 points during his team's three state tournament games in Champaign. Wisman's excellent ball-handling ability allowed Moore to spend most of the time playing the shooting guard position where he was more effective. Wisman, who later played with Thornridge star Quinn Buckner on Indiana's undefeated 1976 NCAA championship team, was dating the coach's daughter Kris Hanks while starring for the Blue Devils. The two eventually wed, although the marriage didn't last.

Six-six Don Sorenson was the only Quincy big man virtually assured of a starting position going into the season. While Kelvin Gott, Mike Sellers, Bob Spear, and Rick Ely competed for the other two starting positions on the frontline, Sorenson started every game when healthy. Sorenson finished second on the team averaging 10.6 points as a senior. Sorenson's mother, who still lives in Quincy, says head coach Sherrill Hanks was very important to her son when Don was in high school. Sorenson's father had some health issues which made it a difficult time for the Sorenson family.

"Yeah, my dad had an eye disease at that point," says Sorenson. "I just turned 16 when he started losing his sight. I had just gotten my [driver's] permit. [I] had been downtown with him getting a haircut. He pulled over the car and said, 'Hey, you wanna drive?' He couldn't see. He didn't tell me that until years later. I remember driving him down to Barnes Hospital in St. Louis for special tests during [my] sophomore year. You know, everybody's got their stuff. [You have to] deal with it."

With his father having trouble seeing, Don was happy that Quincy's head coach made sure the elder Sorenson got to sit close to the court at the Blue Devil's games.

"[Dad] was a big fan," says Sorenson. "He had peripheral vision, so I think he saw [us play]. Hanks pulled some strings and got him decent seats in the gym."

In the early 1970s, high school coaches often took on the role of surrogate father for one or more of their players. Just as Thornridge coach Ron Ferguson had done for some of his team members, Sherrill Hanks helped his players who were in need.

"Hanks always did stuff behind the scenes that people don't know about," remembers Sorenson. "We had to wear a sports coat on the road. One kid couldn't afford it. He bought him one. Remember [1970-71 starter] Tony Ball? He did stuff for Tony. The coaches back in those days, I mean, it was really that old school kind of thing. You know, Hoosiers, Gene Hackman? [Those coaches were] tough as nails. But, then they do this nice thing, and you go, 'Wait a minute. It changes my whole vision of who you are. What's that about?' One thing I was really grateful for, fifteen years after graduation, I was able to talk with Hanks and just thank him for all he had meant to me and had taught me."

Six-three junior forward Bob Spear was hardly a physical presence. He was so thin that his teammates compared him to a skinny frankfurter.

"Wiener. We called him Wiener," says Don Sorenson. "You look at Bob. [He was] skinny as a rail. I was six-six, 175 [pounds]. [I could] turn sideways, stick out my tongue, and I'm a zipper. But, Bob was the same way. He would just wiggle his way in for rebounds or shots. He'd just *wiener* his way in."

Spear was an excellent defender who, after working his way into the starting lineup, was often assigned to guard the opponent's best offensive player. Spear could also score, although he got off to a slow start in 1971-72. He ended the regular season averaging 9.8 points, even though he scored a total of one point in Quincy's first three games. He did not even get off the bench in the Blue Devils' third game of the season. Quincy teammate Kelvin Gott credits Sherrill Hanks with developing Spear into an outstanding all-around player.

"Coach Hanks was a genius at managing people," says Gott. "There may have been people who coached X's and O's better than he did at times. But, he got the most out of everybody who played for him. Bobby Spear was a string bean. He probably weighed 145 pounds soaking wet, and he was captain of the All-State team his senior year. He just became an unbelievable scorer. I don't know how Coach Hanks saw that in him."

Spear had already developed into a fine player by the time the Blue Devils marched into the state tournament his junior season. He and his teammates had to overcome quite a lot to reach the state final. Located in the western section of the state, far from other large towns, Quincy travelled long distances to play all of their road games.

"We traveled fairly extensively," remembers Spear. "What's interesting for Quincy, we are so isolated over there [in western Illinois). Our closest road game, which was Springfield, was 100 miles [from Quincy]. Galesburg, our closest conference game, was 120 miles. All of the other four [conference schools] were up in the Quad Cities which were 160 miles [away]."

The difficult travel schedule helped toughen the Blue Devils. So did playing some primarily black schools that Coach Hanks agreed to schedule. Hanks wanted to play the best competition. He also wanted to make sure his white players would not be intimidated when they went against teams featuring minority players during the state tournament. Spear says because he and his white teammates had played some tough black teams that season, they were not intimidated by the prospect of playing Thornridge.

"We played at Thornton that year," says Spear. "That was an all-black, powerful team. We played some [other] all-black teams. It was not unusual for us. We were not intimidated by that, not at all."

Kelvin Gott was a muscular six-four junior. Gott was the tight end on the football team and a real banger on the boards in basketball. Gott was in the starting lineup at the beginning of the season and scored 17 points in the first game against Ottawa. As the season progressed, he started occasionally, but more often than not, he served as the Blue Devils sixth man. Gott averaged only 6.8 points during the regular season but came up with several huge performances when his team needed him most.

Gott later in life became a high school basketball coach. After playing and coaching in the state, he believes Illinois high school basketball is very special.

"It's that Blue Devil [mascot] coming out with the fire lit at Quincy High School, and the whole place is up for grabs and off the wall," says Gott. "I just can't describe it. You just feel it inside of you. It's Coach [Steve] Goers carrying on the legacy of Coach Hanks and about to become the winningest coach in Illinois basketball history. [Goers goes] from being an assistant of Coach Hanks, and takes the love of the game and the knowledge of the game with him. It's a thousand things like that. It's going to Lincoln High School and knowing that there are 3,000 people in that gymnasium to watch you play every Friday night. That's what people are going to talk about on Monday. That's what's going to be on the radio. And, that's going on at Pinckneyville High School, and Mt. Vernon High School, and Quincy High School, and every one of those schools around the state where you're the only act in town. [It is] where people leave their season tickets in their wills. That's what Illinois basketball is."

Six-four junior forward Rick Ely and senior guard Kimber Gay were the only minority players on the 1971-72 Quincy High basketball team. Gay played sparingly as the season progressed, but Ely saw regular playing time throughout the year. Ely started in the season-opener, but failed to score and began the next game on the bench. Coach Hanks eventually worked the shot-blocking Ely back into the starting lineup because he was such an intimidating presence on defense. Ely finished the regular season averaging 7.4 points a game. Though whites greatly outnumbered blacks on the Blue Devils' squad, Ely remembers being treated well by his white teammates. Ely says color was never part of the equation in the Quincy High School basketball program. That doesn't mean, however, that he spent a lot of time hanging out with the white kids away from the court.

"This was the situation," says Ely. "I came from a poor family, a single parent family. My mother raised me and my two sisters. You had Jim Wisman, Bob Spear, Mike Sellers, all these guys [had money]. Larry Moore's father was a very hard-working individual, but financially they were [all] doing a hell of a lot better than I was doing. As far as hanging together outside of basketball, we never did. They lived in one part of town. I lived in the other part of town. That's not really hanging together. [It was] not because of race but because of socio-economics, the backgrounds that we came from. They were driving cars home from the high school games at night. I was either trying to hitch a ride, or many a night in the winter, I remember walking home all the way across town in the snow. It was probably a good five or six miles."

Anyone who has experienced the bitterly cold winter in the Midwest understands the conditions Ely must have endured as he walked home on those nights he could not hitch a ride. It is hard to understand why Ely would not have asked someone for a lift or why someone would not have offered to take him home. Perhaps the teen was too proud to ask for help. Perhaps Quincy's white fans did not like the idea of driving into the black part of town. Whatever the reason, Ely's long walks in frigid conditions were indicative of the struggles poor blacks had to deal with in the early 1970s, even in small towns like Quincy. Ely also recalls trying to hone his basketball skills on outdoor courts during the winter months.

"Everybody [later] made a big deal of how Magic Johnson would be on the basketball courts in the winter, in the ice and rain and cold," says Ely. "He wasn't the only one. I can remember many times being out there when it was cold [and] when it was raining. Snow? You just shovel the snow off the courts. I didn't live in the projects, fortunately, [but] I *played* down in the projects because that was the nearest decent basketball court from where I lived. You hear different stories, and it brings back memories of a lot of things that you grew up with. I know these athletes nowadays have so many more opportunities, even in high school, than what a lot of us had growing up. I hope they can appreciate what they have because there wasn't much when I was growing up."

Now living in El Paso, Texas, Ely says that his time playing high school basketball for Sherrill Hanks helped prepare him for life.

"There were so many things that were gained from playing basketball there," says Ely. "Coming from Quincy, it was a good thing. I didn't know it then, but as I see things the way they are today, it truly was a good thing. It was one of those experiences that made me a better person leaving high school. It helped me many a time when I was in the military. I went into the Army after college. I was in ROTC, and then subsequently went into the Army. [I've served] 13 years and counting. I'm in the inactive reserves now. The last time I got called up was after 9/11. I'm pushing 55 now, so unless something like 9/11 happens again, I don't see myself getting recalled."

Sherrill Hanks ranks as one of the most successful high school basketball coaches in Illinois history. Hanks finished his 20 years of high school coaching with 446 wins and only 128 losses. In five years at Alton, his teams won nearly 70% of their games. Then, from 1960 to 1975, Hanks won nearly 80% of his games at Quincy, finishing 354-89. Entering the 1971-72 season Hanks' teams had won 20 or more games in 13 straight seasons. He started the streak with a pair of 20-win seasons at Alton, an Illinois town near St. Louis. Hanks' teams then won at least 20 games in his first 11 seasons at Quincy. While many observers felt his streak of 20-win seasons might end in 1971-72, Hanks had been quietly confident that his team had enough talent to surprise the naysayers. He thought Moore would have a breakout season. He believed Wisman had the goods to handle the job at the point despite his inexperience. In addition, with several players six-three or taller, he thought the Blue Devils had the size to be able to compete with most teams. Quincy did manage to win more than 20 games in 1971-72, and the Blue Devils would go on to post 20-win seasons in all 15 years that Hanks coached at the school. Hanks talked tough, and he coached tough. He intimidated many of his players, but they produced for him. His former players remember the times Hanks would halt practice to address a player who had made a mistake.

"Hell's Bells. [That was] Hanks' favorite expression," says Don Sorenson. "'Hell's Bells' this, and 'Hell's Bells' that. Now you're experiencing Hanks. People either liked him or hated him. I think all of us hated him during the season, but that turned around. We all loved him when we got done [playing]. "

Sorenson recalls Hanks would occasionally become very upset. The players knew to watch their step.

"All of us remember ducking erasers in the locker room or the whistle blowing in practice," says Sorenson. "Once in a while when he was not in his shorts and stuff for practice, he'd wear street shoes. It was the '70s, and Hanks always wore these high-heeled things 'cause he wasn't a real tall guy. We'd hear this clickety-clack comin' down the middle of the court, and we'd just be going, 'Oh, here it comes.'"

"I have a lot of admiration for Coach Hanks," says Larry Moore. "This was back in another era. *Now*, somebody would report a coach that talked like that in practice. But he just called it like it was. If you screwed up in a game, or in practice, by God, he was gonna let you have it. And he had such a high, piercing voice you just didn't want to hear it."

Hanks was a disciplinarian. Then again, most coaches in the 1960s and '70s were tough task-masters. Champaign's Lee Cabutti, Pekin's Dawdy Hawkins, and Lincoln's Duncan Reid were just a few of the many high school coaches of that era whose players experienced "tough love." For example, Reid broke a clipboard over the head of the senior captain of the 1971-72 Railsplitters during halftime of a game at Pinckneyville after the senior had blown an uncontested layup at the buzzer. That player continues to love his former coach, just as the Quincy players continue to love Hanks. It does not matter how much he yelled at them in practice and games. Hanks did not pick on any particular player or group of players, and race was never an issue with Hanks.

"He didn't care what color you were," says Rick Ely. "You got your butt chewed no matter what. I'm not kidding. I watched him chew out the principal's son so bad that we all felt like we were gonna be in tears. I think Coach Hanks was a drill sergeant in the Marines. He had the ability to yell so loud. He yelled at us so loud that the cheerleaders and wrestlers up in either of the balcony gyms were quiet. Race was not an issue. He told you that straight up, and he practiced that. I find that unique back in that era."

Hanks had gone directly into the service right out of high school. He was in the Marine Corps for three years during World War ll. Undoubtedly, some of the toughness he learned while serving in the Marines carried over to his coaching. Though tough, Hanks was soft-hearted when it came to caring for his players.

"We were given our [basketball] shoes [and] our practice uniforms," says Ely. "He was giving us multi-vitamins. If we had two-a-days, he would go to McDonalds and grab us lunch out of his own pocket. We would sit there and eat lunch on the basketball floor, watch film, and practice again. [It was] truly a program that was well ahead of its time."

When told that Thornridge coach Ron Ferguson had also treated players to food that they couldn't afford to buy for themselves, Ely said that Ferguson, Hanks, and the other coaches of that era were important role models.

"They were more than coaches then," says Ely. "They had to be coaches first. But obviously [they were] mentors, a keeper of the clan, you know, [watching over] the group of players that they wanted to see succeed. It was different. It was really a unique situation."

The Quincy players were a tight-knit group. Although Hanks kept his players on a short leash, they were able to have fun. On the back of each player's warm-up jacket was the player's nickname. The nicknames included "Weiner" for Spear, "E" for Ely, "Rosie" for Sorenson, and "Hatchet" for Gott, whose physical play and propensity for fouling was well known. Wisman, the team's sophomore point guard, wore "Rookie", and Moore wore "Pistol" as a tribute to his hero, former NCAA scoring champion "Pistol" Pete Maravich of LSU.

"I just admired Pistol Pete Maravich," says Moore. "He was way older than I was, but he was just amazing. Back then, they only had one or two games on [TV] a week. Every once in awhile you'd catch an LSU game when he was [playing]. How in the world could a guy average 44 points a game in college? And again, this was way before the 3-point shot. I really did admire him. I used to wear floppy gray socks over top of our knee-highs because that's what he did."

When the 1971-72 season began, Coach Hanks knew his team would suffer some growing pains. Quincy's youth and inexperience proved costly at times. The Blue Devils made mistakes that prevented them from having many easy games. Even the veteran players were occasionally guilty of making bad decisions. Senior center Don Sorenson made a huge mistake against Ottawa in the first game of the season in the Quincy Thanksgiving tournament. As the game was winding down, the scoreboard clock was not working, so time was being kept on a stopwatch at the scoring table. Larry Moore, who led Quincy with 24 points, had seemingly sealed the victory. Moore made a go-ahead free throw with nine seconds remaining. Although he missed a second free throw, he stole the ball from the Ottawa rebounder and scored a basket with five seconds to play, putting the Blue Devils up 66-63. Remember, this was in the days before there was a 3-point line. Coach Hanks called a time out. He reminded his players that the only way Ottawa could get three points to send the game to overtime would be if a Quincy player committed a foul while an Ottawa player was scoring a basket. Avoid a 3-point play, and the Blue Devils would win. Sorenson has never forgotten what happened next.

"Here's the situation," says Sorenson. "There was a timeout called, and we were up by three. Coach told us in the huddle to 'Just let them go. [Play] no defense.' They'd get their two points, and the game would be over. Dutifully, I ran to my spot as we lined up in a 1-2-1-1. [Ottawa's Keith Clements drives towards me, and] I hear Hanks yelling, 'Let him go!' So I began to move out of his way. Alas, he was quicker than I was, and he ran into me as I was moving. Of course, he made the shot, my best intentions gone horribly awry. Do I remember that play? Coach Hanks ensured that I would remember it for a long, long time. Man, did he chew my backside after that one!"

Luckily for Sorenson, Clements went to the line and missed the potential game-tying free throw. Quincy escaped with a 66-65 win. It was to be that kind of season for the Blue Devils. They had many close games decided in the final seconds. Six of their first seven games were decided by four or fewer points. Following the one-point win over Ottawa, the Blue Devils beat Pekin 76-74 in front of a surprisingly sparse crowd at the Quincy gym. Quincy won another thriller over Champaign Central 53-49 to win its own Thanksgiving tournament. Moore scored a total of 77 points in the three Quincy victories.

Quincy improved to 4-0 the following week with a narrow 70-69 home win over a very strong Rock Island Alleman team. Moore scored

21 points and came up with a key steal to save the game after the Blue Devils missed five consecutive foul shots in the last minute. The next night, Quincy raised its record to 5-0 by rolling past eventual Western Big 6 Conference co-champion Moline 76-57. Moore scored a game-high 25 points and made 13 of 15 from the line. Quincy outscored Moline 34-15 from the charity stripe. Moline was whistled for 30 fouls, 10 more than the Blue Devils.

The following week, Quincy suffered its first loss. The Blue Devils went on the road for the first time and fell to Rock Island 73-70. The Rocks' Jack Riley ended the first half with a basket from half-court. He also drained a 40-footer to end the third quarter. Those four Rock Island points, as well as a dozen missed Quincy free throws, proved too much for the Blue Devils to overcome.

Quincy had a full week to get ready for its next game, a December 17th home game against Chicago's Tilden Tech. However, nobody was prepared for the excitement to come. Quincy somehow found a way to win a game it probably should have lost. After being burned by half-court shots in their previous game against Rock Island, the Blue Devils needed their own miracle against Tilden Tech. With five seconds left in the fourth quarter, Bobby Jones' rebound-basket put Tilden Tech on top 84-82. Quincy's Larry Moore frantically tried to call for a time out, but the officials did not see him until the scoreboard timer read zeroes. One official, Mike Ireland of St. Louis, said the game was over. However, the other official, Harry Anderson of Pekin, said there was still time left since the horn had not sounded. Given a reprieve, Bob Spear threw a long pass to Jim Wisman, who caught the ball at mid-court and launched a shot that found the bottom of the net. The long two-pointer at the buzzer sent the game to overtime. Quincy's Kelvin Gott remembers it like it was yesterday.

"They go up by two. We call time out, and there's zeroes on the clock," says Gott. "Jimmy Wisman came in the huddle. He's a sophomore, and he had thrown the ball away to give them the lead. He's just in tears. Coach Hanks grabbed him by the shirt and says, 'The game's not over. The horn didn't go off. The game's not over. The horn didn't go off.' I'm looking at [Hanks] and thinking, 'Coach, there's zeroes on the clock. The game's *over*.' We threw the ball into Jimmy, and he hit to tie the game before the horn went off. We won it in overtime. Jimmy was on fire from then on. He took over the point guard job which allowed Larry to score [instead of handle the ball]."

Moore finished the Tilden Tech game with a career-high 38 points on 16 of 22 shooting. He still can't believe how the Blue Devils pulled out the victory that helped Quincy go undefeated at home.

"They just dominated us on the backboards," remembers Moore. "They were extremely talented. Jim Wisman threw one in from, I don't know, it was probably 47 or 48 feet. That put us into overtime. I think we won by three. They had to foul us at the end, and we made free throws."

Moore's memory is as good today as his shooting was nearly four decades ago. Neither team missed a field goal in the overtime period. Quincy made four of four while Tilden Tech made all seven of its field goal tries. While outscored from the field in the extra session, the Blue Devils won the game at the line. Moore calmly sank three charity tosses in the final seconds of overtime to give his team a 91-88 win.

Five nights later, just three nights before Christmas, Moore scored 34 points to lead Quincy past East Moline 88-73. The Blue Devils were 7-1 as they headed to Pekin to play four games in three days in the Pekin Holiday Tournament.

On December 28, 1971, Sherrill Hanks picked up career coaching victory number 400, as the Blue Devils opened the Pekin tournament with a 100-69 win over Peoria Limestone. Moore led the way with 24 points. Don Sorenson and Bob Spear added 19 points apiece. The next night Moore scored 28 in a 75-53 win over Toluca. Rick Ely had 13 points, 10 rebounds, and 3 blocked shots. Moore and Ely teamed up again the next afternoon to lead Quincy to a 71-66 win over the host Pekin Chinks. The Pekin school, which has since changed its school nickname to be more politically correct, only trailed by four with 1:48 remaining. But Moore made more clinching free throws on his way to a 30 point game. Ely had a strong defensive game and rejected six shots. After beating Pekin in the afternoon game, Quincy came back that night to hand previously-undefeated North Chicago its first loss. Moore scored 27 points in an 84-53 romp. Although the Blue Devils were the Pekin Holiday Tournament champions, Moore was the only Quincy player named to the 10-man All-Tournament Team.

The next game for the Blue Devils turned out to be one of the wildest of the season. On January 7, 1972, Quincy won 65-62 in front of 3,600 screaming fans at Galesburg. The game began with Galesburg's Brad Wilke scoring a basket at the wrong end of the floor. Also benefiting the Blue Devils were three free throws made by Larry Moore after technical fouls were called on Silver Streaks' coach John Thiel and the Galesburg bench.

Late in the third quarter, Jim Wisman knocked down a 15-footer to give Quincy a 51-50 lead. A timeout was called, and an upset Thiel was assessed a technical foul. Shortly thereafter, Galesburg's top scorer Dave Woodward fouled out. Thiel was hit with another technical. A third technical was whistled by referee Bob Brodbeck when the Galesburg bench interfered on a free throw attempt by Wisman. It was an absolute zoo inside the Galesburg gym and had been for much of the night. Earlier in the game, Thiel had shoved Moore in front of the Galesburg bench which was located underneath one of the baskets. After the third Galesburg technical foul was whistled, Thiel moved into the stands where he could view the game from a spectator's perspective. Fans threw paper and other debris onto the floor after the third technical was called. Calm was restored only after the officials threatened to call a technical foul on the crowd. It was a bad night in every respect for the home team. Four Galesburg starters fouled out, and Bob Spear put Quincy on top to stay 63-60 with a 3-point play late in the fourth quarter. The Blue Devils hung on for a hard-earned road win. Thiel not only lost the game, he was later censured by both the Galesburg High School principal and by the Illinois High School Association for his unsportsmanlike conduct.

The next night, Quincy returned home to its gym at Thirtieth and Maine to play Edwardsville. Moore poured in 38 points to equal his career high. Quincy shot 74% in the first half and led 54-33 at halftime while cruising to an 89-67 win.

The Blue Devils had only one game the following week, but it was a tough one at Thornton High in Harvey. Thornton had finished third in the Pekin Holiday Tournament, and both teams had made sure to scout their future opponent. Now squaring off two weeks later, the Blue Devils trailed by six with less than 1:30 to play, but Moore sparked a late comeback. Quincy pulled even, and the game went to overtime. The Blue Devils, though, were unable to steal the win on the road. Thornton prevailed 77-76. Thornton's Carl Richardson scored 23 points and teammate John Delya scored a season-high 17 to help the Wildcats improve to 12-4. Despite Moore's game-high 33 points, Quincy fell to 13-2. It was a disappointing loss for the Blue Devils who insist they were not intimidated by the hostile crowd and tough surroundings in Harvey.

"We had to have a police escort in and out of Thornton," says Larry Moore. "They said, 'These guys, they'll take pot shots. There's gangs up here.' They ended up beating us in overtime. That was one of those games that just pissed me off because we never should have lost the game. But the black-white thing, it never really entered into it. I looked at a guy, and I didn't really see a skin color. I was trying to size him up to see how I was going to score on him. That was the first thing I looked at. It wasn't so much a color thing."

"We were told that it was gonna be really hard," remembers Kelvin Gott. "We were gonna be under guard, you know, protected going in, [and] protected going out. I don't think any of us thought anything about it. We had a number of black guys in school playing with us. [But], I remember there definitely was a police presence as we went in and out of the building to go play."

The Blue Devils' next game against Rock Island Alleman was played in front of nearly 7,000 fans at Wharton Field House in Moline. Alleman, ranked fourth in the AP and UPI polls, had won 12 straight games since losing by one at Quincy six weeks earlier. During the winning streak, Alleman had won the Pontiac Holiday Tournament, considered by many experts as the strongest of all the Christmas tournaments played statewide. It looked like the Pioneers were going to gain revenge for their early-season loss to Quincy. Alleman led by 11 points in the third quarter, thanks to the scoring of Andy Sottos who scored a game-high 30 points on the night. But, the Blue Devils came back in the fourth quarter. Mike Sellers came off the Quincy bench and banked in an eight-footer to pull his team within one. In the final minute, Sellers hit a pair of free throws to again pull the Blue Devils within a point, this time with only 38 seconds remaining. An Alleman turnover gave Quincy a chance for the final shot. Larry Moore, struggling through one of his worst shooting nights of the season, just 9 of 29 from the field, found the ball in his hands with the game on the line.

"We're down one, and Wisman is bringing the ball down," remembers Moore. "I flashed around up by the top of the key. I knew there wasn't much time left, so as soon as I caught it, I didn't even have time to square myself [to the basket]. I turned to my left shoulder. I was maybe, 20 or 21 feet away. I just went up. I remember one of these [Alleman] kids [fouled me]. It wasn't just a subtle foul. I mean this kid knocked me sideways. [Peoria official] Bob Brodbeck blew the whistle. He was right there. I heard him blow it. The Alleman kids are running all over the floor. Fans are running onto the floor. I said, 'Mister Brodbeck, you got that didn't you?' He goes, 'Larry, I got it. Relax.' You get to know those refs. He worked a lot of those Western Big 6 games. After he told me that, I said [to myself], 'Well, I'm gonna be shooting free throws. I'm not even gonna go walk over by our huddle.' I sat down, crossed my legs, and sat at the top of the key where I was going to shoot my free throws. It just irritated those Alleman fans to no end. They just got louder and louder. They actually made an announcement, you know, trying to clear the floor saying that there was a foul on the last play, and there's gonna be two [foul] shots. These fans were just razzing the officials so bad. Nobody else was out there except me and Bob Brodbeck. Bob handed me the ball, and when he handed it to me, he said, 'Stick this in their ass.' That's exactly what he said. That is no joke."

Brodbeck was one of the most respected referees in Illinois in the 1960s and early '70s. He worked the 1964 Illinois state championship game in which Pekin beat tiny Cobden to end the Apple Knockers' Cinderella season. He also called many major college basketball games throughout the Midwest. But this night, the unruly behavior of the Alleman fans had apparently got under his skin.

Bob Spear's younger brother, Jeff, a member of the Quincy sophomore team at the time, was watching the craziness on the floor at Wharton Field House. The younger Spear is still amazed by the confidence Moore displayed while waiting to shoot the potential game-tying and winning free throws.

"He sat at the free throw line while they were clearing the floor because they thought they'd won," recalls Jeff Spear. "Rather than hanging with the team, he just went out and sat down at the free throw line. As far as the other teams, everybody *hated* him [since] he was such a hot dog. His hair would get all greasy, and he had those thick glasses. People just *hated* him. They really did."

Moore sat on the court, in the midst of the celebrating Alleman fans, knowing that he was going to break their hearts as soon as he was allowed to shoot his free throws. He looked over at the Quincy bench and smiled like the cat that swallowed the canary. Steve Goers, Coach Sherrill Hanks' top assistant during the 1971-72 season, remembers what happened next.

"We're down one, [needing] one to tie, two to win." says Goers. "There's no time on the clock. If you've been in Wharton Field House, there are 6700 people, and it's dark all the way around the floor. As soon as this happens, everybody's over at the benches. Larry is out there with the two officials. Don Morris, a Hall of Fame coach who was at Alleman for years, gets up and walks between the two benches right by the scorer's bench. There's an aisle that goes underneath those upper deck bleachers that goes right into the locker room. He's not standing by his bench. He's standing right there in the middle. Larry says the game's over. He's talking to us saying, 'It's over. Don't worry about it.' They give the ball to Larry, and he swishes the first one. Don Morris walks out. He just left. Then Larry made the second, and it was over."

Moore, sporting a nearly 90% career free throw percentage, calmly ignored the screaming, arm-waving fans and stuck a dagger in their collective heart. His two free throws with no time on the clock gave him 29 points and lifted Quincy to a 74-73 victory over Don Morris' Alleman Pioneers. Moore enjoyed sitting on the court in the midst of the madness knowing that he would soon disappoint those celebrating Alleman fans. It was the kind of pressure situation he relished.

"Don Morris had a comment in the Moline Post Dispatch," recalls Moore. "He said, 'If I had known then what I know now, I would have made an announcement and had the fans be completely silent. I wouldn't have had them yell or scream. I think that would have bothered him more than fans getting up screaming and throwing things, and waving through the back of the [see-through] backboard."

The Blue Devils had escaped with the win, but they had not yet escaped with their lives.

"After I hit the two free throws, everybody's going crazy," says Moore. "I'm just walking off the floor. There is a narrow [aisle]. It couldn't be more than maybe three or four feet [wide] where the visiting team is going in [to the locker room]. We're going in, and I'm trailing most of my guys. Kel Gott was there too. He had picked me up and just squeezed me to death. I remember seeing something come out of the stands. I remember ducking. Gott reached up and grabbed hold of it. It was a purse. It had kind of a long strap on it, and it was attached to a heavy-set older woman. He pulled this thing, and he was yanking her out of the stands with it. The police came over. Coach Hanks came over. It was just so damn funny because this lady was going to smack me in the head with her purse."

One night after the wild win over Rock Island Alleman, Moore set a new career high by pumping in 43 points in an 89-75 win over Proviso East. Moore made 14 of 24 from the field and 15 of 16 from the line. Assistant coach Steve Goers still remembers Moore's big game.

"Larry was the type of guy that, when he went off in a game, there was no stopping him," says Goers. "We were playing Proviso East. Glenn Whittenberg was their coach. Larry ended up with 43 points. This was before the 3-point line. He was like 15 out of 16 from the free throw line. [At one point], Glenn had taken a time out. He was originally from southern Illinois, and you could hear him yelling at his kids," continues Goers, imitating Whittenberg by speaking in a slow, southern drawl.

"'Damn it. He'll miss a couple from the field, but he don't miss from the free throw line. So, quit foulin' him!'"

Moore's 43-point performance tied the school record set by Bruce Brothers who played for Quincy in the early 1950s. You would think the biggest scoring game of his career would be one of Moore's fondest memories. However, the memories of that night are bittersweet.

"I played a really good game that night," says Moore. "But, I need to be honest with you. This is one thing that I may never forgive Coach Hanks for, and I know he did it on purpose. There was probably 1:45 left when he took me out of the game. I sat almost two minutes. The game was still going on when they made the announcement that I had tied the all-time single game scoring mark. Everybody is patting me on the back. Later, I kept thinking, 'You know, if I had stayed out on the floor, there was nobody else out on the floor that could even guard me.' We ended up winning by 14 or 15, but the game was in question until the very end when they had to keep fouling, and we kept hitting our free throws. I guess that makes me mad. I know that sounds like rotten grapes, but when a guy is having a game like that, I don't think you take him out when he *ties* the damn record. Leave him on the floor to break it, or maybe try to get *50* [points] which I think would have been amazing."

Moore upped his season scoring average to 30.1 points when he poured through 39 points the next week in an 88-81 win over Galesburg. For the third straight game, the Blue Devils trailed at the half. But, Moore's 25 second-half points rallied his team to its 16th win in 18 games. Bob Spear also had a big night scoring 23 points. Quincy's win over Galesburg came on the same night Lincoln fell at home to Springfield, the Railsplitters' first loss, after starting the season 17-0.

The next night Springfield played host to Quincy, and the Senators nearly pulled off another major upset. Moore was held to only 15 points, his lowest output of the season to date. Thankfully, the Blue Devils got a timely contribution from senior Don Sorenson. He had a game-high 21 points and 12 rebounds. His tap-in of a Moore miss with four seconds left snapped a 62-62 tie. Quincy was on top to stay. Moore added a free throw after a technical foul was called against Springfield for calling a timeout when it had none available. Quincy snuck past the Senators 65-62. Springfield fell to 5-10 on the season, though the Senators were now playing better than their record would indicate.

"If you played them in their gym, they were a good team," says Moore. "That was a tough place to play. Joe Freymuth was like a six-five, six-six kid. He's one of the few kids that I remember blocking my shots. I hardly ever got a shot blocked. He came out of nowhere and just swatted one. I remember him saying a few uncomplimentary things to me."

Quincy raised its record to 18-2 the following week by beating Springfield Lanphier 95-83. Bob Spear, averaging 7 points a game, exploded for a career-high 36 points, 16 coming in the first quarter. Spear also guarded Lanphier's All-State candidate Jim Kopatz.

"That was my best game that year," says Spear. "[Kopatz] was a man. I mean, there was a guy with a big hairy chest [who] weighed about 210 pounds."

Kopatz scored 20 points but fouled out early in the fourth quarter. Larry Moore was held to only 17 points, far below his average, but the Blue Devils' leading scorer recorded 13 assists against the Lions. Jim Wisman had 11 points and 9 assists, and an active Rick Ely played less than half of the game but finished with 12 points and 9 rebounds.

The Blue Devils travelled to Centralia the following night, and Moore scored 25 points to lead the Blue Devils to a 79-72 win. Sorenson had 24 points and 12 rebounds. Spear added 17 points, as Quincy won its sixth straight game. The Blue Devils were ranked number two in the state by coaches voting in the UPI poll but fell to fifth in the AP sportswriters' rankings.

Quincy's modest winning streak would end the next week. In a game played at the Wharton Field House, Moore was held to 13 points which would be his lowest output of the season. Not surprisingly, the Blue Devils lost to Moline 68-55. Jim Wisman scored a team-high 18 points, but the loss meant the Blue Devils would have to win their last two conference games to finish tied with Moline for the Western Big 6 championship.

Win, they did. Moore scored 28 points to go over the 1000 point mark for his career while leading Quincy to an 87-56 home win over Rock Island. The victory gave the Blue Devils their 20th win of the season. Sherrill Hanks' string of 20-win seasons had reached fourteen including twelve straight at Quincy. The next night at East Moline, Moore scored 27 of his 30 points in the first half to lead Quincy to an 80-64 victory. The win gave the Blue Devils a share of the Western Big 6 Conference title and gave them a record of 21-3 with one game left in the regular season.

The Blue Devils laid an egg in Collinsville in the regular season finale. Spear, Sorenson, Ely, and Wisman all fouled out in an 80-75 loss to the Kahoks. Rich Knarr, who entered the game averaging 21 points a game, scored a game-high 33 for Collinsville. The lone bright spot for Quincy was the 32 points scored by Larry Moore. He passed Bruce Brothers' 1952 Quincy record of 694 points in a season. Moore finished the regular season with 702 points. He would go on to shatter the record since he played eight more games in the postseason tournament. Assistant coach Steve Goers remembers the trip to Collinsville. He said it was an important turning point for the Blue Devils.

"We went down to Collinsville for the first time [to play] in their new purple gym," says Goers. "Virgil Fletcher was still coaching. They were running the press, and they had some good players. [After the loss to the Kahoks], the [Quincy] players, coaches, and staff got together and said, 'We don't want to be remembered as the team that lost at Collinsville. We want to put this together and do what we need to do.' And we did. It was a team effort."

"There were unique personalities," remembers Goers. "Jimmy [Wisman] was a happy-go-lucky guy. Certainly Larry Moore was a very, very, *very* intense competitor who didn't want to be around his teammates before a game. When we rode in the bus, nobody would ride next to him. He was in his own world. He was very, very competitive. He's a great guy, and everybody [in Quincy] loved him. It's just that he was really uptight before a game."

Quincy hosted its own regional, and in the first tournament game, the Blue Devils played one of their worst games of the year. Quincy struggled but defeated Springfield Griffin 65-52. Wisman and Spear scored 16 points apiece on a night Moore scored only 14, just the fourth time he had been held under 20 points since the start of the season.

In the regional final, Moore bounced back to score 26 points, and Kelvin Gott scored a career-high 22. They were the only Blue Devils to score in double figures in a narrow 74-73 win over Jacksonville. Defensive stalwart Rick Ely scored only two points but blocked eight shots.

In their first game at the Springfield sectional in the State Armory, the Blue Devils beat Mattoon 81-63. Larry Moore scored 31 points. Ely had a big offensive night with 18 points. Quincy was anticipating a matchup with Springfield Southeast in the sectional final, but the Blue Devils never got a chance to play the team from the state's capitol city. Springfield Southeast, the team that had upset Lincoln in the regional final, was knocked off by Decatur Eisenhower in its first game of the sectional tournament.

"We had been working on the pressure that Springfield Southeast was supposed to be bringing," says Larry Moore. "Then, we hear they got beat, and we're playing Eisenhower. I remember our coaches saying that we had to call some coaches to get a scouting report because we were not scouting Eisenhower."

Against Decatur Eisenhower in the sectional final, Quincy had to rally from 11 points down with 6 minutes remaining. Wisman, Sorenson, and Ely all fouled out, but seldom-used Kimber Gay came off the bench and delivered the late-game heroics. The senior guard made a key steal with about two minutes to play. He then drained a 24-foot jumper with 50 seconds left to give Quincy an 84-83 lead. Moments later, there was a scramble for the basketball, and Gay forced a jump ball. In the era prior to alternating possessions on held balls, Gay and the Eisenhower player went to the jump circle. The official tossed the ball into the air, and Gay won the tip. Quincy had possession with a one point lead. The Blue Devils held on to win 87-85. Though Moore scored 27 points and Spear added 20, it was eighth man Kimber Gay who made the difference as Quincy won to advance to the "Sweet 16".

"Jimmy [Wisman] fouled out, and we had Kimber Gay on the floor," remembers Blue Devils' assistant coach Steve Goers. "He had started the first games of the year. Then Jimmy took his place. [Kimber] played sparingly the rest of the year. He wore a big brace on his knee. He came in [against Eisenhower] when it was a very, very tough situation. He hit a big shot. Then, there was a loose ball on the floor. There was this scramble, and he came up with a jump ball situation. He won the jump and came down and hurt his knee. He didn't play again the rest of the year. But, he won the jump in the last minute of play. We got control and ended up winning that game."

Gay was just the latest in a long line of Quincy heroes. Throughout the season, one of the players would come through with a big scoring night, a great effort on the boards, or a huge defensive play to help the Blue Devils win. Gay, in his last game in a Quincy uniform, and in his final seconds as a high school basketball player, put his team in the "Sweet 16."

Interestingly, the Blue Devils had reached the "Sweet 16" without defeating a ranked team. When the brackets were first announced, it seemed likely that Quincy would have to battle 4th-ranked Lincoln in the sectional final and would likely face 2nd-rated La Salle-Peru in the super-sectional. However, both of those teams were upset before the Blue Devils had to play them. When Lincoln bowed out in its own regional, Kelvin Gott realized his team's chances of getting to Champaign had improved tremendously.

"I remember seeing those scores from the regional the next morning [in the newspaper]," says the Quincy forward. "We were looking to figure out how to beat Lincoln. We knew Lincoln was gonna be there. [Springfield] Southeast won, and we went, 'Holy Cow! We have a chance of going all the way to Champaign!' There were some tough teams, but [we thought], 'We can really go if Lincoln's not in the way.' And that's the way it actually turned out for us."

To get to Champaign and the state tournament quarterfinals, Quincy would have to beat 16th-ranked Kankakee Eastridge. The Kankakee team had won its last 16 games and had the same 23-4 record as Quincy. But, the Blue Devils picked up their 24th victory of the year by beating Eastridge 76-70. Moore led the winners with 27 points in front of 6.800 fans at the Horton Field House on the campus of Illinois State University in Normal.

"Eastridge was very confident," remembers Moore. "They talked crap with us the entire game. At that point, I thought we really had a chance to do something, to bring some hardware home."

The super-sectional victory sent Quincy into the "Elite Eight" at Champaign. Just three nights later, Quincy met Chicago city champion Crane Tech in the late Friday night game at the Assembly Hall. Moore was ice cold before turning red hot. The streak-shooter missed 10 of his first 11 shots but then made 15 of his last 20. Once he got rolling, Moore lit up the Assembly Hall for 36 points in an 87-71 victory.

In the semifinals against Aurora East, the two teams set scoring records that still stand. Blue Devils' assistant coach Steve Goers remembers being shocked at the amount of offense displayed that Saturday afternoon.

"In the semifinal game, we played one of the most unbelievable games in the history of basketball," says Goers. "In the Assembly Hall, we're playing East Aurora with Ernie Kivisto against Sherrill Hanks, which was a story in itself since they were two fabled coaches. There was a tremendous amount of scoring. We were walking across the court at halftime, and I looked up [at the scoreboard], and I said, 'Coach, we can't keep this up.' It was 50 to 50 in a *high school* game. I'll be damned. It ended up being 107-96. We kept it up, and East Aurora didn't quite keep it up."

Later that evening, the Blue Devils would be trying to keep up with defending champion Dolton Thornridge in the Illinois Class AA final. Few people had predicted the Blue Devils would be the last team with a chance to shoot down the Falcons. The Quincy players might have been a little surprised, but Kelvin Gott had the sense that something magical was happening as his team worked its way through the state tournament.

"Yeah, [I had] lots of *destiny* kind of feelings," says Gott. "The first thing that I remember was Lincoln losing to [Springfield] Southeast because we knew how good Lincoln was, and we didn't know if we could match up. We were pretty sure we could win the regional, but Lincoln was gonna be there in the sectional. Then, Lincoln lost to Southeast, and I remember thinking that fate is lending a hand. Then, we had a super-sectional game [against Kankakee Eastridge] where Kimber Gay came in for two minutes. We were down, and he hit two 28-footers. He was a pure shooter, slower than the devil, but a great shooter. Then, he tore up his knee and never played again. He brings us back [though], and we win that game. Bailey Howell from the [Boston] Celtics shows up in the locker room because he knows Coach Hanks somehow, or maybe he was recruiting Larry. You're seeing a Boston Celtic [and] you're like, 'Holy Cow! What's going on here?' You had this feeling that there was something out of this world going on."

Gott truly believed that Quincy was destined to win the state championship when, Saturday afternoon in that high-scoring win over Aurora East, he looked up in the jam-packed Assembly Hall and was able to make eye contact with one of his biggest fans.

"I did my usual thing and fouled out with about three minutes to go. But, we were up, and I knew we had it," recalls Gott. "I look up in the Assembly Hall. I've never played anywhere that big in my life. I look up, and there's my *dad*. He's lookin' at me, and I'm lookin' at him. How in the hell do you pick your dad out of 17,000 people [in the] first place you look in the stands? I had no idea where he would be sitting, and there he was. He gave me a thumbs-up [sign]. [I thought], 'All right, we're gonna win this whole thing. He knows it too.' That kind of stuff happened all the time. It's that feeling that everything is going your way."

But Quincy was still one victory away from capturing the first Illinois Class AA championship. The Blue Devils would face, by far, their toughest opponent of the season. The defending state champions from Dolton Thornridge were looking to cap their perfect season. It would be a game that players on both teams would remember for the rest of their lives.

CHAPTER 21

I Was On Top Of The World

THE PLAYERS ON QUINCY AND Thornridge had little time to recharge their batteries. Only hours after recording semifinal wins, the players needed to somehow find the energy to return to the Assembly Hall and compete for the state championship. Thornridge likely had a bit of an advantage. The Dolton school had played the first Saturday afternoon game which gave the Falcons two additional hours to rest while the Blue Devils were fighting for their lives against Aurora East. Also, while the Falcons' win over Peoria Manual was hardly a walk in the park, the Thornridge players did not have to expend nearly as much energy as the Quincy players had to use to win the second semifinal game. Thornridge coach Ron Ferguson admits that being the top team in the tournament bracket gave the Falcons an advantage.

"We played the first game all the time," says Ferguson. "We were in the top of the bracket. We played the first game Friday afternoon, then the first game Saturday afternoon. There's no question. That's an advantage, especially on Saturday because of the time element between [games]. You have a little more rest. Quincy had played such a hard game that afternoon. I knew we'd be a little bit fresher than they were. But, you take your team to the motel and tell them to lay down and rest. Hell, they're not doin' that."

The Thornridge players stayed at the Assembly Hall to watch the first quarter of the Quincy-Aurora East game and then headed back to the motel where they watched the rest of the game on TV. Most of the Falcons did lie down and try to rest. Ernie Dunn, though, was a bundle of nervous

243

energy. Most of his teammates had been through this the previous year. They understood how to handle the anxiety prior to a championship game. Dunn had been at Thornton when Thornridge won its first state title. He was experiencing all of the emotions for the first time.

"That afternoon, we were supposed to go back to the room and take a nap," says Dunn. "But, I didn't sleep at all. I just walked around. We stayed at a Howard Johnson, and I just walked around Champaign all afternoon. [It was] not the jitters. I'm not sure what it was. I was just restless."

Dunn's thoughts were on the upcoming game. He had been told he would defend Quincy's top scorer, and he was getting into the proper frame of mind to shut him down.

"I knew my whole game was to stop Larry Moore," says Dunn. "That's all I focused on [just] keeping up with him. I didn't care what happened on offense. My job was to chase him around and make sure that I either had help with him or [that] he didn't get off a good shot because he could shoot. He was a very streaky shooter."

While taking his walk, Dunn thought about what his teammate Greg Rose had said to him while they sat together and watched the first quarter of Quincy's semifinal game. Rose understood that Dunn loved a challenge. He challenged his friend to shut down the Blue Devils' star that night.

"I pep-talked Ernie because we saw Larry just rip'em off [scoring points]," says Rose. "The team he played before us, Larry was something else. We had our eyes on him. I was sitting with Ernie, and I said, "Ernie, that's who you got. You can't let him rip'em off like that, man.' He says, 'No problem.' Ernie was so hyped."

"Oh yeah, that was always the speech to me," says Dunn. "Whoever was on [the opposing] team scoring tons of points, it was always me that had to guard him. So, that's when I told Greg I knew what to do 'cause I'd watched him play. I saw him play in those semifinals, and that was like my fourth time watching him."

Dunn was clearly in the right frame of mind to slow down Quincy's top player. He had begun preparing for this moment two months earlier.

"One little secret I had about him," says Dunn, "that same year Quincy played Thornton. We didn't have a game that night, so, I went to watch my brother [Otis] play. Larry Moore literally shot them out of the gym. He scored like 30 something, almost 40 points (actually 33). So, I'd seen him play before, and I knew exactly what he'd do. He'd run behind a pick and try to get to the opposite side of the court where the ball was. They'd swing it back to him where he'd run off a pick. I'd watched that game, and he just lit up my brother. I dogged him after the game and said, 'How did you guys let this guy burn you?' [Moore] had a lot of pimples on his face, and I said, 'He's the shortest guy on the court, the ugliest guy on the court, and you guys couldn't keep up with him.' My brother called me when we were going to play them, and he said, 'Now see what *you* can do with him.' I told my brother, ' I can't get embarrassed like that.' So, that's how I knew [how to defend him]. I'm not saying I stopped him. I just made it difficult for him in the championship [game]."

While Dunn walked off his nervous energy, the Quincy players had almost no time at all to recuperate from their hard-fought game against Aurora East.

"We played that second game in the semifinal," says Larry Moore. "I remember getting back to the Ramada Inn. We had to be back at the Assembly Hall in like two-and-a-half or three hours. So, we didn't even eat a meal. We ate some oranges. I remember lying down, but we were all just joking around. We were really loose."

"We were having a blast," says Quincy forward Kel Gott. "We were just absolutely having a ridiculous amount of fun. I mean, we scored 107 points in the afternoon and set all sort of state records. I think a lot of them still stand. When you're playing like that, God, it's not even like you're playin'. Everything's clicking. At one point in the quarterfinal, Larry Moore hit like eight shots in a row and none of them were layups. He was just on fire against Crane. If Larry missed a shot, Don [Sorenson] got a rebound and put it back in. It somebody broke down on defense, somebody else took a charge. It was just all working for us. I didn't think there was any way they could beat us."

"I don't think we thought we were gonna lose," says Blue Devils forward Bob Spear. "I don't think we had enough sense to know the reality [of] what was gonna hit us. As a kid, [you believe] anything can happen."

"We had just played Aurora East and set like 26 state records," says Quincy center Don Sorenson. "That was really like a championship game. I think everybody put everything into that game just for the opportunity to play Thornridge. Everybody went back [to the motel] after that game. We had like four hours or something like that. [You] just shut your eyes and, all of a sudden, you had to get up and go again."

***

Before Thornridge and Quincy tipped off the Class AA championship game, Peoria Manual and Aurora East played for third place. Manual seemed to have rebounded from its disappointing afternoon loss to Thornridge. The Rams led at halftime 40-31. However, after scoring 20 points in each of the first two quarters, Manual scored only 26 points in the entire second half. The Rams' All-State center Mike Davis finished with 27 points and 10 rebounds, but Aurora East rallied to win 74-66 behind the 24-point effort of Greg Smith. Peoria Manual captain Wayne McClain remembers it was difficult for his team to get over its semifinal loss earlier that day.

"No disrespect to Aurora, but our guys didn't want to play for third place," says McClain, who scored 10 points in the loss. "I just think we was so let down that we didn't get past Thornridge. They was a nemesis to us. They had dominated us all the way through [our careers], and that was just a bad feeling. I just wish that we would have had a different mindset going into that game and went on and won it. But, I guess our guys just didn't have the energy to play."

When told that many years later Buckner boasted to the author that he would have kicked his ass had Thornridge played Lincoln that year, McClain was quick to respond.

"Yeah, and he ain't lyin' either," laughs McClain. "And you know what? Then, [you] just get in line because that's what he did to everybody."

With back-to-back losses on the final day of the high school basketball season, Peoria Manual finished 26-8 and had to settle for the fourth place trophy. Aurora East finished the season 28-4 and took home the trophy symbolic of a third place finish in the state tournament.

***

While the Peoria Manual-Aurora East game was being played in front of more than 16,000 fans at the Assembly Hall, the Thornridge and Quincy players were inside their respective locker rooms getting dressed for the most important game of their young lives. Sure, the Falcons had won the championship the year before, but this was a chance for Thornridge to make history.

Inside the Thornridge locker room, the players slipped into their home white uniforms with "THORNRIDGE" spelled across the chest in light blue block letters just above the numerals. Quinn Buckner pulled the #25 jersey over his head knowing it would be the last time he would do so while representing Thornridge High School. Fellow senior Boyd Batts' donned his #31 jersey and slipped on his uniform shorts, which in 1972 were indeed "shorts" barely covering the buttocks. And, as the third senior tri-captain put on the Falcons' #23 uniform, he was struck by the realization that he was about to play with his friends for the final time.

"It dawned on me, and maybe Quinn and Boyd at the same time, that this was it," says Mike Bonczyk. "This is the last game of our high school basketball careers."

The Falcons' locker room was very quiet as the players dressed in near silence.

"It was always quiet," remembers Bonczyk. "There was no music, no headphones, no horseplay, no nothin'. When you came in the locker room, it was time to get dressed. We had a game mentality. When we walked into the locker room, it was about business. It was time to play, [time to] put on another show. There's no reruns, okay? This is the show. It's a Broadway musical that's gonna appear one night, and one night only, and you gotta catch it when it's in town."

With the Falcons the heavy favorite to win the championship, Thornridge administrators took steps to make sure that the school would be seen in the best possible light during the victory celebration after the game. Several players recalled the Thornridge principal talking with them about not doing anything to embarrass the school.

"Yeah, he came in and talked to us," remembers Boyd Batts. "We asked him, 'How [are] you supposed to celebrate?' He said, 'Just cut the net and all that stuff.'"

The school officials were concerned because of what had happened after the Falcons won the 1971 state championship game. Some observers were offended by the Thornridge players' jubilant celebration on the court of the Assembly Hall.

"We had a little bit of a problem," says Coach Ron Ferguson. "That's one of the reasons why [good sportsmanship] was a little bit more emphasized by me. Having never experienced that before, I had no idea how our kids would react after the title game with Oak Lawn. We had a lot of black kids, and when they were taking photos during the trophy presentation, they weren't very quiet. You know, they weren't respectful [in the minds of some people]. They were talkin' and laughin' and high-fiving, [and] doin' all that. Naturally, a lot of people, and most of them were probably Caucasians that thought, '[Look at] those black kids jumpin' around like that.' So, we didn't get a real good reputation. There were a few columnists that made remarks like, 'As well as they behaved on the basketball court, when the game was over, they did not behave as well.' A little of [our emphasis on good behavior] was in reaction to what happened that first year."

The Thornridge celebration in 1971 was very mild compared to the way high school, college, and professional players often act today. There was no chest-pounding and no grandstanding for the crowd. The kids had jumped for joy, smiled and laughed, and acted a little silly. One of the players, Quinn Buckner, feels the criticism was unfair.

"We were going to be on our best behavior the second time around," says Buckner. "I think it was a little bit more of, uh, narrow-mindedness than anything because you got *kids* out there. At no point was anybody consciously trying to show up the game, the people of the game, or anything like that. It was some people who were probably disappointed that we won, so therefore anything that we did was not going to be excused. I'm not sure anybody was exactly pulling for us to win either time."

As Buckner and his teammates slipped on their warm-up jackets and laced their basketball shoes, the same scene was being played out in the Quincy locker room. The Blue Devils had not lost a game all season while wearing their home white uniforms. But, in the championship game, they would wear their dark blue road jerseys with "QUINCY" emblazoned in white block letters across the chest above bright white numerals. Quincy's shorts were also dark blue. "DEVILS" was spelled out top to bottom down the side, lined by double white stripes. Each pair of shorts was secured with a belt buckle on the front of the pants. Larry Moore, hoping to play well in his last game as a Blue Devil, picked up his #33 road jersey, slid it over his head, and tucked it nearly into his uniform's tight-fitting shorts. Fellow senior Don Sorenson, put on his #15 jersey for the last time. As Bob Spear slid on his #21 jersey, he thought about where he had been one year earlier. He was in Champaign, not as a player, but as a spectator sitting high above the court in the Assembly Hall.

"I was there the year before as a sophomore sitting in the 'C' section," says Spear. "To watch that team when they won the [1971] state championship, I couldn't envision that a year later I'd be on the floor [playing] against those guys. I'm a skinny kid from Quincy, not even making the varsity, and then a year later, I'm gonna be playin' those guys. What chance do you have against those guys? They were a super team as juniors."

Larry Moore had also been in attendance to watch Thornridge win its first championship.

"I knew these guys were good," says Moore. "I remember going to the state tournament my junior year. We were probably in the 58th row up in the Assembly Hall. I had my binoculars. I remember thinking, 'Boy, these guys are good, and hell, their whole team will be back.' But I thought we had a chance. I never remember thinking that we could lose a game."

Surreal as it was for Spear and Moore to be getting ready to play against that team they had seen win the championship the year before, there was no doubt in Kel Gott's mind about which team would be taking home the first-place trophy. Coming off his tremendous semifinal game, Gott had been informed by Coach Sherrill Hanks that he would start that night in the title tilt. The junior forward was optimistic as he tied the laces on his shoes and prepared to go into battle.

"I was probably as naïve as any human on the planet," laughs Gott. "I thought we were gonna win it. I don't know that many of us felt that way, but I really thought we were [going to win]. I couldn't believe that anybody could beat us after the way we played in the afternoon."

With Gott starting, that meant Rick Ely would come off the bench. Ely, who had started Quincy's last 12 games, can't recall Coach Hanks explaining why he was making the change in the starting lineup.

"I don't remember him talking to me about it at all," says Ely. "I probably wasn't playing to the caliber that he thought I should. Of course, that's what coaches do. They put the best people in all the time. It probably hurt me as far as trying to get in sync with the game. I still say, to this day, that he's probably one of the best coaches I ever played for. To be able to take a bunch of guys from a small town and put them together and make them play at a very high level was pretty remarkable."

Ely was hoping for the best against Thornridge, but in retrospect, he thinks he and his teammates were a little overwhelmed that they were playing this great team in the state championship game in front of a sellout crowd and a statewide television audience.

"I think we were kind of in awe at where we were by then," says Ely. "We beat a lot of good teams on the way to get there. But, Quincy was playing at a high school level. Dolton Thornridge was playing at a college level. That's how good they were."

When the players from both teams took the court to begin warming up for the championship game, Quincy star Larry Moore knew right away that he had not recovered from the high-energy game he and his teammates had played just hours earlier.

"We played the Friday night game and then the Saturday afternoon game," says Moore. "We were walking out on the floor, and I very seldom ever felt tired. But, my legs felt tired. During the warm-ups, I noticed that all of my shots were just a little bit short. Even though you want to say you weren't tired, I think we were."

"I wish Larry could have had fresh legs against Thornridge," says Bob Spear, "just so he could have shown what he was capable of. Larry was just a super player. Obviously, we were banking on him."

Thornridge coach Ron Ferguson did not know Moore was feeling fatigued. Maybe he would not have been as concerned about having to play a team he had just seen put up 107 points in its semifinal win.

"Sometimes you look at another team, and you get scared," says Ferguson, "because they look so good that you don't know if you can compete that well with them."

The Thornridge players were not scared. Nee Gatlin remembers how he felt as warm-ups concluded and the Assembly Hall's scoreboard clock ticked down towards the opening tip.

"Just the anticipation, you know, closure," says Gatlin. "[You think about] the last year for the seniors, the final game. Focus. There was no kind of bantering, no bragging. There was no cockiness or nothin'. From Coolidge [Elementary] to Thornridge, we always won. So, we knew what we had to do."

CLASS AA STATE CHAMPIONSHIP IN CHAMPAIGN (SATURDAY NIGHT, MARCH 18, 1972) QUINCY

The Assembly Hall was completely sold out as fans from around the state came to witness the phenomenon that was Thornridge basketball. 16,128 fans were in the building that night. No Illinois high school basketball game has had as many people in attendance since Thornridge and Quincy took the floor to start the Class AA championship game.

FIRST QUARTER

The officials selected to work the game, Robert Burson of Western Springs and Otho Kortz of Oak Lawn, waited patiently for the players to break out of their respective huddles. As the players moved toward the center of the court for the jump ball that would start the game, Thornridge point guard Mike Bonczyk looked around and soaked it all in.

"Awesome. Awesome," remembers Bonczyk. "Everything's on the line, the repeat championship, the undefeated season. You're playing a quality team that can light it up. Larry Moore can light it up. They got some players that are good. Everything has been put into play up to this point. This is what we strived for all year long. We were seniors. This is it, the last game. What are you gonna do? What do you want to be remembered for? You're talkin' about 16,000 people [at the game]. To come out and play in that type of atmosphere, it was awesome."

Fellow senior Boyd Batts walked to the center jump-circle. Just before the ball was tossed into the air, he remembered what his mother told him before he left Phoenix for Champaign.

"My mother couldn't go because she couldn't hear or talk," says Batts. "She said, 'When you go to play, you make sure you play the best, and show me what you are made of.' I went out to play as hard as I could."

It was loud in the Assembly Hall. In homes around the state, fans were settled in front of their television sets to watch the first Illinois Class AA basketball championship game. Veteran announcer Tom Kelly was calling the play-by-play. He was assisted on the broadcast by Jim Bolan, Vince Lloyd, and Evanston High School coach Jack Burmaster.

Boyd Batts of Thornridge and Don Sorenson of Quincy leaped high as the ball was tossed in the air, and the game was on. Batts won the tip, sending it back to Mike Bonczyk. Not long afterwards, Thornridge took the first shot of the game, a 16-footer by Quinn Buckner. The ball bounced off the rim and into the hands of Quincy's Kel Gott. Larry Moore missed the Blue Devils' first attempt, but the ball went out of bounds off Buckner, and Quincy retained possession. Moore missed again from 15 feet but hurried back on defense to intercept a Buckner pass intended for Ernie Dunn. Quincy's young point guard, Jim Wisman, missed an open 17-foot jumper from the left wing, and Greg Rose of Thornridge hauled in the rebound. Thornridge went to the other end and scored. 68 seconds into the game, Batts rattled in a short jumper in the lane. The Falcons would lead the rest of the night.

Both teams were struggling to find the rhythm offensively. Rose scored a rebound-basket on a Bonczyk miss to put Thornridge on top 4-0. Two and a half minutes had passed before Quincy got on the scoreboard. Wisman beat Bonczyk on a crossover dribble and rose up from the right side of the free throw line to score over Buckner who was late getting there to help on defense.

After Batts and Bob Spear exchanged free throws, Thornridge held a 5-3 advantage. The Falcons doubled their lead when Rose hooked a lob pass over Quincy's Gott to Buckner who caught the ball on the low blocks on the left side of the lane and laid the ball off the glass and in. Thornridge went to its full-court press after the made basket, and Moore lost the ball as he tried to dribble through four Falcon defenders. Bonczyk picked up the loose ball and led the Falcons on a 3-on-2 fast-break. Rose was flying down the left side with Buckner on the right. Bonczyk passed to Buckner, who momentarily fumbled the ball in the lane, before regaining possession and shooting a successful five-foot bank shot from the left side of the lane. It was 9-3 Thornridge and, with 4:37 left in the first quarter, Quincy coach Sherrill Hanks called a timeout, hoping to slow the Falcons' momentum.

After Hanks calmed his players, the Blue Devils got their second basket of the game. Gott took a pass at the high post, made a strong move past Batts, and shot the ball off the backboard and through the hoop. Rose then missed a right-side jumper at the other end. Dunn grabbed the offensive rebound but missed the put-back. Gott grabbed the rebound for Quincy. Batts made a steal at the defensive end giving the ball right back to the Falcons. Thornridge worked the ball around before Batts missed a 12-foot jumper from just outside the lane on the right side. Once again, Dunn beat the Quincy players to the rebound, and Dunn scored while being fouled by Wisman. Even though Dunn failed to complete the 3-point play, Thornridge led 11-5.

Quincy was looking for a basket, but Sorenson was sent to the line when he was fouled by Rose. This was in the day teams were awarded a single free throw attempt prior to getting into a one-and-one bonus opportunity. Sorenson made the foul shot to trim Thornridge's lead to five.

The Falcons then tried to work the ball inside to Batts, but when Rose could not make the entry pass, he took one dribble toward the line and rose up for an 18-foot jumper that swished through the net for a 13-6 Thornridge lead, its largest of the game to that point.

Quincy, though, was not going to go quietly into the night. Buckner was called for traveling after hauling in a defensive rebound on a Wisman miss. The Quincy point guard then inbounded the ball to Moore who caught the ball in rhythm and swished an 18-foot jumper from the right wing with 2:51 left in the first quarter. Spear made a steal at the defensive end, and Moore came right back with a jumper from the right side of the lane to make it 13-10.

Thornridge again tried to go inside to Batts. The Falcons' six-seven center was fouled from behind by Sorenson who picked up his second foul of the game. The Batts free throw made it 14-10. After the made foul shot, the Falcons were quickly in their 1-2-1-1 full-court trap. Quincy barely got the ball across the midcourt stripe in time to avoid a violation. The ball was sent ahead to Gott, whose 5-foot baseline jumper rattled around the rim and in. Quincy was within two at 14-12 with 1:58 left in the period. It was the last time the Blue Devils would be that close.

The key play of the game came moments later. Thornridge worked the ball to Buckner who took a jumper from the left wing. Buckner's shot was long and bounced off the right side of the iron, high into the air. The ball went to the top of the backboard and appeared to touch a basket support, but there was no whistle. When the ball came down, it bounced off the hands of Batts onto the court, where it was picked up by Dunn. The guard quickly put the ball up and in while being fouled by Sorenson. It was the senior center's third foul of the game, and there was still 1:38 left in the first quarter. Dunn added the free throw to complete the 3-point play and give Thornridge a 17-12 lead. Sorenson left the game six seconds later, and Quincy would sorely miss him. Dunn's 3-point play was the start of a 21-3 scoring run for the Falcons, part of an even-larger 43-9 scoring blitz that assured Thornridge its second straight state championship.

Rick Ely replaced Sorenson with 1:32 left in the quarter just before Spear missed a free throw. Buckner grabbed the defensive rebound and dribbled quickly to the other end. He rose up at the free throw line and fired a jump-pass to Batts who had beat Ely down the floor. Batts scored on a reverse-layup to give his team a 17-12 lead. After the basket, Thornridge again went to its 1-2-1-1 full-court press. Dunn, causing Quincy all kinds of problems, knocked Moore's inbounds pass out of bounds. Moore again tried to inbound the ball, and again, Dunn was there to create havoc. The Thornridge guard knocked the ball to Buckner, who took one dribble towards the basket before rising up and banking in a jump shot. It was 21-12 in favor of Thornridge.

Moore sank a free throw for Quincy, but Buckner came right back with a 17-foot jumper from the left side and the Falcons had their first double-digit lead. After Ely was called for travelling with 35 seconds left in the period, Bonczyk saw Batts work himself free between Ely and Gott. A lob inside to Batts resulted in another basket and it was 25-13.

Quincy got the last points of the first quarter when, with three seconds remaining, Spear rebounded a Moore miss and laid it in. Thornridge led 25-15 after the first quarter.

There was no question that the momentum had swung in Thornridge's favor when Sorenson went to the bench with his third foul. Nearly four decades later, the Quincy players still believe the ball hit the basket-support and should have been whistled dead. The Blue Devils would have had the ball and a chance to tie. Instead, the game began to slip away from them.

"They took a shot that went up and over the basket and hit the guy wire," says Bob Spear. "Everybody in the place saw it except the refs, and Burson was right there. The rebound comes down, and Rose or somebody gets a layup. Don fouls him, so it's 17-12 instead of 14-12. It would have been a hugely bad non-call in *any* game. It was pretty visible. It actually went over the backboard and came back. That's kind of when it started and, you know, it ended quickly."

"We were going back and forth scoring with them and staying with them," says Kel Gott. "Don going out sure didn't help."

"Don Sorenson already had two fouls," remembers then-assistant coach Steve Goers. "There's a shot that hit the basket and bounced up and hit the wire above the basket. It bounced down and hit the floor. Nobody moved because they thought it was a dead ball. A Thornridge kid picked it up and put it in. Sorenson reacted, and fouled him. That made it 17-12, and Sorenson had to sit down. When the first half was over, the game was over. That was a young [Quincy] team, and he was one of two senior starters, him and Larry. Don was the biggest kid we had, and he was strong enough to hold off Batts inside. It might have been more psychological than anything else. Now we're down 17-12, and our center's on the bench with three fouls. [It was as if the players said], 'What are we gonna do?'"

"We used Don as a safety valve," says Larry Moore. "If you threw the ball to him, he had a good chance of grabbing onto it because he wanted it. Rick, being a junior at the time, was kind of a timid player. We didn't really want to throw the ball to him because we figured he's either gonna get [it] stripped or he's gonna fumble it around. They're gonna be going the other way shooting layups. When Don went out, we lost our safety valve. Then, we ended up trying to make passes we couldn't make, and they just picked us apart with that press. They scored three or four straight times, and the rout was on. Nothin' felt quite the same after that."

SECOND QUARTER

The second quarter began with a jump ball between Ely of Quincy and Batts of Thornridge. Batts tipped the ball back to Bonczyk giving the Falcons the first possession of the period. The Thornridge point guard dribbled quickly across the mid-court line and passed ahead to Greg Rose who was open along the left baseline. Rose drove hard to the basket but missed a right-handed layup. Batts grabbed the offensive rebound and laid it off the glass and in, making it 27-15 in favor of Thornridge. After a Jim Wisman miss at the other end, Ernie Dunn hit a bank shot for the Falcons. With his team down by 14 and feeling the game starting to slip away, Quincy coach Sherrill Hanks called a timeout. Hanks was not the only one who could sense the Blue Devils were in trouble.

"I was probably more pissed off than anything," says Larry Moore. "I was a very emotional player. I remember in the huddle, I was just *mad* thinking, 'How could we let this slip away like this?' Actually, it didn't slip away. It rolled away. That was just one of those games we were just outmatched, period."

Since Sorenson left the game, the Blue Devils had been outscored 12-3. The senior center was frustrated at being relegated to observing from his courtside seat as Thornridge pulled away.

"You're feeling helpless when you're on the bench," says Sorenson. "If you're a player, you don't wanna be on the bench."

While Sorenson continued to sit following the timeout, Moore was promptly whistled for a traveling violation. At the other end of the court, Batts took Ely to school. Ely was defending Batts at the high post. Batts backed into Ely who stumbled backward trying to draw an offensive foul. Instead, Batts dove down the lane and Bonczyk found him with a lob pass on the left side of the basket. Batts rose up and his 4-foot fall-away baseline jumper found nothing but net. Batts had scored 12 points in a hurry.

"Boyd could shoot," says his teammate Greg Rose. "I was saying, 'Don't let him get warm.' When one guy's hot, we would feed him. Boyd got hot in that championship game."

The score was 31-15, and Quincy continued to struggle. Ely was fouled but missed the free throw. The next time down, Moore missed a jumper from the left side of the lane while being contested by Dunn and Rose. The long rebound came out to Bonczyk, and the Thornridge point guard quickly pushed the ball up the court. Bonczyk took just one dribble, then saw Dunn and Rose streaking up the floor, Dunn on the right, Rose on the left. Bonczyk passed ahead to Dunn who caught the ball about eight feet from the basket. When Jim Wisman came up to defend, Dunn dropped a bounce pass to Rose who laid the ball softly off the glass and in. Ely, flying back in a vain attempt to help on defense, hit the front of the rim as the ball dropped through the net. When the whistle blew with 6:30 left in the period because of Ely's goaltending, play was stopped momentarily. Sherrill Hanks could wait no longer. He sent Sorenson back into the game. The Falcons had just completed a stunning 21-3 scoring run, most of it coming with Ely on the floor in place of Sorenson.

"I think we were shell-shocked," says Ely. "I know Coach was pretty frustrated too that we couldn't execute a lot better against a team like that. This was a mind-boggling experience trying to get our game on, and we just couldn't do it. For me, it was a lot of personal frustration, frustration that I couldn't play better. [I was frustrated] that we got this far, and I wasn't playing how I was used to playing. I think I was harder on myself as to why I couldn't get up and down the court and do the things that I had been doing all season."

Looking back after nearly four decades, Thornridge coach Ron Ferguson analyzes just how important Sorenson was to the Quincy team.

"You remember what the rebound statistics were?" asked Ferguson. "26 to 6, or something like that, at the half. I think that's where they really missed him. We might not have gotten as many offensive rebounds. We got a lot of second chances right under the basket. I think that it definitely hurt them because he was probably their best rebounder. They were getting only one shot. We were getting more than one shot. I'd like to think it wasn't going to make a difference in who won the game, but it might have kept the score closer in the first half which gives a team a little more incentive."

Though Sorenson was back in the game, the Falcons continued to pull away from the Blue Devils. After a Quincy turnover and a Wisman miss, Thornride looked to score again. Rose rebounded the Wisman shot and dribbled the ball to the other end of the floor. He passed to Bonczyk at the top of the key. Bonczyk quickly passed to Buckner on the right side 20 feet from the basket. Buckner zipped a two-handed chest-pass to Batts who rose up from the right corner and launched a long one. The ball hit the front of the rim, bounced off the glass, and through the hoop. Batts had 14 points and Thornridge led 35-15.

Thornridge was dominating at both ends of the court. Batts rejected a jumper by Kel Gott. As the ball sailed out of bounds under the Quincy basket, Greg Rose leaped high into the air, grabbed the ball, and threw it back over his head to Batts. Batts gave the ball quickly to Buckner who threw a two-handed chest-pass the length of the floor to Bonczyk. The pass was a little long, and Bonczyk caught up to it with his momentum carrying him out of bounds under his own basket. He threw a no-look, over the shoulder pass towards Buckner, but Wisman knocked the ball out of bounds. A foul was called on Larry Moore who bumped Bonczyk as he flew over the end-line. Two Bonczyk free throws made it 37-15.

Quincy then worked the ball inside to Sorensen, but his layup attempt was rejected out of bounds by Batts. After the Blue Devils inbounded the ball, Moore missed another jumper. Buckner grabbed the rebound and dribbled quickly in the direction of the Thornridge basket. As he crossed the mid-court stripe, Buckner zipped a two-handed chest-pass to Rose who had already sprinted into the right corner. Rose swished a 15-footer to give him 10 points and his team a 39-15 advantage.

Quincy finally got its first points of the second quarter with 4:57 left in the period. Moore was fouled in the act of shooting by Dunn, and the Quincy guard sank both free throws.

At the other end, Rose threw a lob inside to Batts whose easy layup gave the Falcons a 41-17 lead. The Quincy coach called another timeout with 4:39 remaining in the half. Sorenson says, try as they might, the Blue Devils just didn't have much energy left after having to play so hard earlier in the day.

"Everybody wanted to do better," says Sorenson, "and wished we had a week to recover [from the afternoon game]. But, the tank was just dry. I remember the speed of the game. I thought, 'Okay, I gotta get here.' But the legs are saying, 'What, are ya nuts?'"

The Blue Devils' woes continued after the timeout. Moore was short on a jumper in the key, and Batts was fouled at the other end while attempting a put-back. Batts sank both free throws to up the lead to 43-17.

Wisman drained a 15-footer for Quincy's first field goal of the second quarter with 4:10 left in the period. But, Batts rebounded a Buckner miss and laid it in. At that moment, Batts had 20 points, one more than the entire Blue Devils' team.

Wisman missed a runner at the Quincy end, and moments later, Buckner made one of the most impressive and athletic plays of the championship game. Rose missed a short jump shot, but Buckner crashed to the basket, leaping high into the air over Moore who failed to box out. Buckner ripped the ball down with his right hand, and in one fluid motion, quickly switched it to his left hand. He laid it off the glass and in while being fouled by Gott. Buckner added the free throw. His 3-point play gave him 11 points and his team a 48-19 advantage.

Rick Ely, who had come in for Spear before Buckner's free throw, swished a short left-handed baseline jumper to make it 48-21 with 3:11

left in the half. Ely picked up a personal foul moments later when he was trying to box out Batts on a shot by Bonczyk. Batts, his slender, muscular legs spread wide, toed the line, dipped down, and then lofted the first free throw cleanly through the net. He also made the second, and Thornridge led 50-21 with almost three minutes still to play in the first half.

Quincy's Gott was called for shuffling his feet, and Thornridge continued to dazzle. Rose swished a corner jumper. Moore missed a shot for Quincy. Then Batts leaped high over Wisman to secure an offensive rebound before rising up and swishing an 8-footer on the left baseline. Ely had a shot partially deflected by Rose, and Gott picked up his third foul while going for the rebound. Batts made the front end of the one-and-one. He badly missed the second free throw, but Ely did not block out and Rose grabbed the ball. Rose stuck it back in the basket. Thornridge led 57-21 with more than a minute and a half remaining in the second quarter. The Rose basket capped a 43-9 scoring run by the Falcons over a stretch of less than eight minutes.

Radio announcer Lanny Slevin was covering the game for WPRC in Lincoln. Slevin has seen or called play-by-play of every Illinois high school championship game since Thornridge and Quincy met in 1972. Slevin could not believe his own eyes while watching Thornridge score 43 points in what amounted to less than a full quarter of a high school game.

"That's crazy," says Slevin. "You can't even imagine that, you know, unless you're playing some junior high team. You're playing in a championship game. I mean, that just doesn't happen."

"We shot the ball from outside pretty good during that run," remembers Thornridge coach Ron Ferguson. "We were throwing them in from the bus. We normally didn't shoot the ball that well from the outside. And we didn't have to because we were able to get the ball pretty close to the basket. It was just like a steam-roller. The shots were going in. When they kept hitting them, I said [to myself], 'Just don't coach anymore. You might be better off.' We shot better than we normally do. We usually got a lot of layups and easy baskets off the press, but we were shooting the ball from wherever. It was just one of those games where everything goes right for one team, and at the key time, didn't go right for [Quincy]."

"There was a reality like, 'Oh, God,'" says Quincy forward Bob Spear. "It's not like we were playing bad. We weren't doing anything wrong. We'd just miss a shot, and they'd go down and power it in. A couple quick passes and Batts was dropping it in the hole. We realized that there wasn't anything we could do. It wasn't like we could fix what we were doing wrong. It was that they were doing everything right. You're just getting steam-rolled by probably the greatest team ever. It's conceivable that if you took Larry out of the equation, they had the five best players on the court. In a pickup game, Larry probably would have been picked third behind Buckner and Batts. They had all the horses."

Quincy added a pair of free throws, one by Gott and one by Sorenson, before Sorenson sank a baseline jumper at the buzzer to pull Quincy within 31 points at the break. Thornridge led 57-26, and Batts was leading the way with 25 points.

"I was on top of the world," says Batts. "It seemed like I couldn't miss. I felt like I could do anything."

"I hope they don't take offense to this," says Quinn Buckner slowing to make his point. "Boyd was kickin'... their... butt. Oh, I'm tellin' you, he was wearin' 'em out! He was making anything and everything. He was rebounding the ball. He'd bring it down and shoot it. Somebody would shoot and miss, and he'd get a tough rebound in traffic, go back up, and put it in the basket. He'd make kind of a no-look pass. I mean he was flat-out wearing them out."

HALFTIME

What does a coach say to his team that trails by 31 points at halftime in a state championship game? Quincy's Sherrill Hanks jokingly told reporters after the game that he was looking for a back exit so he might sneak his team to the bus. Exactly what he did say has never been revealed. But, when you ask the Blue Devils' players, they all have a slightly different recollection of what transpired in the locker room at halftime.

"I played college ball for four years and have been involved in sports in different ways," says Bob Spear. "It was the only time where at halftime that we actually conceded. We went in [to the locker room]. There were some guys yelling, 'Come on! We can do better than this!' [Coach] Hanks just said, 'Quiet down. Take it easy. We don't have a chance.' You know, it wasn't in a bad way. It was like the reality [of the situation]. We were getting throttled."

"I think it was more like, 'Let's just try not to embarrass ourselves,'" says Don Sorenson. "He may have said, 'Let's have some fun out there. Hey, let's mix it up. Let's go press them.' I think it was in that context versus [Hanks saying], 'Well guys, we're out of it.' He knew what was going on. I think everybody did. We didn't want to speak it. You know, one thing I learned from Hanks is you work hard and don't give up, and you're gonna achieve a whole lot more than expected. It was that drive to be just absolutely the best you could be."

Forward Kel Gott fesses up to being the player who was trying to fire up his teammates inside the Quincy locker room at halftime.

"Oh, there was some hot-headed junior who knew we could come back and win," laughs Gott. "It was me. [My teammates] had gotten in there before me, and I went in and hit a locker and said, 'Damn it! We can do this!' Coach Hanks was right on my heels. He was right behind me, and I didn't know it. I yelled, 'We can come back! Get your heads up!' Coach Hanks said, 'Damn it, Kelvin. Sit down.' It was like he said, 'You've had a great year. We're gonna go home with a nice trophy.' It was over, and everybody knew it was over but me."

"After we all filed in, I remember Kel [being fired up]," says Larry Moore. "I was just totally amazed. We were down at least 30 at halftime. Kel really got fired up about stuff, and he was screaming, 'C'mon, we can get back in this. These guys are not that good.' And that's when Hanks said, 'Kel, sit down. Shut up. These guys *are* that good. We could play them ten times and might never get closer than 20 points.'"

"At halftime, we just said, 'Go out and do the best you can. Just play every possession," remembers then-assistant coach Steve Goers. "But, we knew that it was basically over."

THIRD QUARTER

As Don Sorenson and Boyd Batts moved to the center-jump circle to start the second half, the two players gave each other a "soul handshake" and offered good luck wishes. Sorenson won the tap, but the ball went to Rose. Thornridge scored just 17 seconds into the third quarter. Mike Bonczyk swished a 19-foot jumper, and the Falcons led 59-26.

But, the Blue Devils did have some fun in the third quarter. They pressed and forced several Thornridge turnovers. Quincy more than held its own in the period. In fact, the Blue Devils outscored the Falcons 26-21 in the quarter. Yet, the outcome was never in question. Any hopes of a Quincy comeback ended when Gott fouled out less than three minutes into the second half. Though his statistics were not as impressive as they had been in that afternoon's semifinal, Gott had been active at both ends of the floor. He hated the idea of having to leave the game with so much time left.

"I was really irritated," remembers Gott. "We're down 35, and I'm headed for the bench. Somebody grabbed my shoulder. I'm pissed, and I've got my jaw set. I turn around and it's Quinn Buckner. He grabbed my shoulder to turn me around and shake my hand. I mean, I knew how good he was. We all knew what a phenomenal player he was. I had no idea he was that kind of a human being. He went out of his way and came over to get me, a lonely peon junior who just got his ass kicked. Here he is coming to tell me, 'Great job' and to congratulate me. Wow, it was an eye-popper for me at the time."

One eye-popping play midway through the quarter brought the Thornridge fans to their feet. Buckner stripped the ball from Spear just as the Quincy forward was starting to go up for a shot. Buckner frantically dribbled from the back court into the front court. He passed off the dribble, zipping the ball between Moore and Ely, into the hands of Bonczyk who was racing down the right side. Bonczyk caught the ball and took one dribble to the top block on the right side of the lane. He stopped, and with his back to the Thornridge basket, threw a behind-the-back, no-look pass to Rose who sank a short jumper over Sorenson. The Assembly Hall crowd rose as one to cheer a play that, in 1972, was far ahead of its time. That play gave Thornridge a 70-37 advantage. In the final 3:33 of the quarter, Buckner played a key role, either scoring or assisting on every Falcons' point. Although Quincy scored as many points in the third-quarter as it had in the entire first half, Thornridge led 78-52 heading to the final period.

FOURTH QUARTER

The fourth quarter of the 1972 Illinois Class AA championship game was all about making history. There was no doubt that Thornridge would soon be crowned the king of Illinois basketball for the second straight year and that the Falcons would extend their state-record winning streak to 54 games. It was a certainty that many state championship game records would fall as well. When Nee Gatlin blew past Don Sorenson for a layup to make it 86-56, Thornridge broke the record for most points in a state championship game set by Mt. Vernon in 1950 in an 85-61 win over Danville. Not long thereafter, Boyd Batts took a feed from Buckner and scored to break the record for title-game scoring by both teams. Batts' bucket with 5:47 left gave the Falcons a 90-58 lead and broke the record of 146 points scored by Mt. Vernon and Chicago Du Sable in 1954.

Midway through the fourth quarter, Thornridge coach Ron Ferguson began removing his starters. He took them out one at a time so they could receive individual recognition from Falcons' fans at the Assembly Hall. Ernie Dunn was the first to leave the game. He enthusiastically slapped the palm of Gatlin and was greeted in front of the Thornridge bench by Ferguson who wrapped his arms around the junior guard and gave him a big hug.

Greg Rose soon left the game after scoring a basket which gave him 26 points and Thornridge a 96-63 lead. When Bill Redman checked in for the high-scoring junior, Rose slapped the open palms of Dunn who met him in front of the team bench. Ferguson, standing beside Rose, put his left arm around his player's waist, then with his right hand, reached around and patted Rose on the chest. As Rose turned around to find his seat on the bench, an exuberant Ferguson slapped him on the buttocks two times. Yes, in the 1970s, a coach could pat a player on the butt to show appreciation for a job well done.

Of the Thornridge starters, only the three seniors were still on the court. Batts was next to leave the game. After Batts hit a fade-away jumper to give Thornridge a 98-63 lead, Keith Hutchinson subbed for the six-seven center. Boyd had wanted to make his mother proud, and he finished with a championship game record 37 points to go with 15 rebounds. As he left the court, the senior big man clenched his fists and threw both arms high into the air. He slapped hands with Buckner before reaching the bench where he was met by Rose and Dunn. Coach Ferguson, who had gone through many trials and tribulations with Boyd through the years, buried his face into the front of Batts' jersey and gave his player a huge hug.

Point guard Mike Bonczyk was soon replaced by Dave Anderson. As he left the court, Bonczyk walked towards Buckner with his arms out and palms facing upward. Quinn raised both of his arms then brought them down quickly to give his friend a hard two-hand slap. As Bonczyk moved towards the Falcons' bench, Quincy players Jim Wisman and Larry Moore offered handshakes. Greg Rose then gave his teammate a "low-five" slap on the palm of one hand. So-called "high-fives" were not yet popular. Players in that era usually extended one hand with the palm up while saying, "Gimme five" or both hands extended with palms up while saying, "Gimme ten" to describe the number of fingers each person would involve in the hand-slap. Before Bonczyk took his seat on the bench, he walked to Ferguson and wrapped both arms around his head coach. The two enjoyed a long embrace while Ferguson patted Bonczyk on the back.

Buckner, the team's most celebrated star, was the only Thornridge starter still in the lineup. With Ken Kremer waiting at the scorer's table to check in for the senior All-American, Buckner scored on a pass from Hutchinson to give Thornridge a 100-65 lead. Moments later, Buckner made an eight-foot bank shot, giving him 28 points to go with 11 rebounds and 7 assists. Twenty-four seconds later, with 1:01 remaining, Bill Redman made a baseline jumper to round out the Thornridge scoring. To get Buckner out of the game, Ferguson had Redman foul a Quincy player in order to stop the clock. A happy Buckner ran to the bench and jumped into the arms of Bonczyk as the two friends shared an emotional embrace for the last time as teammates. Dunn and Rose then patted Buckner on the back while Coach Ferguson joyously hugged his star. Batts walked over and slapped Buckner's hands. Quinn then walked to his seat on the bench with both arms raised high. He was holding up the middle and index fingers of each hand signaling "V" for victory, or perhaps signifying the number "2", symbolic of a second straight state championship.

When action resumed on the court, Quincy coach Sherrill Hanks walked in front of the scorer's table and went to the Thornridge bench to congratulate his friend, Coach Ron Ferguson. The clock stopped with 37 seconds left, at which time Joe King and Fred Knutsen checked in for Thornridge which meant that every eligible Falcons' player would appear in the box score of the championship game.

At the same time, Larry Moore walked towards the Quincy bench while receiving a nice ovation from the fans at the Assembly Hall. It wasn't Moore's finest hour. He had made only 5 of 22 from the field to finish with 15 points which was well below his season average. Even so, players on both teams understood that Moore had given everything he had while playing his third game in 24 hours. By the time Moore reached the Quincy bench and plopped down in his chair, Quinn Buckner had left the Thornridge bench and was there extending his right hand. He was followed closely by Dunn, Rose, Bonczyk, and Gatlin who also offered congratulatory handshakes. The impromptu act of good sportsmanship was appreciated by the Quincy star.

"Yeah, pretty classy," says Moore. "That just shows classy those guys were. I don't think I would have been able to think happy, or had the shoe been on the other foot. I think I would have been there and too emotional, to gather the other four starters and [that]. They say, 'Congratulations on a great season.' But, there was no trash talking. played the game the way it should be played. T

I think that's a reflection on their coach too. I just think that was a classy group of guys."

"I remember it vividly," says Kel Gott, who was on the bench when the Thornridge players congratulated Moore. "I was stupefied. I'd never seen anything like it. It was the coolest thing. It gives me goose-bumps right now thinking about it. They were phenomenal and a classy group of people. It was just impressive. They beat the hell out of you then told you how wonderful you were. And you believed that they were thrilled you came out to compete. They knew they were better than you, but they [acted like] they were thrilled that you were there. It was cool. It just speaks well to what kind of people they were. A lot of that carried over for us the next year at Quincy High School. We made a point of being that kind of team. When the game was over, or if somebody had been special, we made a point of going over and talking to them after the game. It was very much inspired by what happened that day against Thornridge."

"Man, you appreciate effort," says Thornridge sixth man Nee Gatlin. "If the dude on the other squad is giving everything he's got, [you] respect it. That's all it was about, respect."

"Larry Moore had a tremendous state tournament," says Thornridge guard Mike Bonczyk. "I think it was led by Quinn. He said, 'Hey, let's go down there and congratulate him and give him his respect.' That was something we did on our own. It was appropriate to acknowledge a guy that was a heck of a basketball player. That's the bottom line."

"He had played his heart out all those other games," says Falcons' guard Ernie Dunn. "It wasn't sympathy. It was more like, 'You had a great ar. You're still a great player. We want to congratulate you.'"

"It also had a lot to do with Coach Ferguson," says Bonczyk. "I think s what's lost in athletics today. Everything is about me, me, me, of we, we, we. Even when I coached, it was, 'Shirttails stay in. I ed any lip. I don't need frowns. A guy makes a call, that's it. You it because that's what you're supposed to do.' When we played [at , we were very driven. We were very businesslike. Fergie always be classy in everything we did. The response to Larry Moore e floor, the way we dealt with officials' bad calls, [playing ils out, that's just part of a class way to do things."

Ron d to death when they did that," says Thornridge coach eir o did not have anything to do with it. They did that on ear e started out the year, we talked about the situation state championship game in '71. I told them, 'You're the defending state champions. People are gonna watch you as closely as they can. We want to keep a good reputation on the floor, off the floor, and in the public. So we're going to be good people. We're gonna be good sportsmen. We're gonna congratulate other players. We're not gonna let happen what happened last year.'"

The final points of the game came when Quincy's Bart Bergman banked one in from straightaway at the buzzer. The final score was Thornridge 104, Quincy 69. No Illinois high school team had ever scored 100 points in a state championship game, and no team has done it since.

Buckner says you should not be fooled by the lopsided score.

"We just pounded them," says the former Thornridge star. "But listen, they were a good team. Frankly, sometimes the stars align."

POST-GAME

After his players quietly and respectfully accepted the 1972 Illinois Class AA championship trophy, Coach Ron Ferguson met with reporters to talk about his team's impressive performance. Even though the Falcons had acted with proper decorum during the trophy presentation, just as they had during the game, the media found something to criticize. It was not a knock on the players. It was a subtle knock on the head coach of the two-time state champs.

"I did get a question in the media room after the game about not getting the [starting] players out a little faster," says Ron Ferguson. "I wanted to take them out one at a time and give each a chance to get an ovation with Buckner [coming] out last. If I had to do it over again, I'd probably take them all out at the same time. I probably made a mistake [in judgment]. There weren't enough whistles to get the clock stopped to make the substitutions as quickly as I wanted to make them. I thought I could get them out a lot faster. In retrospect, I probably goofed up. I probably shouldn't have done it that way. [Quincy coach] Sherrill Hanks never ever said one word about the score or anything about that. He was a class guy."

The Thornridge players were thrilled to have finished the season a perfect 33-0. Boyd Batts had a double-double in each of his last four games, from the "Sweet 16" to the championship game. Indeed, he had saved the best for last. Batts made 14 of 18 shots from the field and 9 or 10 from the line. He set a championship game record with 37 points. The

37 points still remains the most points scored by a player in a Class AA championship game.

"It was very special," says Batts. "The reason it was so special was because we were undefeated. I wanted to go out with a bang. That way, I know I did somethin' that a lot of people hadn't done."

"You have to understand that Boyd wearing them out was big [for the team], but it was also important for Boyd," says Quinn Buckner. "And I *knew* it was important to Boyd. I don't think he'd ever say it, but I always thought that he felt he was given less credit [for our success] because of the credit that was passed on, candidly, to *me*. So, I always had a sense of, 'I gotta make sure Boyd's okay.' I didn't ask for the credit, and I wasn't trying to get the credit. But, he felt like he needed the credit. I'm telling you, from a pure skills' standpoint, Boyd was the better player. Therefore, the logic suggests he should have gotten more credit for what we did. I was sensitive enough to Boyd to understand that. So, for him to have that good game made it so much easier on the rest of us."

It is easy to understand why Buckner has received so much credit for the success of the Thornridge team. His numbers in the title game were awe-inspiring; 28 points on 11 of 17 from the field, 6 of 6 from the line. He had 11 rebounds, nearly twice as many as Quincy's top rebounder in the game. Buckner's 7 assists were three more than the Blue Devils had as a team. Batts and Buckner were both sensational in the championship game, but so was Greg Rose. Rose made 13 of 21 shots for 26 points. He pulled down 8 rebounds which helped Thornridge outboard Quincy 49-28. Mike Bonczyk and Ernie Dunn had less impressive statistical lines, but both were key to the Falcons' victory. Bonczyk, who had 4 points and 5 assists, displayed great floor leadership. Dunn, who had 5 points and 6 rebounds, did a stellar job of defending Quincy shooter Larry Moore. Holding the Blue Devils' sharp-shooter to 5 of 22 from the field was one of the most important factors in the Falcons' win.

"Ernie had the length and the size to make Moore shoot over him," says Bonczyk. "And I had the opportunity to guard him a little bit. If he was bringing the ball up the floor, I could challenge him, make him work, tire him out. Moore was the key guy we were concentrating on. That's why Ernie drew the assignment, and Ernie did a tremendous job."

The Falcons had it all; talent, athleticism, and a maturity that exceeded their years. It was hard to believe Thornridge was a high school team.

"We were in awe," says Quincy's Bob Spear. "I was in awe with what they could do. We were watching men to a large extent. I was a skinny junior. Larry was a five-nine senior. We were watching men play basketball at a level that we'd never seen before. It seemed like they scored every time they brought the ball down. They would make nice crisp passes. They would move it around until the guy had a layup. Then, they just went back to the other end of the court or set up their press. They were very businesslike, and they took care of business. They were mature, well-coached men out there. It was an honor to be out there [playing them]. You were lucky if you were in the other bracket because you had a chance at second place."

Second place was pretty good for a team that was supposed to be a year away from being a championship contender. Nearly four decades later, the coaches and players reflect back on the feelings of disappointment.

"There wasn't a lot of disappointment," says Quincy head coach Sherrill Hanks. "That team was so talented, with so many good players. It was just realistic that finishing second was pretty damn good."

"You're always disappointed when you get to the championship game and don't win it," says Quincy assistant coach Steve Goers. "But, only two teams ever get there. We were young and had great aspirations and high goals for the future."

"I'd say I got over it immediately," says Spear, who scored 12 points in the final. "Honestly. I think people from Quincy would look at that as like we won the state tournament that year. We did everything we possibly could. We won every game that we possibly could win. The last one wasn't one of them."

Spear thought it was great just to have a chance to have played the team regarded by many as the best team in Illinois high school basketball history.

"To be eliminated by Thornridge, there wasn't any disappointment,'" Spear continues. "It was like you got a chance [to play against greatness]. You actually got to go out there and play a practice round with Tiger Woods or something. You got to go out there and do it. Once you got out there, you realized you didn't belong out there, but you had earned the right to be out there. So, there was no disappointment."

"I think being a junior on the team was different because we knew we had another year to go," says Kelvin Gott, who had 5 points and 6 rebounds before fouling out of the championship game. "I remember getting back home, and they had a big pep assembly to welcome us back. The guys who were juniors and sophomores were saying, 'Hey, we're going back next year. [Buckner and Thornridge] won't be there next year. We can get back [to Champaign].' We knew we were losing Larry, but everybody knew Jimmy Wisman was going to be really special. We were losing Donald [Sorenson], but we had me to replace him. We had a couple young kids that really could play. We had that to look forward to, so it wasn't as disappointing for us. I think it really hit Larry hard because, God, he had been such a great basketball player. To finish up on that stage and have the kind of game he had, I think it bothered him a lot."

"It bothers me more now than it did back then," says Larry Moore. "I see now that even though we had a really good run up to the state title game, we got lucky. We got lucky with some wins and some teams that we thought we'd be playing who were better teams than the teams we played that ended up getting beat. Lincoln, [Springfield] Southeast, La Salle-Peru all ended up getting beat. It makes me mad because any other year, [with no Thornridge], we probably would have won the state title."

"I think the embarrassment was there," says Don Sorenson, who scored a team-high 16 points in the final, two points more than Jim Wisman. "We're going, 'This isn't who we are.' We weren't really competitive in that game, so we felt a little cheated by it. I think that piece gnaws at ya. You know three games in 24 hours, that's a pretty good feat for anybody. I guess I wish we'd had some time to recover and really had an equal footing. But, as far as feeling bad about being beaten by that team, I think [Coach] Hanks enabled all of us to get through that. He said, 'You know, they would be a competitive collegiate team.' And they were [that good]. Holy cow, everybody on that starting five could jam the ball. That was unheard of in high school back in those days."

"It took a couple months [to get over the disappointment]," says Rick Ely who had 5 points and 3 rebounds in the championship game. "I thought about it a lot, about what we could have done, if anything. It took a couple months, and then life goes on. I think what helped us was our trip back to Quincy. I still remember that just outside of Jacksonville, Illinois, is where the line started forming. All of our supporters, our fans and students, met and formed a car caravan that followed us all the way back to Quincy. I remember looking out the back of the bus. You could not see the end of the line for miles."

Also dealing with disappointment in March of 1972 was Thornridge sophomore basketball coach Ron Bonfiglio. He, of course, was thrilled that the Falcons completed their perfect season and won a second straight state title. But Bonfiglio could not attend the game at the Assembly Hall that fateful night.

"I never made the game," says the man who would serve as Thornridge's Athletic Director for 16 years starting in 1979. "I was in a hospital bed. I was 33 years old, and I ended up with stomach surgery in February. I watched the state championship game with [Thornridge sophomore] baseball coach, Carlos Medrano, while in my hospital bed. I fell asleep. When I woke up, he said, 'You won't believe what we did.'"

CHAPTER 22

The Best Team Ever

NEARLY FOUR DECADES AFTER QUINN Buckner, Boyd Batts, Mike Bonczyk, Greg Rose, and Ernie Dunn raced through their undefeated and rarely challenged season, the question is often asked. Has there ever been an Illinois high school basketball team as good as the 1971-72 Thornridge Falcons? Each March, when another state champion is crowned, basketball fans ask, "Well, how does this team compare to Thornridge?"

In the minds of many, Ron Ferguson's 1971-72 team continues to be the gold standard of Illinois high school hoops. Thornridge was only the second Illinois team, joining 1949-50 Mt. Vernon, to go undefeated while defending a state title. In the many years since, only (Class A) Lawrenceville in 1982-83 and (Class AA) Proviso East in 1991-92 have been able to successfully defend an Illinois state championship while going unbeaten. Those four teams were all outstanding, but Thornridge went through an entire season without ever being in serious jeopardy of losing a game. It is significant to point out that only one team finished within 14 points of Thornridge that year. Only four teams got within 20 points of the Falcons.

In more than 100 years of Illinois high school basketball, only ten schools have won consecutive state championships. Elgin, Mt. Vernon, and Rockford West were the only schools to do so prior to Thornridge in 1971 and 1972. The only schools to win consecutive titles since are Lawrenceville, East St. Louis Lincoln, Proviso East of Maywood, Peoria Manual, Peoria High School, and Chicago Simeon. East St. Louis Lincoln won three straight state titles in the late 1980s. Peoria Manual won a state record four in a row from 1994 to 1997.

There is no question that Illinois has seen its share of great high school basketball teams through the years. It would seem an impossible task to decide with absolute certainty which team is the best of all time. Some would even consider it unfair to compare teams of different eras. The game and its rules have changed through the years. Today's athletes run faster and jump higher. Teams today are often made up of players who have made a conscious decision to play together. High school players transfer from one school to another in order to play with friends or to be part of a superior team.

Thornridge coach Ron Ferguson has never been one to say that his team is, without question, the best of all time. He does, however, believe his 1971-72 team was special.

"There have been a lot of great teams," says Ferguson. "I don't know whether it's really fair to compare our team in 1972 with the teams now. I think maybe the teams now are probably bigger, faster, and probably *better*. But, you can't ever really prove that. I'm just satisfied to say that our team was probably the best team in our era and let it go at that."

When trying to determine the best high school basketball team in Illinois history, any team with a loss surely must be eliminated from consideration. It would seem no matter how great a team might have been, if it suffered a loss, it does not match up to the teams that managed to fight off every challenge and go through a season undefeated. That said, special consideration must be given to a pair of one-loss teams thought by many to be among the best in the state's history.

The 1990-91 Maywood Proviso East team was led by future college stars Michael Finley, Sherrell Ford, and Donnie Boyce. The "Three Amigos" were joined by talented underclassmen that went unbeaten the following season. But, as good as this team was, Proviso East did suffer a loss and also barely won its state semifinal 47-44 over Libertyville. That doesn't measure up to Thornridge.

Another one-loss team that often gets mentioned in discussions about the all-time greats is the 1997 Peoria Manual squad that won the school's fourth straight state title. Despite having a loss, Manual was still recognized that season as the best team in the country. Wayne McClain, who lost three times to Thornridge in 1971-72 while playing for Manual, was the head coach of his high school alma mater in 1997.

"We lost one game and was USA Today national champs," says McClain. "I'm not taking anything away from [Thornridge]. I'm just saying our schedule was really brutal that year. In the state championship semifinal, we played against Thornton, the number two team in the country. We were number one, and they were number two. We're not talkin' about the state. We're talkin' about the *country*."

McClain coached the last three of Manual's four straight championship teams following the retirement of Dick Van Scyoc in 1994. McClain's son Sergio was a star on all four of the Rams' championships. Wayne McClain was ecstatic to win a state title while coaching his son.

"It was an unbelievable feeling," says McClain. "The thing that just totally took me over as a coach was the fact that I was doing it with my son. [Winning a state championship as a player], he got to do something I never could do."

McClain believes if his 1997 Peoria Manual champions played the 1972 Thornridge champs, it would be a great game. He knows from first-hand experience just how good Quinn Buckner and his teammates were in the early 1970s. But, he hesitates to call Thornridge the best ever because it is difficult to compare teams from different eras.

"They dominated the state of Illinois [in 1972]," says McClain. "Now, you get a chance to go all around the country and play the best everywhere. My teams played Oak Hill [Academy]. We played teams out of New Orleans. We played the state champions in Missouri. That's the only thing that makes it a little hard for me to say, 'Yes, they're the best of all time.' Things are different now. Maybe Thornridge could have traveled all over the world and beat a lot of teams. Maybe they could have done it."

McClain believes one reason so many people consider Thornridge the best ever was the way the Falcons handled Quincy in the state final.

"It was incredible how they annihilated them," says McClain, who watched the game in the Assembly Hall after playing in the third place game. "To beat a team that bad in a championship game is probably second to none. Nobody is beating teams like that in championship games. That gave them an aura of invincibility."

Dick Van Scyoc, who at the time of his retirement had won more games than any coach in Illinois high school history, has said he considers Thornridge a great team, probably the state's best. However, he now qualifies his earlier comments so that he does not offend any other teams or coaches.

"I have to say Thornridge was the best team that I saw," says Van Scyoc. "Now, I'm not saying they were the *best* because they're all good. And on a given night, one team might beat another. But, position through position, Thornridge just had an outstanding ball club."

When asked if he believed Thornridge would have success today, Van Scyoc did not hesitate for a second.

"Oh, I'm sure they'd be successful today," says Van Scyoc. "I think my ballclub would have been successful today because of the clinics and the camps being held today. Now that they all got weight rooms and conditioning coaches, the kids are just so much bigger and stronger than they were going back 20 or 30 years. If we'd had that same program they have today, our guys would still be competitive."

Longtime Champaign News-Gazette Sports Editor Loren Tate is one who believes it would be difficult to rate any team over the Peoria Manual teams that dominated Illinois high school basketball in the mid-1990s. But, he was very impressed with the 1972 Thornridge championship team. Like most every newspaper writer of the era, he was absolutely sure that the Falcons would beat Quincy to take home the first-place trophy.

"They were really a mature team," remembers Tate. "They were really good both offensively and defensively. They were just way better than everybody else. In that period, there would be two games played in Champaign on the final day. They would have the semifinals in the afternoon and the finals at night. We [writers] would always be in a heck of a position because the [second] game would be late. There was a third place game that preceded the championship game. We were always against deadline. I would have to try to put together something that would stand up [as accurate] in the paper the next day. I just kind of went out on a limb because I wasn't worried about them losing. I'd basically write a column almost before [the game] was over. That's how much confidence I had that they would win. That was my big concern, getting a column out that would hold up on deadline. With them, you could do that."

There have been 17 undefeated Illinois teams since the state began playing the state championship tournament in 1908. Taylorville was the first to go unbeaten racking up a state-record 45 wins in 1944. Mt. Vernon (1950), La Grange (1953 and 1970), Chicago Marshall (1958), and Collinsville (1961) also went undefeated prior to Thornridge in 1972. Since the Falcons turned the trick, only ten championship teams have finished the season without a loss. In the small-school classification, only Lawrenceville (1982 and 1983), McLeansboro (1984), Teutopolis (1986), and Seneca (2006) have been undefeated state champions. In the large school classifications, the only unbeaten champions since Thornridge are Lockport Central (1978), Quincy (1981), Chicago King (1990), Maywood Proviso East (1992), and Chicago King (1993). It should be noted that Illinois went to a four-classification system in 2007-08 to give more schools the opportunity to win state championships. Prior to the change, Illinois had been a two-class system for 36 seasons (1972-2007).

So, which of those teams could claim to be as good, or better, than Thornridge? Even though today's teams might be bigger, stronger, and faster, no large-school in Illinois has gone undefeated since Chicago King in 1993. Among the Class A schools, only the Lawrenceville teams of 1982 and 1983 could seriously enter into the discussion. With smaller enrollments, it is rare that a Class A school could contend against a larger Class AA school. Those unbeaten Lawrenceville teams might have been able to play with the big boys. Ron Felling's teams won a record 68 straight games which broke the state mark set by Quincy in 1982. The 1944 Taylorville team with Johnny Orr should be seriously considered based on its state-record 45 victories. Those who saw Max Hooper and Mt. Vernon in 1950 will argue the Rams should also be in the discussion of all-time great teams. There are those who will argue for the 1961 Collinsville team led by Bogie Redmon, the 1970 La Grange team led by Owen Brown, or even the 1953 La Grange Lions that allowed no team to finish closer than nine points all season. Let's face it. Any team that went undefeated can stake a claim as the best. But, two high schools, Chicago King and Quincy, seem to have viable arguments.

Chicago King went unbeaten in both 1990 and 1993 with Rashard Griffith figuring prominently in both championships. Griffith was a freshman on the 1990 team that was named national champion after winning the Illinois Class AA title. The state's "Mr. Basketball", Jamie Brandon, led King that season, but he had plenty of help from Griffith and senior Johnny Selvie. However, the 1990 champions were not dominating in the same fashion that Thornridge had dominated every opponent. Three years later, however, Chicago King did dominate with a pair of seven-footers in the lineup. Seven-four Thomas Hamilton was part of King's "Twin Towers" joining the seven-one Griffith who was named "Mr. Basketball" in his senior season. Chicago King won its "Sweet 16" game by 25 points then proceeded to dominate its opponents in Champaign, winning the three games in the Assembly Hall by 28, 31, and 37 respectively. In its 79-42 championship game romp over Rockford Guilford in 1993, King broke open a tight game by outscoring its opponent 32-2 in the fourth quarter. With that kind of dominance, it is easy to see why some consider the 1993 King team to be one of Illinois' very best teams of all time.

But, most will say the best argument for state supremacy can be made by the 1980-81 Quincy team coached by Jerry Leggett who took over at Quincy after Sherrill Hanks left in 1995. In March of 1981, the Blue Devils won their "Elite Eight" games by 25, 31, and 29 points. In each of those games, Quincy exhibited Thornridge-like domination breaking out to first quarter leads of 24-2, 19-2, and 19-8. The Blue Devils beat Proviso East in the championship game 68-39. Six-eleven senior Michael Payne and the Douglas brothers, Bruce and Dennis, were the key players on a team that, like Thornridge in 1972, was named the national champion. Quincy averaged 77 points a game and allowed only 50. Those numbers are strikingly similar to the Thornridge averages of 87 points scored and 55 allowed. The 1972 Thornridge team provided 33 wins as the school won a state record 58 consecutive games over parts of three seasons. In the 1980-81 season, Quincy won 33 straight as part of a 64-game winning streak that broke the Thornridge record. Based on the numbers, you can understand why most longtime observers believe the 1972 Thornridge and 1981 Quincy state champions are considered the best high school basketball teams in Illinois history. You would think that anybody from Quincy would favor the Blue Devils over the Falcons, but most of the players from the 1971-72 Quincy team say the edge goes to Thornridge.

"I knew all those kids on that '81 Blue Devil team," says Larry Moore, who still lives and works in Quincy, "and they were not the players that the Thornridge players were. I don't take anything away from that team, but Batts was every bit as good as Payne. Quinn Buckner was better than Bruce Douglas. The other three players for Thornridge, I know, were better than the three supporting players for Quincy High. They were not in the same league as Thornridge. They're probably in the top five high school teams of all time. USA Today did some kind of a poll, and they ranked the top 25 high school teams of all time. They had Thornridge number three."

While USA Today was unable to produce a copy of the poll mentioned by Moore, there was an article written in the Chicago Sun-Times a few years ago ranking Thornridge fourth among all of the nation's top high school teams. The article was written by Taylor Bell who is still considered Illinois' top prep sportswriter and has written several books on Illinois high school basketball.

"I've always said they're the best team this state ever saw," said Bell during a September 2007 radio interview on 1190 KEX in Portland. "I think most people agree. I never got an argument from Jerry Leggett even though he had the '81 [Quincy] team. He never argued [the point], and that's the only team that you could almost argue [was as good]. There's one fact I always bring up that separates them from virtually everybody else, including other teams from other states. In the course of winning 33 games, no opponent came [closer than] 14 points of them. And I don't think, whether you're talking Quincy of '81, or you can think of your own state and your own teams, that you're going to find a program that was so dominant that nobody came [closer than] 14 points during an entire season."

Other 1972 Blue Devils' players join Moore in putting aside their hometown pride to favor Thornridge over the 1981 Quincy squad.

"That's hard for me," says Bob Spear, now a specialist in intensive care and pediatric anesthesia in a children's hospital in San Diego. "Obviously, I think talent-wise they had a lot of talent on the floor with Leggett in those years. My honest answer is I don't think they would have measured up [to Thornridge]. Bruce Douglas and Quinn Buckner, there could be comparisons there. Michael Payne and Batts [could be compared]. Douglas and Payne could match up in a 2-on-2 game with Buckner and Batts. Maybe. But then Mike Bonczyk, Greg Rose, and Ernie Dunn? Jeez. Those three guys, they'd be a great nucleus of a team. I just don't think the other three guys [on the '81 Quincy team] measure up. You take a Greg Rose. He'd be one of the best players that ever played for Quincy, and people don't remember him. Mike Bonczyk was a great floor leader, and Buckner led the defense. They were unselfish. They throttled so many good teams. I think the proof is in the margin of victory, and in such big games. How could you compare? They didn't just beat somebody by three points before they clobbered us. They clobbered people all the way through from start to finish. A 14-point margin of victory was the lowest [for the season]. If you use that as any kind of a bench mark, who compares to that? And they played great competition in a great conference."

Kel Gott, now a teacher in Chicago suburb Crystal Lake, believes Thornridge ranks number one of all Illinois high school basketball teams.

"Yeah, there's no doubt in my mind," says Gott, "and I loved that team with Bruce Douglas and Michael Payne. That was a phenomenal team.

That's the definition of heaven. You get to watch those two teams play each other for the rest of eternity. That would be heaven."

The former Quincy assistant coach, Steve Goers, and Gene Pingatore of Westchester St. Joseph, both moved ahead of former number one Dick Van Scyoc on the state's list of all-time winningest coaches in 2008-09. Goers considers Thornridge the best high school team in Illinois history.

"I think it is because they were so good together," says Goers. "They had great coaching. They had some smart kids who ended up being coaches like Buckner and Bonczyk. Batts was just a great shot-blocker, and Rose was an outstanding athlete. There were teams more physically imposing, but they didn't play with the energy and the focus that Thornridge did. They just seemed to be able to respond both physically and mentally. It was just unbelievable. It's kind of hard to say one team was the best ever, but there was nobody better than Thornridge."

Rick Ely now lives in El Paso, Texas, and works for an airline company. Even though he has not lived in the state for a number of years, he cannot conceive how any team could possibly have been as good as the 1971-72 Thornridge Falcons.

"At that time, I equated them to a major college team," says Ely. [With] their style of play, the way they played together, and their talent, they could have beat many a college team back then. They were that good."

"What I'll tell you about our team," says Quinn Buckner, "and this is me just kind of going through it here almost 40 years later, all of us were probably better athletes than basketball players. We've got some instinct that we can make plays that most people are not going to make. We make them, not because we're basketball players, but because we're athletically gifted enough. When we pressed, I played in the middle like a free safety. That's what I played in football. So I'm using athletic ability. Some intelligence I'm sure, but athletic ability. Boyd was long and athletic. Greg was a great athlete. Ernie too, and Mike was a good athlete. We had really good athletes, and what Coach Ferguson got us to do all the time was, and this is probably why we were undefeated my senior year, we played hard."

"Everybody asks how we would stack up [to other teams]?" says Mike Bonczyk. "'I guess the question should be, how would everybody else stack up against us? We've already proven what we've proven."

While Coach Ron Ferguson is hesitant to talk about his team's place in history, his former assistant coaches are willing to say that the 1971-72 Thornridge team stands the test of time as the best ever.

"Oh, without a question," says then-varsity assistant Dave Lezeau. "I don't think there's any doubt. I know there were a number of great teams through Illinois history, but I don't think there's any doubt that that group, led by Buckner, was the best ever."

"Yes, I do [think the team ranks as the best]," says Ron Bonfiglio, the Thornridge sophomore coach. "There were some other great ones. Proviso East had some great players and great teams. That Chicago Simeon team [with Derrick Rose], they get mentioned in the same breath. But, I just think our press was so devastating, and we seemed to adjust to everything."

"They all get compared to that team," says 1971 Thornridge assistant coach Al Holverson. "The versatility of that team was unbelievable. They would still stack up with any of these teams. I think they would beat them all."

One person who has seen them all, at least since the 1972 state tournament, is radio broadcaster Lanny Slevin. Slevin worked at WPRC radio in Lincoln, Illinois, when Thornridge won its consecutive championships. In fall of 1973, he moved to WLPO radio in La Salle-Peru and has called play-by-play of more than 3000 games in the years that followed. Slevin, who has broadcast or watched every state championship game since the early 1970s, is one who thinks nobody was better than Thornridge in the perfect 1971-72 season.

"I've seen a lot of great teams, wonderful teams that were thrilling," says Slevin. "The Lawrenceville teams in Class A were very good teams. Quincy had some great teams. It would be thrilling to watch Jerry Leggett's team that had the Douglas Brothers and Michael Payne. I'm not so sure that Quincy could win [against Thornridge]. Oh yeah, there are teams that could have pushed them. There are teams that possibly could have beaten them on any given day. Chicago King had some wonderful teams, but when it comes down to head to head, full strength, put the ball up, play the game and see what happens, the "Three Amigos" at Proviso East probably would need two more Amigos, or three more, in order to beat Thornridge. Thornridge had something intangible that every coach is looking for. No team has been able to duplicate the same kind of chemistry, or togetherness, love, or family, or whatever you want to call it.

I remember hearing Coach Ferguson saying, 'My biggest concern was that I would get in the way and screw it up.' That's like Phil Jackson saying, 'Yeah, I just had to get out of Michael Jordan's way and try not to mess up the Bulls,' when they were on those great runs. But, Thornridge had a similar kind of thing because everybody knew their role, and each person did what they did best for the common good. That's what makes teams like that so unique."

"Thornridge got primed for it the year before [when it won the state title]," continues Slevin. "They didn't go unbeaten, but that started the run. They went 33-0 the next year. Everybody had a job to do. They practiced hard. They played hard. They were focused. They answered every challenge. It didn't seem like they could play a bad game. They just blew everybody away. Their opponents at Champaign fell by the margins of 31, 29, 19, and 35 points. The win over Quincy in the championship game is a standard that everybody else compares now and will for the rest of time. They led by 31 at the half and went on to win 104-69 over a pretty good Quincy team, a team that could have won it another year, but not that year. There was nobody close to Thornridge that year."

Slevin believes that most Thornridge opponents were convinced they were going to lose even before the ball was thrown in the air to start the game.

"I remember reading a quote from the great hurdler, Edwin Moses," says Slevin. "He was unbeaten in like eight years. He won like 120 straight high-hurdles races. They asked him, 'How do you keep doing this? What's your secret?' He said, 'Every time I go out there, I do the same thing that I've always done. For somebody to beat me, they'd have to do something that they've never done before.' He gets out there on the track with so much confidence that he knows that he's the winner because he *always* wins. It's kind of like super-confidence. Everybody else is lined up, and they look over at Moses and say, 'This guy never loses.' As far as the psyche is concerned, that's gotta enter in. Buckner says, 'We're not gonna lose.' They knew coming in that they were gonna win, and the other guys were going, 'This is the team that never loses.' Whether they say it or not, they think it."

The veteran radio broadcaster is not among those who believe Thornridge would fail to beat today's high school teams. He thinks if the Falcons were put in a time machine, they would be able to do just fine.

"Unlike a lot of sports, I think basketball, from 1972 to [now], is not as dramatic a gap as it could be in the National Football League or the NCAA Final Four," says Slevin. "In other words, if you take that Thornridge team, the 1972 [Class] AA champion, and you put them in there today, they would probably win every year. If they're in their prime, and they're playing this year, they'd probably win it again because they had the size.

They had the athleticism. They had the shooters. They had the coaching. I'm not so sure any team could beat them. Now, they're not going to win the championship game by 35 points every year. They're gonna be pressed. There have been great teams and great individuals. There have been better players individually: Marcus Liberty, Darius Miles, and some of those guys. Farragut had Kevin Garnett and Ronnie Fields on one team, and they didn't even win state. So, take this [Thornridge] team out there today, they would probably win the state tournament. They might have to go into overtime in a game, but they would probably win it. They were so good and so dominant. They were so much better than everybody else for that moment in time. They came together for that one peak moment. And, if they would have stayed frozen in that time, they could have come back in 1988 and 1995, and probably won the state championship. Nobody knows because it's never happened and never will. But, that's my gut-level feeling."

Many of the coaches who saw Thornridge continue to believe that Ron Ferguson's 1972 champions were a once in a lifetime type of team. Frank Nardi, Ferguson's long-time assistant who coached at Thornwood that season, believes that the Thornridge team stands the test of time.

"In my opinion, they do," says Nardi. "They didn't have a weakness. They played defense. They had so many guys that could hurt you scoring and rebounding. They were so quick. I know there were some other good teams around there at the time, but none of them compare to Thornridge."

Gene Pingatore is in his 40th season as head coach at Westchester St. Joseph. Pingatore, who coached future NBA star Isiah Thomas in the late 1970s, entered the 2009-10 season with 840 wins, more wins than any coach in Illinois high school basketball history. Pingatore believes Thornridge is a team for the ages.

"The best team ever," he laughs, "I mean, I can't remember them ever having a close game. They were just unbelievable. They had everything that would qualify them as a great team. Everyone on the team was capable of scoring. They played great defense. They had a great point guard in Bonczyk, and yet Buckner could run the point also. Quinn's leadership was just fantastic. The big people, Batts [and Rose] could score. They had everything and were well-coached. Ferguson did a great job with them. I watched them on a number of occasions, and they just took people apart. When they bring that up about, 'Who's the best team?' I say, 'No contest!'"

Having coached a great player in Isiah Thomas at St. Joseph, Pingatore knows that a talented star can make all the difference on a high school team. He believes Buckner was the key to Thornridge's success.

"He was the glue," says Pingatore. "He was so, so important to that team. His leadership was unbelievable. He could run the point. He could play big. He was such a strong kid. He did everything, and you need a player like that. The mental part of it, that's what made him [great], and that usually is the difference between the great ones and the good ones."

Duncan Reid, who won 643 games during his high school coaching career at Lincoln and Rock Island, agrees that Buckner is the deciding factor when trying to determine which team ranks as the best in Illinois history.

"Because of Buckner, I think Thornridge would beat [the other contenders]," says Reid. "He was the glue, and he was a stud. He was just so mature and could run the team. You couldn't take the ball from him. He was just that kind of player. Even though they had guys go [play] Division One [college basketball], other teams couldn't match up to Thornridge because of Buckner. He was a man among boys, just so mature and so strong. Except for the one position, that 1981 Quincy team might have been as good or better than Thornridge, but because of Buckner, Thornridge would win. Buckner was so good that you couldn't press him. He would just dribble through [defenders] and throw it underneath for layups. But hey, the other guys weren't chopped liver. They were all good players. Rose could shoot the ball outside. Dunn could slash. Batts could go outside and inside. Bonczyk played point guard a lot on that team. But, when it came to [crunch] time, Buckner had the ball."

Chuck Rolinski coached 34 years at Toluca High School and won 649 games while losing only 262. Rolinski, who pushed hard for Illinois to move to a two-class basketball system so that small schools like Toluca would have a better chance of winning a state championship, knows a great deal about winning basketball. Currently the President of the Illinois Basketball Coaches Association, he has many friends in the coaching community. But, he is not afraid to say Thornridge is the number one team of all time.

"It was an awesome team," says Rolinski. "They had just unbelievable talent and great coaching. They played well together. In my mind, and I saw all those teams from 1958 on, by far, it was the best team I've seen, even today. Everybody has their own favorite. The Quincy team was outstanding, no doubt about it. Chicago Marshall was great back then, [as was] La Grange with Owen Brown and [Coach] Ron Nikcevich, and the Proviso East teams. There were a lot of great ones, but I'm just sort of prejudiced for Thornridge. In my opinion, they were the best."

Between them, Lee Cabutti and Bob Basarich won 1024 high school basketball games. Cabutti won 528 games at Illinois high schools, Herrin and Champaign Central. Basarich won 496 games and lost only 99 at Lockport Central. Both coaches have watched other teams come and go, but they both believe Thornridge remains the cream of the crop when it comes to Illinois high school basketball.

"As soon as somebody wins the state title, they say, 'Well, this team might be as good as Thornridge,'" says Basarich. "They're not, but they like to think they are. That goes on constantly. There have been a lot of good teams, but there's been no team as dominant as that one. They never feared anyone, and of course, they beat the hell out of everyone. They had the chemistry. There was nobody on the team that wanted to be the star. They wanted to be a team that was a star. They just did so many things well in addition to having great physical talent."

"They were the best high school team I ever saw play," says Cabutti. "They just had it all. They had leadership, good defense, could score, and they had a good coach. Ferguson was a very outstanding person and a great coach. They proved it. When you go through a whole season undefeated and the closest game was 14 points, what else can you say? I remember them playing Quincy at the state finals, and Sherrill Hanks was a great coach. You don't beat Quincy too often, but, my God, by the half that game was over. You're lucky if you get one team like that in a lifetime. Ferguson will be the first one to tell you. You really do a lot of coaching when you *don't* have any talent. When I retired, they asked me which was my greatest team, and I gave them a team that finished with a .500 winning percentage. They pointed out, 'They only won half their games.' And I said, 'They shouldn't have won any.'"

Cabutti says Buckner made all the difference for the Thornridge championship teams.

"Without Buckner, those guys probably would have had an average team," says Cabutti. "I think they'd a been a good team, but they wouldn't have won no state championship. You can see what [Buckner] did at Indiana also. There are certain guys that just have it. You don't teach that type of stuff. Hell, I had years I didn't even have a captain because I felt there wasn't a damn leader in the bunch. But, guys like [Buckner and former Champaign star Clyde Turner], they make a good coach out of you."

A name that will be familiar to many basketball fans in Illinois and around the nation is Ernie Kent. Kent was a Parade All-America player at Rockford West High School in 1973 before heading to the University of Oregon where he became one of Dick Harter's famed "Kamikaze Kids." Kent was hired as his alma mater's first African-American coach in 1997 and has since won more games at Oregon than any other head coach. Kent was still in high school when he went to watch Thornridge play in the Rockford Thanksgiving tournament.

"I just remember what a dominant team they were," says Kent. "They were like a college team, maybe even a pro team, because they had so much size and so many skilled players and skilled athletes. Of course, Quinn Buckner was the leader of that group, and [Boyd] Batts was an incredible, incredible player as well. They had a demeanor about themselves, a mystique that they were a great team, and you were not going to be able to get on the floor and play with them because they were just so talented. You understood what a dominant team they were. That was the most impressive thing about them. It was not that they were winning games but how badly they were beating people. No one could get close to them. That tells you just how good they were. They were kind of a mini-version of the [Olympic] Dream Team. No one could play with them. They were a very dominant basketball team, and when you mention their five names, people will know that's one of the greatest, if not the greatest, team that came out of that state."

The last word on the subject will go to Thornridge head coach Ron Ferguson. He has always found himself in a bit of a pickle trying not to sound boastful while still supporting his players who naturally would like to be considered part of the best team in Illinois history.

"Well, naturally I am proud," says Ferguson. "But, I have a tough time trying to brag about it or get too carried away. It's not my personality for one thing. I like to give other teams credit. The only thing I gotta be careful of is, I would be doing a disservice to my players if I hesitate and say, 'I don't know if we were the best or not.' But, I also don't like to brag about it. People ask, 'Are you the greatest team?' I say, 'I think I'm the wrong guy to ask.' You don't ask the coach because if the coach says he doesn't think so, then his kids are mad. [1981 Quincy coach] Jerry Leggett, I'm sure he campaigned saying that they were the greatest team, and that's fine. He should. It's really for other people to evaluate."

"[As far as being regarded as among the best ever], I'm tickled to death," continues the coach, "and I certainly think we belong with all those teams. But, it's hard to compare teams from different eras. I suggested that they just stop [comparisons] at the year 2000 and start over. That would be the fairest way, you know, to just start over and say 'For the last century, Thornridge was the best team. Let's start over again and get another team for this century.'"

EPILOGUE

THE DAY AFTER WINNING THE 1972 Illinois Class AA basketball championship, the Thornridge Falcons drove north from Champaign and arrived to a heroes' welcome in Chicago's south suburbs. The welcoming party was huge. First, cars began falling in line behind the automobiles carrying the players and coaches until the caravan was nearly six miles in length. By one estimate, 100,000 fans lined the streets of Harvey, Phoenix, South Holland, and Dolton to wave at the players and coaches as they made their way towards Thornridge High School where at least 5000 fans were gathered for the championship celebration. One year earlier, school officials had learned there was not enough room in the school gymnasium to hold all the happy fans who wanted to celebrate with the team. On a cold Sunday afternoon in March of 1972, fans bundled up and waited outdoors for the team to arrive at the high school's football field where the ceremony would take place as soon as the team arrived.

Huge cheers rang out when the team made its appearance. The players and coaches were all smiles, and they thanked the fans for their support. Boyd Batts, wearing a long overcoat, presented the championship game ball to retiring Athletic Director Frank Froschauer, while fellow seniors Mike Bonczyk and Quinn Buckner, each dressed in a sport coat and a shirt with an open collar, looked on and smiled for the photographers. The players proudly displayed the 1972 state championship trophy which coincidentally is the last boys' basketball trophy Thornridge High School has won. The only two trophies the Falcons have ever won at the state tournament are the 1971 and 1972 championship trophies.

Two months after winning his second state title, Coach Ron Ferguson stepped down to take the job as the school's Athletic Director. Still, he remained very close to the coaching community. He and Quincy coach Sherrill Hanks become very good friends and even worked together in basketball camps. Ferguson is saddened that Hanks is now in poor health and living in a nursing home in Alabama near his son Mike. He misses his friend and remembers when he went to Quincy to work in Hanks' basketball camp in the summer of 1972, just months after beating the Blue Devils by 35 points in Champaign.

"I almost felt guilty going over there," laughs Ferguson. "I kept waiting for somebody to say, 'Why did you run up the score?' Some of their guys who graduated were working the camp. They were just as nice as could be. You could see that Sherrill had a great program going there. The kids were all real nice to me."

Ferguson has not been back to Thornridge High School for many years. He tried to visit the school not long ago, but was made to feel unwelcome by the local authorities.

"I went there about two or three years ago," says Ferguson. "I was meeting a friend of mine out near Chicago Heights. I had a little extra time and I said, 'I'm gonna drive through there and then drive by the cemetery where my mom and dad are, you know, just take my time. I drove through downtown Dolton and then out one of the side streets. I was going pretty slow because I was just looking around to see if there was anything new, the buildings and stuff like that. All of a sudden, I'm getting flashed over by a police car. Then, another police car passes and goes in front of me. So, there's one behind me and one in front of me, [and I stopped]. "They said, 'Stay right where you are.' The weather was nice so I had the window down. I said, 'What's the problem, officer?' He says, 'Let me see your registration.' I had to give him all the stuff so he can see if I stole the car. At the time, I guess they had a lot of drug dealers going through town. The fact that I was going so slow made them suspicious. I tried to explain to them who I was and why I was there. They wouldn't buy it. They were young black cops, and they didn't know Ron Ferguson from a hill of beans. I told them I used to work at the high school and all that stuff. Another police car came, and they had me delayed for an hour. They were checking with the state and everything else. They were kind of nasty at first. [Finally, one of the policemen] said, 'If you don't have business to be here, I think it would be good advice for you to probably not drive through here. We have a lot of problems, and there's no sense you getting involved in something like that.' I said, 'Well, I'm sorry. I thought I was going to go by the high school, but now I don't have enough time because I have to meet a guy for lunch. So, that's the last time I've been through there."

The area has definitely changed since the 1970s when Ferguson and the Thornridge High School basketball team were making headlines. Former Phoenix resident Nee Gatlin, now living in Kokomo, Indiana, sees the change in his old neighborhood every time he goes back to visit his mother.

"I see the changes," says Gatlin, a key member of the 1972 championship team. "There were never any gangs in that neighborhood. There were never any shootings or things of that nature. It was fairly safe. Do I have to watch my back [now] as much as I watched my back then? I watch it now. It's a different era now. Things have changed that much. A lot of the whites have moved out. Blacks have moved from the city and into the suburbs. A lot of the blacks who have moved out there moved to get away from the crime [in Chicago]."

"It's amazing how the public housing in Chicago affected the boom to the suburbs," continues Gatlin. "When they tried to get rid of the public housing, they had to find a place for people to stay. The people just moved to the suburbs. Along with that came their baggage, whatever it might have been. You just have to adapt. Survival is the ticket. In the '60s and '70s black folks could not even be around [Dolton and South Holland]. Now here we are in the 21st-century, and they have a black mayor. It had done like a 180-degree turn. It went from one extreme to another."

The demographics at Thornridge High School prove that things have definitely changed in Dolton and South Holland, communities that used to be nearly all-white. The school district was unable to provide specific numbers from the 1971-72 school year, but looking through the 1972 Thornridge High School yearbook from that year, it is clear that a majority of the nearly 3700 students attending Thornridge were white. A rough estimate, drawn from the yearbook's class photos, indicates approximately 83% of the students were white and only 16% black. Quinn Buckner's senior class looked to be approximately 94% white and 5% black based on the yearbook photos. In the 2008-09 school year, numbers provided by the school reveal that 97.9% of Thornridge student were African-American. 1.3 % were Hispanic, and only 0.1% of the Thornridge students were white. That is not a typo. White flight from Dolton has left few white families in that community. South Holland is now also primarily African-American.

Kamala Buckner, the District 205 Superintendent, says the makeup of students at Thornridge, Thornwood, and Thornton has changed in dramatic fashion since her brother Quinn was in high school.

"It is primarily a minority school district," says Dr. Buckner. "If there are 6400 children, I can almost assure you that 6390 are minority children. I have lots of Latinos and children from India. It's really become a different kind of diverse school district."

In recent years there have been rumors that Thornridge, or one of the other high schools in District 205, might have to close due to a lack of funding. Kamala Buckner downplays those rumors.

"That was never on the Superintendent and the board's agenda," she says. "There were parents in the community who were concerned, and that became part of *their* discussion. But to close a school has not, or *is* not, part of my, or the board's agenda."

Jessica Buckner, the mother of Kamala and Quinn, continues to live in Phoenix in the same house in which she raised her kids. The 86-year old Buckner has watched her community change even as she stays involved in education and works within the community to care for its children. It might not be as safe to live in Phoenix, Harvey, Dolton, or South Holland as it was decades ago, but as Mrs. Buckner will tell you, it has been, and will continue to be, her home.

Jessica Buckner, a woman who actively demonstrated in the 1960s seeking better educational opportunities for her own children and the black children of Phoenix, experienced the same emotions as most African-Americans when Barack Obama was elected President of the United States in November, 2008. Proud that America had elected a President of color, Mrs. Buckner imagined what that would have meant to her father.

"I did not think that I would see this day," says Jessica Buckner. "My first thought was that I wish my father had been here because he was an activist in getting people to vote when he lived in the southern communities. He lived in Texas and Florida, and was really involved in a lot of that stuff, registration for voting and the problems that they had there. So, I really thought about him first."

The Buckner name still means a great deal in Phoenix and the surrounding areas. While many of the Buckners chose to serve in education, Quinn did his part to instruct when he taught blacks and whites to get along while leading Thornridge to consecutive state championships. It was a special time, and Phoenix residents have never forgotten what those kids did for the community during the perfect 1971-72 season.

"A while back, we asked residents about the most memorable events in the history of Phoenix," says Phoenix Mayor Terry Wells. "That is number one. That is the event that is just so special to our community. Quite frankly, when you go in town and you talk about the [1972] Thornridge team, everybody knows [the players]. Everybody talks about it. I don't know if it's as important to the school as it is to this community. In fact, I can say that it's not. Some of the tradition that Thornridge had is gone now. It's just not the same. I think part of it is because the school boundaries changed [again]. The kids from Phoenix no longer go to Thornridge. I just don't think that it's as important to this particular group of kids in school now as it is to the village of Phoenix."

Kamala Buckner, like all the local residents who enjoyed the ride as Thornridge won the back-to-back state titles, believes very few people really noticed that the team was bringing the black and white communities together.

"What we were looking at was primarily athletics at its very finest and purist," says Kamala. "It was a great time, a great spirit. But, I don't think anyone understood what was happening then. I guess we can look back now and say what a difference it made."

Last but certainly not least, Quinn Buckner can look back on a lifetime filled with individual and team achievements. He takes great personal pride in the championships he won in the NBA, at the Olympic Games, and at Indiana University. But it all started when he was still a teenager living at home with his mother and father in the Buckner home in Phoenix. It all started with a bunch of his friends at Thornridge.

"It was a good time," says Quinn Buckner. "People easily remember my college, Olympic, and NBA championships. I always make sure people understand that my high school teammates would be a little disappointed with me if I didn't mention we won in high school twice. It was an important part of my athletic career. It molded me, not only athletically, but personally, in a way that I still am able to deal with and do some things that I wasn't sure I could do as a kid."

When my interview with Buckner concluded, and as we said our goodbyes, Quinn thanked me for taking the time to write a book about his high school basketball team.

"Thank you very much," said the former Thornridge star, "and thank you for remembering my guys. It's important to me, but it's *very* important to them."

Nearly four decades after leading Thornridge to a perfect season, Quinn Buckner remains a perfect teammate.

Thornridge Game by Game 1971-72

DATE	LOCATION	OPPONENT	SCORE	RECORD	LEADING SCORER
11/19/71	Dolton	Rich East (Park Forest)	70-52	1-0	Buckner 22
11/26/71	Rockford	Batavia	97-71	2-0	Dunn 24
11/27/71	Rockford	Manual (Peoria)	107-60	3-0	Batts 40
11/27/71	Rockford	Guilford (Rockford)	88-57	4-0	Buckner 27
12/04/71	Dolton	Waukegan	75-50	5-0	Buckner 20
12/10/71	Dolton	Eisenhower (Blue Island)	75-52	6-0	Rose 24
12/17/71	Harvey	Thornton (Harvey)	71-54	7-0	Buckner 20
12/18/71	Maywood	Proviso East (Maywood)	89-59	8-0	Buckner 26
12/28/71	Carbondale	Marian Catholic (Chicago Heights)	86-52	9-0	Rose 27
12/29/71	Carbondale	Eisenhower (Decatur)	89-63	10-0	Buckner 31
12/30/71	Carbondale	Manual (Peoria)	92-65	11-0	Rose 29
12/30/71	Carbondale	Carbondale	85-47	12-0	Buckner 29
01/07/72	Dolton	Bloom (Chicago Heights)	99-65	13-0	Buckner 27
01/08/72	Racine, Wisc.	Washington Park (Racine, Wisc.)	83-39	14-0	Buckner 30
01/14/72	Arlington Hts.	St. Viator (Arlington Heights)	102-64	15-0	Buckner 32
01/21/72	Oak Lawn	Richards (Oak Lawn)	95-42	16-0	Buckner 28
01/22/72	Dolton	Rich Central (Olympia Fields)	106-68	17-0	Buckner 27
01/28/72	Blue Island	Eisenhower (Blue Island)	76-42	18-0	Buckner 22
01/29/72	Chicago	St. Patrick (Chicago)	70-56	19-0	Buckner 25
02/04/72	Dolton	Thornton (Harvey)	73-52	20-0	Buckner 28
02/05/72	Dolton	Homewood-Flossmoor	89-53	21-0	Batts 24
02/11/72	Chicago Hts.	Bloom (Chicago Heights)	90-62	22-0	Rose 26
02/18/72	Dolton	Thornwood (South Holland)	103-57	23-0	Batts 19, Rose 19
02/19/72	Chicago	St. Ignatius (Chicago)	90-52	24-0	Buckner 27
02/25/72	Dolton	Richards (Oak Lawn)	90-53	25-0	Batts 26
02/29/72	Dolton*	St. Francis de Sales (Chicago)	113-59	26-0	Rose 26
03/03/72	Dolton*	Thornton Fractional No. (Cal. City)	101-68	27-0	Batts 33
03/07/72	Chicago Hts.*	Bloom (Chicago Heights)	65-42	28-0	Batts 20
03/10/72	Chicago Hts.*	Thornton (Harvey)	71-43	29-0	Buckner 28
03/14/72	Crete-Monee*	Lockport	74-46	30-0	Batts 18
03/17/72	Champaign*	Collinsville	95-66	31-0	Batts 34
03/18/72	Champaign*	Manual (Peoria)	71-52	32-0	Rose 20
03/18/72	Champaign*	Quincy	104-69	33-0	Batts 37

*-- Illinois High School Association Tournament Game --

Thornridge 1971-72 Season Statistics

PLAYER	G	FGA	FGM	FG%	FTA	FTM	FT%	Points	PPG	Off Reb	RPG	APG	TO/ G	PF/ G
Buckner	33	577	312	.541	181	124	.685	748	22.7	92	9.2	5.4	3.6	2.5
Batts	33	507	254	.501	171	122	.713	630	19.1	166	11.9	1.3	1.1	2.2
Rose, G	33	496	273	.550	110	52	.471	598	18.1	90	5.5	2.0	1.6	2.5
Dunn	33	293	133	.453	127	77	.606	343	10.4	99	6.0	2.7	1.8	2.4
Bonczyk	33	182	89	.489	38	22	.579	200	6.1	15	1.6	8.2	3.2	2.7
Gatlin	31	131	49	.374	69	40	.579	138	4.5	22	2.5	1.2	1.3	1.5
Hutchinson	30	41	20	.488	10	4	.400	44	1.5	12	1.5	0.1	0.4	0.7
Redman	29	26	12	.462	29	18	.621	42	1.4	4	0.5	0.9	0.7	0.7
Anderson	27	36	14	.389	16	12	.750	40	1.5	4	0.6	0.6	0.4	0.4
King	25	26	10	.385	11	8	.727	28	1.1	7	0.8	0.2	0.4	0.3
Rose, K	15	32	12	.375	5	2	.400	26	1.7	5	0.5	0.1	0.3	0.4
Knutsen	21	25	11	.441	1	0	.000	22	1.0	1	0.4	0.2	0.2	0
Lewis	15	24	5	.208	7	3	.429	13	0.9	5	0.7	0.1	0.3	0.5
Kremer	6	7	3	.429	10	6	.600	12	2.0	5	2.2	0	0.8	1.2
T-Ridge	33	2403	1197	.498	785	490	.624	2884	87.4	527	40.5	22.5	14.6	16.1
Opp.	33	1857	696	.375	730	440	.603	1832	55.5	293	25.8	8.7	22.6	16.7

Glenn Dreesen photo

1971-72
THORNRIDGE
FALCONS

Front row (L-R) Gary Ferguson,
AD Frank Froschauer,
Mike Bonczyk, Quinn Buckner,
Boyd Batts, Greg Rose,
Ernie Dunn, Coach Ron
Ferguson, Brad Ferguson
Back row (L-R) Manager
Dean Reszel, Joe King,
Bill Redman, Ken Kremer,
Keith Hutchinson, Nee Gatlin,
Fred Knutsen, Dave Anderson,
Assistant Coach Dave Lezeau
(Not pictured –
Ken Rose, Sidney Lewis)

ACKNOWLEDGMENTS

I could not have written this book without the help and support of dozens of people who generously gave of their time to assist a first-time author. For their willingness to be a part of this, I am eternally grateful.

I cannot possibly thank everyone, but I must, first and foremost, recognize Ron Ferguson who allowed me to enter his home and sift through his scrapbooks and memories of his Thornridge days. He and wife Linda were gracious hosts and have been supporters through the entire book-writing process. Special thanks also to every person I interviewed whose name appears in the book. I particulary want to thank all of the former players and coaches for their willingness to share details of their lives.

Thanks to the many people who helped me track down the players and coaches who now live around the country. Fergie, Al Holverson, Chuck Rolinski, and so many more, I couldn't have done it without you. Thanks to Bob Spear and Don Sorenson for the loan of the Quincy basketball scrapbooks and to Thornridge Principal Kim Walker and Registrar Michele Powers for the loan of the Thornridge yearbooks. Kudos to IHSA Assistant Executive Director Scott Johnson, and the rest of the Illinois High School Association, for providing a wealth of information on the IHSA website (www.ihsa.org), the best in the nation.

Thanks to Tom Dreesen for providing keen insight into what life was like in the neighborhood back in the day. I always loved him on the Tonight Show. I love him even more now.

Thanks to Mike Downey for writing an exceptional foreword and to Downey, Jack Ramsay, Mike Rich, Jim Durham, and Bill Walton for writing back-cover testimonials. I'm humbled by their words. Thanks to Buzz Bissinger, John Feinstein, Peter Golenbock, and Curt Smith for taking the time to offer advice to a first-time author.

Thanks to Glenn Dreesen and Frank McCully for permission to use their photographs, including McCully's back-cover photo of Fergie and the five starters.

To Becky Redding and Nuria Hansen, a *huge* thanks for providing the maps of Illinois and the south suburbs of Chicago. And, thank you to my friend Rich Patterson his wealth of knowledge about the music and TV industries.

Special thanks to my own personal webmaster Adam Crowell for putting the website together. Without you, there would be no www.thornridgebook.com. You are the best!

Thanks to my surgeon Rehan Ahmad, my oncologist Frederick Ey, the 8th floor nurses at St. Vincent Hospital, and everyone at Pacific Oncology for keeping me alive so I could finish the book.

Thanks to my college basketball coach Jim Dudley for giving me a scholarship at SIU-E when I found out I wasn't good enough to play at SIU-C. Thanks also to Coach Fred Wehking who recruited me to Carbondale, then helped me land in Edwardsville.

Special thanks to my high school basketball coach Duncan Reid for believing in me as a player back in the '70s and 38 years later as an author.

On an even more personal note, even a first-time author can tell you that without the support of friends and family, a project like this just wouldn't get done. I thank all of my friends for being there for me over the past 16 months. Although I can't name all of my friends and neighbors, (I'm paying by the word after all), heartfelt thanks go to Al Bell, Mike Rich, William and Jan Thun, Mark and Angie Kattelman, Rich and Deb Patterson, Kathleen Gaylord, John Lashway, Al Egg, Terry Durham, Carl Wolfson, Christine Alexander, Thom and Louise Hartmann, Shawn Taylor, Chris Brown, J.R. Hellman, Manda Factor, Jim Taylor, Michael Convery, Brad Ford, Paul Linnman, J. D. Fort, Mary Loos, Michael Anthony, Jim McLaren, Felicia Heaton, Jeff Kirsch, Mark Mason, Dave Anderson, Mike Oaks, Brenda Lichtenberger, Melissa Ives, Mike Dirkx, Robert Dove, Tommy Austin, and the entire gang at KEX Radio.

A special thank you is reserved for Genevieve Smith. A lifelong school teacher, Genevieve served as the editor for my book. She spent countless hours trying to prevent me from making grammatical and punctuation mistakes. She did a wonderful job, and if you see a mistake, it was me that goofed up in a rewrite.

Finally, my thanks go out to my many relatives in Lincoln and New Holland, Illinois, and also in Iowa, Florida, Arizona, and California. Thanks for providing the kind of support one only gets from family.

And most importantly, thank you to my loving wife Sharon and to my great kids Adam and Kelsey. Thanks for believing in me, now and always. I love you all.

SCOTT LYNN (BETZELBERGER) is an award-winning Radio/ TV Sportscaster who has worked the last 33 years in Illinois, Florida, and Oregon; the last 20 years as Sports Director of KEX Radio in Portland, OR. He has been recognized as the Oregon Sportscaster of the Year seven times and has won a prestigious regional Edward R. Murrow Award on three occasions.

Lynn was born and raised in Lincoln, Illinois. He captained the 1972 Lincoln High School team that was ranked second in the state, and he was a scholarship basketball player at Southern Illinois University before graduating from SIU-Edwardsville in 1976. He and Sharon have been married for 32 years and live in Beaverton, Oregon. They have two children.

Scott Lynn is a colon cancer survivor. He wrote much of this book while undergoing chemotherapy in 2009. This is his first book.

LaVergne, TN USA
16 December 2009
167198LV00004B/2/P